FIBERGLASS

& COMPOSITE MATERIALS

AN ENTHUSIAST'S GUIDE TO HIGH PERFORMANCE NON-METALLIC MATERIALS FOR AUTOMOTIVE RACING AND MARINE USE

FORBES AIRD

HPBooks

HPBooks
are published by
The Berkley Publishing Group
200 Madison Avenue
New York, New York 10016

First Edition: April 1996

© 1996 Forbes Aird
10 9 8 7 6 5 4 3
The Putnam Berkley World Wide Web site address is http://www.berkley.com

Library of Congress Cataloging-in-Publication Data

Aird, Forbes, 1944—.
   Fiberglass and composite materials: an enthusiast's guide to high performance non-metallic materials for automotive racing and marine use/ Forbes D. aird.– 1st ed.
         p.   cm.
   Includes bibliographical references and index.
   ISBN 1-55788-239-8
   1. Reinforced plastics. 2. Glass fibers. 3. Ocean Engineering–Materials.
4. Automobiles–Materials. I. Title.
   TA455.P55A34   1996
   620.1'923–dc20   95-25236
                                                                        CIP

Book Design & Production by Bird Studios
Interior photos by the author unless otherwise noted
Cover photo courtesy DuPont

ABOUT THE AUTHOR

Born in Britain, Forbes Aird moved to Canada at the age of nine. He is gradually getting used to the climate. For several years, Forbes' career alternated between administrative/research work in various academic institutions, and self-employment–which included several years operating a small specialty reinforced plastics shop, and a financially doomed attempt to build a limited production sports car using RP stressed skin construction.

First published in 1965, he began writing full-time in 1986. Despite strong evidence to the contrary, he retains the conviction that he can make a living in this way. Over 100 of his automotive, aeronautical, and science articles have appeared in more than a dozen different magazines in Canada and the U.S. In 1991 he received a Science Journalism Award from The Canadian Science Writers' Association; in 1992 the International Motor Press Association bestowed on him the prestigious Ken Purdy Award. Fiberglass and Composite Materials is his third book.

Forbes works and lives in Toronto with his wife, Kate. When not slaving over a hot keyboard, he spends much of his time cooking Thai and Indian curries.

ACKNOWLEDGMENTS

A great many people provided information, illustrations, and helpful advice during the preparation of this book. My thanks to all the companies and individuals who contributed so generously. In no particular order, they are:

Tex Turnier, Knytex Corp'n; Patricia Espinosa, the Escom Advertising Group Inc; Ray Lukich, TR Industries; Larry Ming, Progress Plastics, Toronto; Don Poland, DOW Chemical (Canada), Glendorah Lawrence, DOW Chemical (US), and Jo Albers, Gibbs and Soell, Inc; The Standard Products Company; Dr Huy Nguyen, Allied Signal, Fibers Division; Robert D. Hillard, Fein Power Tools Inc; William R. Donaldson, The FRP Division of Ashland Chemical; Mary Siotkowski, Sue Burkette, and Jim West of Owens-Corning; John Oncken and Dominic Mammoliti, Shell Canada, and Robert Street, Shell Chemicals (USA); Dr Hal Loken, DuPont; Mr. Herb Oughton, Binks Manufacturing Co; Starlite Industries; Gerry Crawford and Glas-Craft, Inc. Especially helpful were Bob Lacovara, Sally McKinney and Rob Ryan of the Composites Fabricators Association; and Gougeon Brothers Inc, particularly James R Watson.

I wish to express special thanks to Randall Rodine, proprietor of Aerodine Composites Group, for opening his shop to photographer Jack Gladback, and to Jack himself for his artful pictures which contribute so much to this book.

Finally, to Colin Fisher, Manager, Public Relations, Bombardier Regional Aircraft, for not merely inviting me to spend a most informative morning in a tour of de Havilland Inc.'s composites shop, but in arranging that the tour should be conducted by one of the world's leading experts in the field of aerospace composites—Leonard John of de Havilland. As if this were not sufficiently generous, Mr. Fisher also volunteered the services of staff photographer Guy Levesque, whose fine work also graces these pages. Thanks also to Spyro Cacoutis of de Havilland for additional help. I am deeply grateful for (and not a little astonished by) the extraordinary assistance so graciously extended by Bombardier/de Havilland.

CONTENTS

INTRODUCTION

At its worst, a composites shop is a brutally nasty place, where millions of glass particles hang glittering in an atmosphere filled with the howl of chopper guns and the stench of styrene. There, under-supervised workers stumble around red-eyed, tripping over hardened resin spills, reeling from the fumes, cranking out heavy, clumsy, third-rate goods, for a third-world wage. Thankfully, there are fewer such hellholes these days. Some, not surprisingly, have been shut down by Federal or local agencies. But you can still find them.

At the other extreme is a modern aerospace composites facility. The air is clean, with just the barest hint of an odor, as if the floor had been recently waxed. Lab-coated workers move calmly and methodically through this almost antiseptic space, where the only sounds that rise above subdued conversation are the noise—like a zipper being opened—of a knife slicing through pre-preg, and the occasional hair-drier hum of a heat gun. No slopping, stinking liquid resin; no sparkling clouds of particles. All this and union wages to boot!

Ironically, for someone just getting into composites work, either as a hobby or in working to establish a small business, one of the appeals of this class of materials is the possibility of getting into operation with negligible investment in facilities and equipment. Working with a primitive *plant*, though, limits you to the least demanding materials—polyester resin and glass reinforcement. That, in turn, means that the finished goods will necessarily be heavier than a metal part of comparable strength and stiffness. It also means working conditions closer to the first example.

However, if you endure the grimmer aspects of this most basic combination of materials for a while, you can develop sufficient skill (and sufficient business) to justify moving to premium materials—typically epoxy resin and a high-performance reinforcement like aramid. When you reach that point, two things happen. First, working conditions become notably more pleasant; second, you are now in a position to make composite goods that can match or surpass metal ones on the basis of strength and weight, and that opens up a whole new world of applications, especially in the performance automotive field. While an amateur or small shop operator cannot hope to produce, say, a monocoque tub or composite wing that will outperform those of an Indy or Formula 1 car, it is possible to produce something which will outperform a metal part, and at potentially lower cost, especially if only a few are being made.

It is perhaps a bit like being a fighter pilot in wartime—if you survive the first few combat missions, you will learn some lessons they can't teach in flight school, so your chances of staying healthy improve dramatically. At the same time, you start to score victories. Unfortunately, there is no substitute for being shot at—you need the experience in order to learn the lessons.

Similarly, while later parts of this book are spent in describing "state-of-the-art" processes, we begin with the basics, in the belief that this is where you should start. The book is a mix of theory and how-to. The theoretical parts will help you decide what types of goods are appropriate for composite construction, and how to design them; the how-to sections are sufficiently detailed that even a novice should be able to successfully fabricate those goods. Once you experience the magical reward of popping out of a mold a shiny new part that you made yourself, you'll soon want a repeat dose of the rush of satisfaction and pride. And you can get that payoff without threatening your health; with practice and improved processes, the work can be positively pleasant. Here's how. ∎

"While an amateur or small shop operator cannot hope to produce, say, a monocoque tub or composite wing that will outperform those of an Indy or Formula 1 car, it is possible to produce something which will outperform a metal part, and at potentially lower cost, especially if only a few are being made."

THE WHAT AND WHY OF COMPOSITES

In general terms, a composite is a material made up from two or more other substances which give properties, in combination, that are not available from any of the ingredients alone. By this definition, concrete, laminated safety glass, and enameled bathtubs are all composites. In the automotive and aerospace fields, though, the term usually refers to a combination of strong fibers of some sort, encapsulated in a plastic resin.

FRP's

Until recently, this sub-category of composites was called fiber reinforced plastic—FRP for short—with various sub-sub-categories according to the particular kind of fiber employed, such as carbon fiber reinforced plastic (CFRP), aramid fiber reinforced plastic (AFRP), and glass fiber reinforced plastic (GFRP). In common usage, GFRP is also known as fiberglass, which can be a bit confusing, because fibers by themselves, whether glass fibers or any other kind, are only one half of the story; the resin is the other half. Don't make the mistake of thinking that fiberglass (that is, GFRP) is one thing and composites are another—fiberglass, in this sense, is a composite material. (The term "Fiberglas," with just one "s," is Owens-Corning Fiberglas, a registered trademark for the glass fibers themselves.) There are a couple of likely reasons for the term composite tending to replace the term FRP. First, fiberglass had been around for several years before fibers

In addition to being strong enough to withstand incredible g forces, Funny Car bodies must be lightweight too—light enough for one person to lift the entire body as shown here. That is the magic of FRP's. Photo by Michael Lutfy.

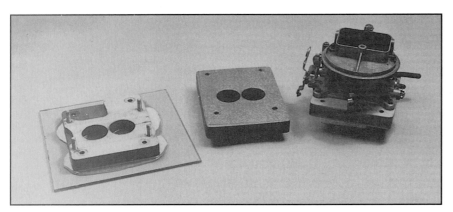
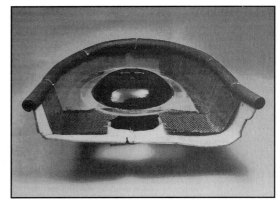

Carb spacers and air plenums are both constructed of FRP's. These are units from a race car built by James Watson. Photo courtesy Gougeon Brothers, Inc.

were developed that were stronger and stiffer than glass fibers, and so could be worked—together with a plastic resin—into composites that were also stronger and stiffer than those made with glass. To distinguish them from GFRP's and to suggest their superiority, composites made using these new fibers were called advanced FRP composites, which soon got shortened to just *composites*. The other reason may have to do with the idea implied by the second half of the expression; "reinforced plastic" suggests that it is the plastic that is doing the

job, and that the fibers just help a bit by reinforcing it.

If there is only a small amount of fiber reinforcement, then the properties of the end product—the combination of plastic and fiber—will be closer to those of the plastic than to those of the fiber. On the other hand, if there is a lot of fiber and only a little plastic, the resulting combination will vastly outstrip the strength and stiffness of the plastic resin by itself. Though there is no hard dividing line, at some point the concept shifts from a piece of plastic whose strength

FRP technology has been, of course, used to build boats for decades. Photo courtesy Escom Advertising Group, Inc.

Another use for FRP's: Water storage tanks. Photo courtesy Escom Advertising Group, Inc.

and stiffness are improved somewhat by the inclusion of some strong fibers, to a material in which the mechanical properties begin to approach those of the fibers, and where the plastic exists simply to hold the fibers in place—the reinforcement provides the strength; the plastic provides the shape; we might better call these *plastic matrix stabilized fibers*. *(Matrix means, approximately, "surrounding"; the lump of rock surrounding a gemstone in nature is called the matrix.)*

In truth, this last statement is somewhere between a gross oversimplification and plum wrong; we deal at some length with the structural properties of these materials in later chapters. For now we want to talk in general about their usefulness, and how they fundamentally differ from more familiar materials.

COMPOSITE CONSTRUCTION

We are accustomed to buying materials either as sheets (a sheet of aluminum, a 4x8 sheet of plywood), or as long stock (a length of one inch steel tube, an eight-foot 2x4), then turning them into some useful end product by cutting and other shaping operations, and by joining individual parts

"In truth, this last statement is somewhere between a gross over-simplification and plum wrong; we deal at some length with the structural properties of these materials in later chapters."

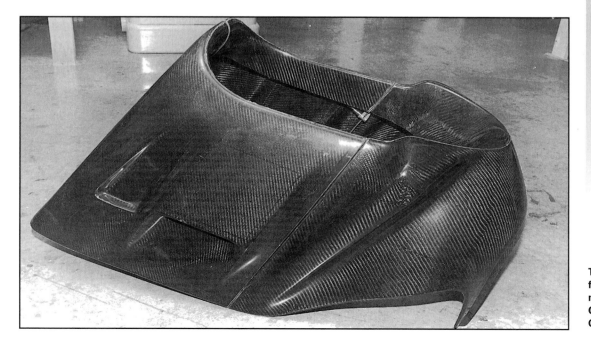

This is a racing motorcycle fairing built of carbon fiber, manufactured by Aerodine Composites. Photo by Jack Gladback.

FRP's are also used extensively in the construction of power generating windmills, and for airplane props as well. Photo courtesy Escom Advertising Group, Inc.

"Using this process as described, we can make planters, furniture, boats, automobile bodywork, shower stalls, machinery enclosures, even airplane parts."

together by nailing, gluing, welding, etc. In the case of formable metals, we can also bend and stretch the raw material into new shapes. When we're done, we can improve the appearance of the final product, and give it protection against weathering, by covering the outside with some sort of finish coating, like paint or electroplating.

Composites—FRP's, if you like—are quite unlike that. The raw materials comprise a thick, sticky liquid plus (usually) a roll of some floppy fabric. To make a useful product from these shapeless materials, the fabric is soaked in the resin, then set into a mold that defines the final contours. As just stated, all we've got is a mold full of gooey cloth, but if a certain second liquid is mixed into the plastic resin before using it to saturate the cloth, in the course of a few minutes or hours, the plastic magically transforms from a liquid to a solid. In this way we can produce any shape we have a mold for, with no nailing, no gluing, no welding and, except for a little trimming around the edges, no cutting.

Laminate

And if we want something thicker, all we have to do is add another layer of the same materials. In fact, the nature of the process allows us to vary the thickness from one area of the part to another, if we choose, by adding an extra layer (or several) in high stress areas. This process of building up a part by applying one layer of reinforcement and resin over another is called *laminating;* the end product is called a *laminate.* (Actually, even if there is only one layer, it is still called a laminate.) Because the resin perfectly captures all the surface detail of the mold, the surface of the finished product (at least the surface that was in contact with the mold) will be smooth and shiny, assuming the mold was also smooth. Depending on the particular kind of plastic resin we used, this finish surface may also be self-colored and completely weatherproof, so no painting or plating is required; FRP goods do not rust or rot.

Using this process as described, we can make planters, furniture, boats, automobile bodywork, shower stalls, machinery enclosures, even airplane parts. In fact, we can make anything that consists of a shaped thin shell, from palm-sized to hundred-foot-plus sailboats, more or less all in one piece, more or less all in one operation, with only the simplest kinds of tools and equipment, using comparatively low-skilled labor. Little wonder, then, the explosive growth in the use of fiberglass, starting from the end of World War II, when the resins were first developed.

Fiberglass Drawbacks

For all of these attractions, fiberglass has some drawbacks. Although it is fairly strong, it is only barely competitive with metals on that score—at least, that is the case when using the most popular variety of plastic resin and the most common arrangement of the glass fibers. Perhaps worse, conventional fiberglass compares poorly to metals in its stiffness—it is easy to bend, and so

In order for FRP's to compete with metals for uses in applications like this Indycar nose, where weight is important as well as strength, combinations of fibers and resins are needed that offer equal or better strength and stiffness than metals, in comparison with their weight. Photo by Michael Lutfy.

"That breakthrough occurred about twenty-five years ago, and since then we have seen a revolution in the way aircraft and race cars are made."

Large autoclaves are pricey items! But they are necessary for making high performance components, such as aircraft wings and race car tubs. Guy Levesque photo courtesy deHavilland, Inc.

springs around a lot in use unless it is made heavier than a comparable metal part. Neither of these considerations matters much for planters, or shower stalls, or furniture, where the other attractions of fiberglass are overwhelming. But for FRP's to compete with metals in mobile applications like automobiles and aircraft, where weight is important, combinations of fibers and resins are needed that offer equal or better strength and stiffness than metals, in comparison with their weight.

Modern Materials

That breakthrough occurred about twenty-five years ago, and since then we have seen a revolution in the way aircraft and race cars are made. Almost as dramatic are changes in the construction of weight-critical sporting goods, like tennis rackets and skis. Now, a small shop operator or amateur hobbyist cannot hope to make a composite chassis tub for an Indycar that could compete with last year's winner, or part of the wing of a passenger aircraft that would pass muster with the FAA, just by substituting advanced modern fibers and resins for traditional fiberglass materials, used in the way described above. To make state-of-the-art FRP composites, you need some fairly sophisticated facilities—the large autoclaves (think pressure cooker) used for heat-curing some of the modern resin systems are particularly pricey items. We discuss some of this in Chapter 8. Nevertheless, using little

Large trailer beds can be lightened considerably with FRP construction. This, of course, helps to improve fuel economy. Photo courtesy Escom Advertising Group, Inc.

more equipment than it takes to make a shower stall in traditional fiberglass, but substituting these advanced materials, it is possible to produce something which will match or beat the performance of a metal structure, at potentially lower cost! And there's still no welding, no machining, and certainly no nailing! (Even though these modern materials can be pricey, very little of them is used, and the capital investment in equipment is really very modest, compared with metal working).

There are at least half a dozen distinctly different kinds of fibers used to make FRP goods, and an equal number of basic types of plastic resin. Several of these, however, are so specialized and require such complex and expensive facilities for their fabrication that they lie far out of the mainstream. Outside of military contractors and research labs, the vast majority of FRP composite work (certainly more than 90%, probably more like 99%) employs one of three basic kinds of resin and one of three basic fiber types; we talk about each of these, and a couple of others, in the next two chapters.

In practice, the number of possible combinations is reduced even further, since two of the three fiber types are not compatible with one of the resins; that leaves six or possibly

seven material combinations. Nevertheless, it is not sufficient to simply identify that small handful of mixtures of materials and enumerate their properties; certain other factors can have as large an effect on the physical nature of the finished composite as the initial selection of material types. The proportion of fibers to resin is one of the more important of those factors; the geometric arrangement of the fibers is another—do they all lie in parallel lines, or are they woven into a cloth that has two principal axes? Or are they just randomly scattered about?

We discuss these issues in later chapters. The point we want to make here is that the various kinds of composite material differ enormously in properties, according to the particular combination of fiber and resin employed, and the way the fibers are arranged; to say "composite" without further explanation is like saying "metal" without specifying what kind of metal.

HOW TWO BRITTLE MATERIALS MAKE ONE TOUGH ONE

When cured hard, the resins used in FRP construction form a solid chunk of plastic that, by itself, is quite weak and brittle. Most

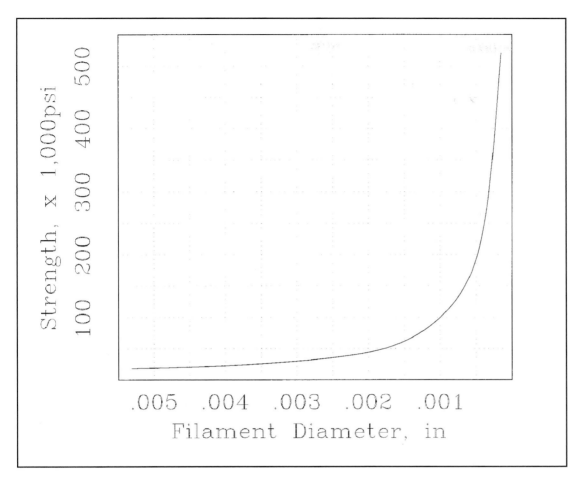

The strength of a filament increases dramatically as the filament is made smaller.

of the fibers used are also made from brittle materials—glass, for instance. How can one brittle material combine with another to pro- duce a tough, reliable composite?

We will use glass as an example here because it is not only the most common rein- forcing fiber material, it is also a notorious- ly brittle one. And, yes, it is real glass, chem- ically very similar to window glass, which we think of as not merely brittle, but also weak. In fact, glass is an enormously strong material, as long as it has a flawless surface. Even the best quality plate window glass, however, develops microscopic surface scratches and other invisible flaws starting from the moment it is made, just in the course of ordinary handling.

These flaws spell death when the glass is exposed to any significant load, because they form the starting point for cracks that, given half a chance, will spread through the bulk of the glass at, literally, the speed of sound. (Why some materials, like metals, can tolerate surface flaws, while others, like glass, cannot, is a subject that lies outside the scope of this book. Interested readers may wish to consult some of the references listed in the bibliography.)

When the glass is drawn out into very fine filaments, though, cracks become a much less significant problem for two reasons. First, the very fineness of the fiber means that, if contacted, it will just bend out of the way, rather than resist and get scraped as a result. Second, there is a minimum size of crack which glass will tolerate without its very high natural strength being affected. Although that minimum crack size is very

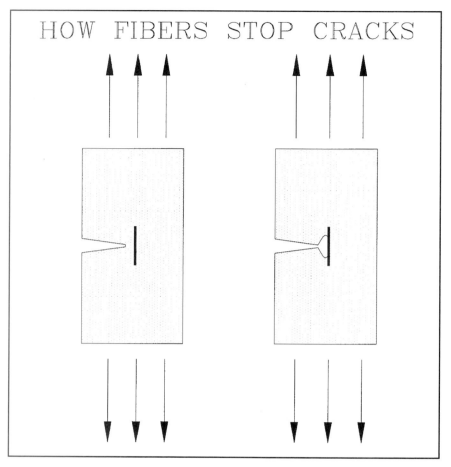

HOW FIBERS STOP CRACKS

Weak bond between fiber and resin matrix breaks at tip of crack, halting progress of crack. It is, in effect, blunted in the same way as a hole drilled at the end of a crack will serve as a stop.

incorporate some brittle fibers into the brittle resin, paradoxically we get a tough material. Here's why. Imagine, first, a surface crack in the resin. As it tries to advance deeper into the material, it soon encounters a fiber lying across its path. To make progress, the crack has to either break the fiber, too, or else detour around it. The fiber is very long, however, compared to the radius at the tip of the crack, so any attempt by the crack to skirt around the fiber means it has to grow much larger in radius. It is, in effect, blunted, in the same way as a hole drilled at the end of a crack will serve as a stop.

How about busting right through? Remember that the crack is in the resin; the fiber is intact. To break the fiber, the crack has to stress the fiber lengthwise, which it can only do via the surface connection between the two. This fiber-to-resin bond is much less strong than the fiber itself, so the bond breaks, leaving a gap between resin and fiber that likewise blunts the crack.

What is vitally important here is the strength of the bond between fiber and resin. It has to be weak enough to allow this crack-stopping mechanism to work, yet strong enough to carry the load from one fiber to another (see *How FRP Composites Carry Loads*, in Chapter 14), if we are to realize a useful fraction of the inherent strength of the fibers.

(Incidentally, the basic idea behind all this is by no means new; it dates back at least to the ancient Egyptians, who added straw to their clay bricks to reduce their brittleness. The biblical admonition to "make bricks without straw" was intended as a punishment—without the straw fibers to prevent them from splitting, the sun-dried clay bricks were uselessly weak and crumbly.) ∎

small, it is generally larger than the diameter of a single fiber, so the mere fact that the fiber exists in one piece means it probably does not contain any flaws above the critical size. Of course, if the surface of the fiber does become damaged, it is doomed. One job of the plastic matrix, then, is to shield the fibers from scratches. (It also protects the fibers from moisture, UV light, and other harmful factors in the environment.)

The matrix is also brittle as a bulk material; it, too, is unable to stop a crack from spreading right through it. But when we

FIBERS & FIBER FORMS

2

Fibers of a great many different materials—including jute, flax, asbestos, and fine metal wires—were used in the past to reinforce a plastic matrix; now, carbon, aramid, polyethylene and boron fibers grab the headlines. Yet by far the most common reinforcing fiber used in FRP composites over the past fifty years has been (and remains) E-glass—the same glass as used for electrical insulation.

TYPES OF FIBERS

E-Glass

There are many reasons for this predominance. Unlike organic fibers, glass is not subject to rot or other decay; unlike asbestos, it is not an inherent health hazard; unlike metal wires, it attaches strongly to many resin matrices. Glass fibers are also very low in cost and extremely strong.

The fibers are manufactured by first melting glass marbles in an electric furnace, then forcing the molten glass through hundreds of tiny holes in the base of the furnace. These fine, still fluid threads are further reduced in diameter by the tension applied to them as they are wound onto a storage reel. The result is a strand of filaments, each from 1/10,000 to 5/10,000 of an inch in diameter.

Strength—Virgin strands of E-glass are two to three times as strong as alloy steel. Subsequent operations of twisting them into

Chopped strand mat is commonly used in a variety of ways. This photo was taken at Hallett Performance Boats, a custom builder of high performance speed boats. Photo by Michael Lutfy.

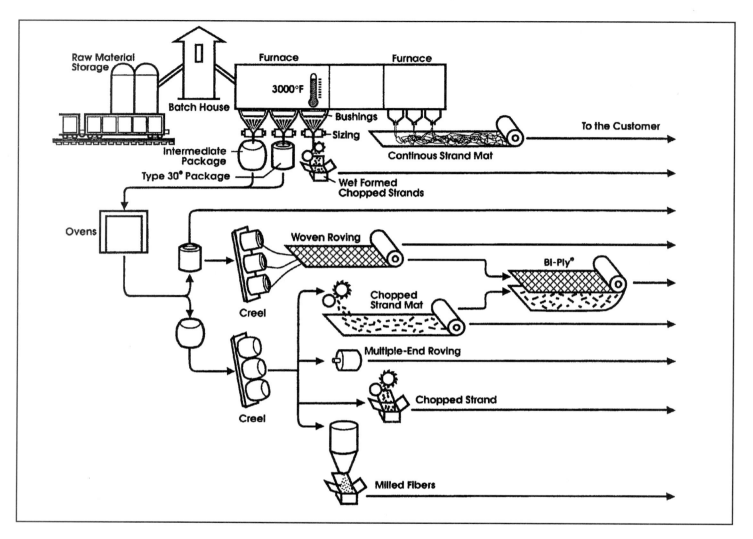

This schematic details how fiberglass reinforcements are made. Courtesy Owens-Corning.

yarn and weaving these yarns into a fabric reduces their strength; this plus the fact that a large fraction of any composite is the plastic resin matrix, which contributes little to strength, means that a finished laminate will exhibit no more than a quarter of the tensile strength of a single filament. Nevertheless, properly fabricated E-glass laminates compare very favorably to metals both in terms of raw strength and in the ratio of strength to weight.

Drawbacks—In another important respect, though, E-glass fibers are inferior to metals—they are less stiff. Although they will withstand a very large force before breaking, they deform considerably under load. (This subject is discussed more fully in Chapter 13.) On this basis, a laminate based on woven E-glass fabric is, at best, about one quarter as stiff as a part of comparable size made from aluminum, and barely one tenth as stiff as a steel part of the same dimensions. When the comparatively light weight of the glass laminate is taken into account, the picture improves somewhat; about forty percent of the stiffness-to-weight of a metal part can be achieved. While there are ways to address this shortcoming (as discussed in Chapter 13), considerable effort has been spent over the past few decades to develop fibers having greater stiffness than E-glass, as well as greater strength.

S-2 Glass™

To meet the demands of high performance aerospace and military applications during

Carbon fiber fabric looks just like black fiberglass. Photo by Jack Gladback.

the cold-war era, a chemically different form of glass was developed that was as much as one third stronger and more than 20% stiffer than conventional E-glass. Because this material, called "S-glass" (a trademark of Owens-Corning Fiberglas), was designed for the aerospace community, it was produced in small quantities and its cost reflected this fact, plus the lengthy and expensive certification process required for such applications.

The same material is now marketed for commercial use under the name S-2 glass fiber, without the accompanying paperwork that helps make aerospace stuff so costly; it remains, nevertheless, several times the price of E-glass. S-2 glass fiber is used commercially in filament wound pressure vessels, such as for the self-contained air supply used by firefighters. In its certified form, it is seen in such specialized aviation applications as helicopter rotor blades and the floor panels of some commercial aircraft.

Carbon Fiber (CF)

While S-2 glass fiber represented an advance over E-glass, it was by no means the final answer, and the search for even stiffer and stronger fibers continued. One result of this research effort—carbon fiber—became available in small quantities in the 1960's. An early application was as localized reinforcement in race car bodywork.

Carbon fiber is now the principal component used in Indycar chassis tubs. Photo by Michael Lutfy.

Tubs aren't the only items utilizing carbon fiber on an Indycar—it can also be found in brake cooling ducts (left) and rollbars. Photos by Michael Lutfy.

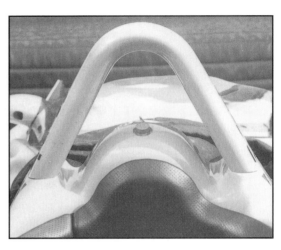

"Carbon fiber is now the principal material used in the construction of the chassis tubs of all Formula One and Indy race cars."

Different methods of producing carbon fiber have been developed, and there is much argument about their relative merits. Depending on the processing variables, the fibers can have their properties tailored toward greater strength, while giving up some stiffness, or toward greater stiffness, at the expense of strength. These variants are sometimes termed HS (high strength) and HM (high modulus) carbon, respectively but, in fact, the trade-off point in this exchange of properties can be struck anywhere, so this nomenclature may be misleading. There is even disagreement about what to call the stuff—some makers insist on the term "graphite"; others call it carbon. Whether it is made by high temperature processing of a fine filament of polyacrilonitrile (PAN), or by a less expensive method that uses coal tar as the starting point, the resulting product is more than twice as strong as ultra-high-strength alloy steel and, more important, three times stiffer.

Strength—Even when the fiber properties are diluted by the presence of the weak plastic matrix, carbon fiber incorporated into a structural laminate results in a product with superior strength to alloy steel, and only slightly inferior stiffness, when the comparison is done on the basis of volume. When weight is taken into account (finished laminates weigh about the same as magnesium), laminates based on carbon surpass all metals, and most other fiber reinforced plastics.

Brittleness—Despite concerns about the brittleness of carbon fiber (again, see Chapter 13), large sections of the rudder of the DC-10 aircraft were built in the 1970's using carbon fiber reinforced plastic (CFRP) composites. After many years of trouble-free experience in that and many other aircraft applications, the use of CF is now expanding rapidly. A substantial fraction of the Aerospatiale Airbus and of the Boeing 767 now involves CFRP. In the race car world, small amounts of CF were used as early as 1968, to provide local stiffening in the glass fiber body panels on the Ford GT40 that won the 24-hour race at LeMans that year. Carbon fiber is now the principal material used in the construction of the chassis tubs of all Formula One and Indy race cars.

Aramid (Kevlar™) Fiber

The generic name for this stuff is aramid, but since DuPont is the only outfit making it, everybody calls it "Kevlar"—DuPont's registered trademark for aramid. Kevlar fiber was introduced in the early 1970's, and its first major application was for ropes and other cordage, including tire cord; ballistic body armor (such as bulletproof vests and jackets) soon followed.

Variations—Like carbon fiber, aramid can have its properties adapted during manufacture to favor either stiffness or strength. The original tire cord ("stronger than steel," as claimed, though not spectacularly stiff) was Kevlar 29; the latest body armor uses an even higher strength version called Kevlar 129. A high modulus (high stiffness) version, Kevlar 49, is widely used for high performance composites; Kevlar 149 is a comparatively rare variation with even greater stiffness than Kevlar 49, but correspondingly less strength.

Features—Some versions of Kevlar are even stronger in tension than some kinds of carbon fiber, though they are less stiff. The compression strength of a Kevlar laminate, however, is limited by the apparent inability of any resin matrix to wet the fine fibrils that make up the fiber bundle; the outside of the bundle gets surrounded by the resin and attached to it, but individual fibrils do not. As a result, when a laminate using Kevlar reinforcement is loaded in compression (i.e. pushed on rather than pulled), the individual fibrils buckle and split away from the bundle when the stress exceeds about one fifth of what it would take in tension. Thus, the properties of the laminate become dominated by the characteristics of the resin matrix, and a Kevlar laminate's strength in compression is limited to relatively low values.

On the other hand, the gradual buckling of the fibers acting under the restraint of the matrix means that an aramid laminate does not fail in a brittle manner like those made from other structural fibers, but "yields," much like metals (see Chapter 13). In the process of failing in this way, a substantial amount of energy gets absorbed, which makes it attractive to manufacturers of aircraft and race cars. This property together with its all 'round toughness (which is why Kevlar is very difficult to cut cleanly) also makes it very popular for lightweight canoes and kayaks.

Kevlar can be used by itself or in combination with other fibers, either as one or more separate plies, or woven together with other fibers into a hybrid fabric. Combined in these ways with CF, it is widely applied in

race car construction as a hedge against the brittleness of carbon. Indeed, much of the credit granted by TV race announcers to "the incredible strength of carbon fiber chassis" following a race car accident should, in fact, be attributed to the aramid that is almost always visible flapping around the crumpled parts of the car. You won't see much crumpled carbon fiber in such cases—it just explodes into dust when it is grossly overloaded in this way.

Another significant feature of Kevlar is its light weight. An aramid-based laminate will typically wind up about twenty percent lighter than a part of the same thickness made using glass or, for that matter, carbon. Used as a direct substitute for glass reinforcement in lightly stressed body panels, Kevlar cloth yields a part that is about one fifth lighter yet stronger than the panel it replaces. A minor drawback of Kevlar not shared with glass or carbon is that it deteriorates slowly when exposed to ultraviolet light, so some sort of paint or other covering is needed to exclude UV from a Kevlar laminate. This hardly matters in practice because Kevlar is invariably combined with epoxy resin, which itself needs protection from UV, no matter what the reinforcement.

Composites made from Kevlar 49 com-

Aramid is better known to the public by its DuPont trademark, Kevlar™. The stuff is commonly used in bulletproof vests, tire cords, and items like kayaks and canoes. Photo courtesy DuPont.

"On a same weight basis, a Kevlar 49 laminate will give one half to one quarter the stiffness of one made from carbon fiber, depending on which version of carbon fiber it is compared with."

Yarns of two or more different fibers can be woven together to form a *hybrid* fabric. Here carbon fiber (black stripes) is *hybridized* with glass. Guy Levesque photo courtesy deHavilland, Inc.

pare unfavorably to carbon fiber composites in terms of stiffness, both on a per-volume and a per-weight basis. On a same weight basis, a Kevlar 49 laminate will give one half to one quarter the stiffness of one made from carbon fiber, depending on which version of carbon fiber it is compared with. On the other hand, its strength-to-weight ratio falls between that of HM and HS carbon and is many times better than that of steel, and it is at least as stiff in compression—per unit of weight—as high strength aluminum alloy.

Spectra Fiber™

This is a trademark name of a thermoplastic fiber material produced by Allied Signal, Inc. Thermoplastics are versatile materials that find widespread application in everyday life, largely because of the ease with which they can be formed to shape by heating until they become fluid, forced into a mold, then cooled until they return to a hard solid. Some thermoplastics, like nylon for instance, are also reasonably strong. Unfortunately, as a rule they seriously lack stiffness, which virtually excludes them from use in high performance structures where stiffness is usually as important as strength.

The reason for this lack of stiffness is that the long molecules that make up the material are folded or coiled, so forces that tend to extend the molecule do not actually work directly against the atomic bonds holding the molecule together; rather, they simply straighten out the kinks. A good way to visualize this is to think of a typical coiled telephone cord—it is very springy when tugged on, until all the coils are straightened out.

For polyethylene, at least, ways have recently been found to straighten out these molecular kinks during manufacture (by analogy, the phone cord is pulled straight), resulting in dramatically increased stiffness. Single strands of this material, called Spectra fiber, are comparable to glass in strength and to aramid in stiffness. Spectra, however, is very lightweight stuff (it floats!), and when this is taken into account, both strength and stiffness per-unit-weight are closer to the values associated with carbon fiber.

As with other reinforcing fibers, the numbers drop very substantially when finished laminates are considered, rather than individual fibers or strands. A unidirectional Spectra/epoxy laminate is likely to be a little less strong than one of glass or aramid, and about comparable to a glass laminate in stiffness. Again, however, when its light weight is factored in, the same unidirectional laminate will exhibit a strength-to-weight ratio slightly superior to one of glass or aramid, and a stiffness-to-weight ratio somewhere between the two.

Like Kevlar, but unlike glass and carbon, laminates made with Spectra fiber are weak in compression, and the effect is even more severe than in the case of Kevlar—about one tenth of the tensile strength is about all that can be expected. For this reason (and as explained in Chapter 13), its bending strength is low, too. Also like Kevlar, how-

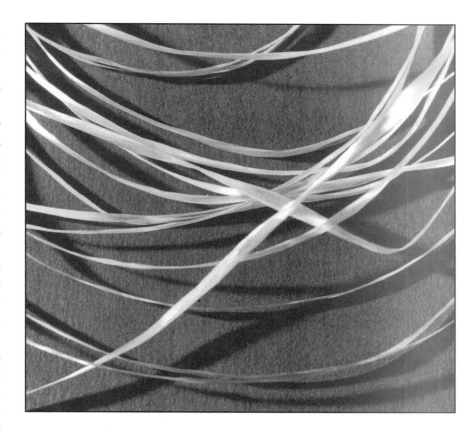

Continuous glass roving. Photo courtesy DOW Plastics.

ever, a very large amount of energy is absorbed when the material is failed in compression or buckling, so Spectra might be considered as one component in a hybrid fabric or laminate to perform the same kind of fail-safe function that might be achieved by aramid in the same application. Other drawbacks of Spectra are its low working temperature limit and its tendency to creep under load. Although it will tolerate the temperatures involved in the post-curing of epoxies (see Chapter 8), and recover almost all of its properties when again cooled to room temperature, if it is subjected to loads while hot it will run away from the load.

There are two versions of Spectra on the market at this writing, identified as "Spectra 900" and "Spectra 1000" (trademarks of Allied Signal, Inc.), the latter being slightly stronger and much stiffer, and is the version considered in the above comparisons. Unidirectional and woven bi-directional Spectra fabrics are available from a few weavers.

> "In the case of S-2 glass, carbon, aramid and Spectra, heat cleaning cannot be used, as the fibers would be damaged or destroyed by the extreme temperatures involved."

FIBER FINISHES

All the strong fiber materials discussed above tend to be rough on looms and other processing equipment, simply because they are so strong and stiff. Glass is particularly bad, as it is also highly abrasive and rapidly wears any surface it scrubs against. The fibers, too, tend to be damaged by contact with processing equipment, which is one reason why laminate properties always fall far short of the strength and stiffness numbers associated with individual strands. To minimize both effects, a *size* is usually applied to the surface of the fibers early in the manufacturing process.

In the case of glass, this material is often a mixture of oil and starch, which must be removed before the fibers are incorporated into a laminate, to ensure adhesion between the fiber and the resin matrix. The traditional way this is done is by burning the size off, leaving a heat-cleaned surface. Although such heat-cleaned glass can be made into an apparently satisfactory laminate, the bonds between the fibers and the plastic gradually deteriorate, so the laminate steadily becomes weaker. To overcome this problem, a coupling agent or finish is applied to the surface of the fibers immediately after heat cleaning. This ensures a more or less permanent set of properties for the finished laminate. Various coupling agents are used, each intended for use with one type of resin system, but "Volan A" is one common finish for glass which gives good results with polyester, vinylester and epoxy resins.

Cautions—There are many other finishes for glass cloth, and some of these are deliberately designed to prevent adhesion between fiber and resin—some peel-ply fabrics (see Chapter 7), for example, use exactly the same woven E-glass that makes strong laminates, but with a different surface finish. Also, dirt and moisture can degrade the finish. You must determine that the material you buy has a surface finish appropriate to the task at hand: materials should be bought from a reliable supplier that deals with the composites industry, not from surplus stores or dry-goods suppliers; fabrics should be kept stored in a dry cool place, wrapped to prevent contamination with dust, and used within a year or two, as the finish may deteriorate over time if left exposed to the atmosphere.

In the case of S-2 glass, carbon, aramid and Spectra, heat cleaning cannot be used,

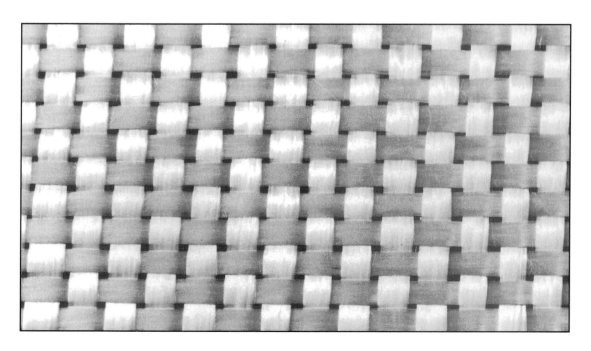

Here is a close-up of woven roving. Photo courtesy DOW Plastics.

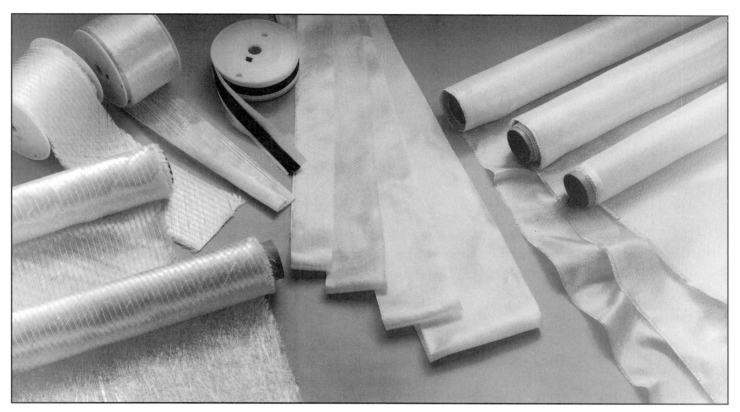

A few of the wide variety of glass fiber fabrics and tapes available. Photo courtesy Gougeon Brothers, Inc.

as the fibers would be damaged or destroyed by the extreme temperatures involved. Kevlar is cleaned by washing, producing a scoured fabric; no subsequent surface finish is applied. In the case of carbon and S-2 glass, the fibers are given a very thin surface coating of epoxy resin immediately after manufacture, which helps lubricate the passage of the fibers through subsequent processing operations and serves as the coupling agent in the laminating process.

WOVEN ROVING & FABRICS

In a later chapter we discuss some production processes, such as *pultrusion* and *filament winding,* which use individual fibers or strands as their starting point, and transform them directly into a useful product. Apart from these few situations, and the manufacture of ropes and other cordage, making use of continuous lengths of strong fibers requires that these one-dimensional goods be rearranged into a two-dimensional material; this is commonly achieved by weaving or knitting them into a fabric. While there are comparatively few primary manufacturers of the kind of strong fibers we are discussing, there are hundreds of independent weavers who work these fibers into a huge variety of woven sheet goods.

If bundles of untwisted strands, called *roving,* are woven together, the result is *woven roving*—a heavy, coarse product that allows thick laminations to be laid up quickly. Woven roving is used mainly in comparatively large scale articles like boats and highway transport trailers. Because of its thickness, woven roving is more difficult to wet out than thinner fabrics, and it does not readily conform to rapid changes in curvature. When a more drapeable material is needed, smaller strands are twisted together into yarns before being woven into a fabric.

"If bundles of untwisted strands, called roving, are woven together, the result is woven roving—a heavy, coarse product that allows thick laminations to be laid up quickly."

Woven roving is used mainly in comparatively large scale articles like boats and highway transport trailers. Photo by Michael Lutfy.

weave at wide intervals to hold the whole thing together. This yields a "unidirectional" fabric having all its strength in one direction. Others have an equal number of yarns running in both the lengthwise direction (called the warp), and the crosswise direction (the fill), producing a balanced, bi-directional fabric with equal strength properties in both the lengthwise and crosswise directions. (At angles between 0 and 90 degrees, though, the strength and stiffness is lower than when the load is exactly aligned with either the warp or the fill yarns.)

Weaves—For any basic type of weave, the strength and stiffness of the finished product depends on the volume fraction of fiber. Tight weaves give the best strength and stiffness values, but are more difficult to wet out; open weaves are easier to saturate, but yield a laminate which is less strong because of the greater proportion of weak plastic in relation to the amount of strong reinforcement.

(Basically, it is the twisting of the strands into yarns that distinguishes a fabric from woven roving.)

Fabrics—There is a whole galaxy of different fabrics, varying in properties according to the number of filaments in each strand, how many twists per inch the strands are given, how much space is allowed between consecutive rows of yarn, the pattern of the weave, and a number of other factors. Some fabrics have most of the fibers running one way, with just a light cross

One problem with woven goods of all kinds is the crimping of the yarns that occurs as they cross over and under each other. When loaded in tension the yarns try to straighten out, creating high local stresses where they cross yarns running in the opposite direction. This reduces the strength of

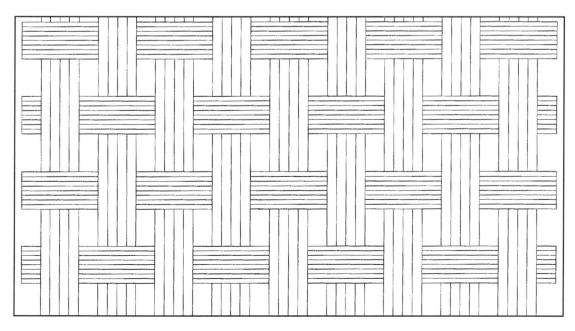

An illustration of a plain square weave.

woven fabrics considerably, in comparison with the same amount of fiber loaded in a perfectly straight line. Things are even worse under compression loads—the zigzag path of the yarn means that it is much more inclined to buckle when pushed on.

To some extent this problem is a function of scale—it is a matter of how far each strand or yarn is displaced sideways from a straight line path, in relation to its basic diameter or width. The problems are worst for fine weaves, especially in compression; coarse weaves do better. Woven roving, for instance, is distinctly stronger in compression than fabric, pound for pound. And weave patterns that vary from a simple over-one-under-one pattern also tend to show superior strength and stiffness than a simple *square weave*, as it is termed.

Satin and Other Weaves

Crimping of the yarns is reduced if each warp yarn crosses over more than one fill yarn before crossing under one. Such patterns are generally termed *satin weaves*, and are further identified by the number of successive fill threads that are skipped over; thus there are "five harness" and seven harness satins, etc. Because of this more advantageous geometry, laminates made using satin weave fabrics generally show slightly superior strengths than those made from square weave materials, especially when loaded in compression. Because the yarns in a satin weave can skew more easily than in a square weave, they have superior drapeability—it is easier to get them to conform to tight curves, especially ones with complex changes in radius. Also, satins yield a smoother surface finish than a square weave of the same weight. Taken together, these advantages often justify the slightly higher cost of satin weave fabrics.

Weave Patterns—Apart from conventional satins, there are also a couple of fairly common irregular weave patterns that deserve description. A satin weave with an

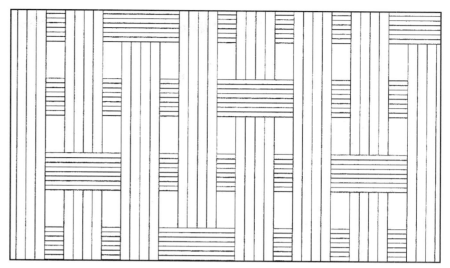

FIVE HARNESS SATIN WEAVE

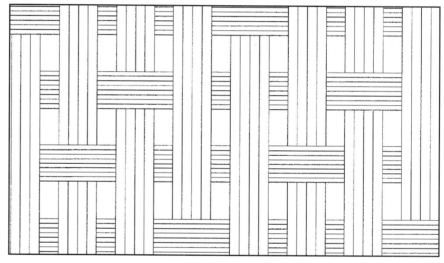

CROWFOOT SATIN

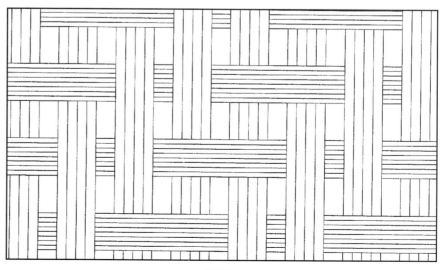

TWILL

Unidirectional aramid *pre-preg*. **Close packing of fibers offers maximum strength.** Guy Levesque photo courtesy deHavilland, Inc.

"*Despite the drawbacks, cloth woven from high performance fibers is widely used in aerospace, race car and marine applications, especially for complex shapes and for parts requiring strength in many directions.*"

over-three-under-one pattern is called a *crowfoot satin*, or sometimes just *crowfoot;* a *twill weave* has an over-two-under-one sequence that produces a distinctive diagonal pattern on the surface. Then there is a variation on a plain square weave in which both warp and fill are made up of pairs of yarns that parallel each other through the repeating pattern of the weave; this is known as a *basket weave*.

Compared to forms of reinforcement consisting of randomly oriented fibers, like mat (see below) and those produced with a chopper gun (see Chapter 9), the systematic arrangement of strands in woven products permits much closer packing of the fibers, with a corresponding improvement in mechanical properties. Nevertheless, the inevitable spaces between warp and fill means that, of the weight of a finished laminate made with woven fabric, 40% or more consists of resin. This is far more than the amount needed to carry loads from one fiber to another; the additional resin is just extra weight going along for the ride. Also, as already noted, each strand within the fabric is pre-buckled as it snakes through the weave, so much of the theoretical strength of the strong fibers goes unused, especially under compression loads.

Unidirectional (UD) Reinforcement

Despite the drawbacks, cloth woven from high performance fibers is widely used in aerospace, race car and marine applications, especially for complex shapes and for parts requiring strength in many directions. When the shape of the part and the pattern of loads permit it, however, there is a great advantage to be gained from the use of unidirectional reinforcement. When all the fibers run in the same direction they can be packed very closely together, so a fiber volume fraction of 75% or more can be achieved with unidirectional fabrics. (If the width of a roll of this material is greater than twelve inches, it is still called fabric, even though there may be no fill yarn whatsoever; narrower UD goods are termed tapes.) The high fiber loading allowed by the compact arrangement of the yarns, together with the absence of any of the kinking that characterizes woven fabrics, means that unidirectional goods yield the strongest and stiffest laminates.

Even when the principal loads in a structural part lie in one straight line, such as the vertical bending loads that predominate in a wing, there are almost always some secondary loads acting in other directions. (The drag forces on a wing, for example, act horizontally backwards). Because a purely unidirectional laminate cannot deal with these off-axis loads, it is common either to form some layers of such laminates with a woven fabric (often with its weave oriented at plus and minus 45 degrees to the axis of the UD material), or else to apply multiple layers of UD at an angle to one another, in somewhat the same way as plywood is arranged.

Mat and Veil

Even though woven glass cloth (in particular) is remarkably cheap, on the basis of pounds of load carried per dollar, the weaving process nevertheless adds something over the cost of the raw material in the form of roving or yarn. A cheaper form of reinforcement is *mat*, which is a felt-like material consisting of fibers chopped into short lengths, and held together with a resin-soluble binder. As soon as the mat is saturated with resin, the binder dissolves, which allows the fibers to be easily nudged around, so mat will conform to much tighter curves than fabrics, especially when the material has to be stretched to reach into an inside corner or other depression. Woven materials simply will not stretch at all. This makes working with mat easy, so it is naturally very popular with small shops and hobbyists.

Strength & Stiffness—The random orientation of the fibers in mat means that laminates made from this material have *isotropic* strength and stiffness characteristics— meaning they are equal in all directions. While it is in many cases advantageous for a material to exhibit the same response whatever the direction of the imposed loads, this benefit is only obtained, in the case of mat, by accepting very low levels of overall strength. The inferior strength and stiffness is partly due to the short fiber length, but mostly because the random arrangement of the fibers prevents them from being packed tightly together, as in woven goods.

Appearance—Appearance counts, of course, so it is common for a product to be judged on the basis of both how well it performs and how good it looks. While a laminate made using only woven (or unidirectional) reinforcement is always going to be stronger than one made with random reinforcement, such as chopper gun work (see Chapter 9) or mat, the slight shrinkage of the resin that occurs on curing tends to telegraph the weave pattern through to the visible finished surface, impairing its appearance. To prevent this *print through,* it is common practice to make the first layer immediately adjacent to the gel coat (see Chapter 4) out of mat, even when most of the laminate is made using the stronger woven goods.

It is also usual to use a layer of mat

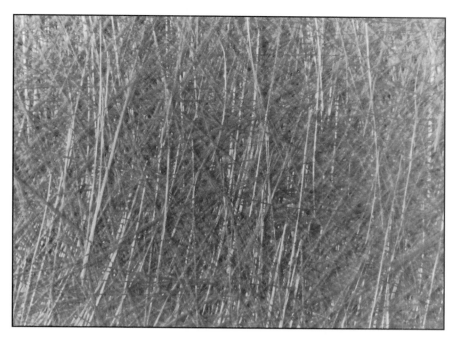

between consecutive plies of woven roving, and occasionally other forms of woven reinforcement. When multiple layers of woven goods are laminated together, a resin rich zone is created between layers because the tiny humps and hollows of the weave do not mesh perfectly. A layer of mat helps to bond the adjacent layers of woven material, reducing the risk of *de-lamination*—the splitting apart of the separate layers that make up the laminate.

Needled Mat—A variation of mat is available which has been *needled*, producing a fuzzy surface with some fibers sticking out from the surface at near right angles. Because the protruding fibers provide a more solid connection between layers, needled mat is sometimes preferred for these cushion layers. A light spray of chop from a chopper gun (see Chapter 9) is also sometimes used for this same purpose, and some combination materials have been introduced fairly recently that consist of a layer of woven material (usually roving), with a layer of mat either lightly stitched or needled to its surface, or else simply attached by the same resin-soluble binder that holds the mat together.

Mat is produced in a continuous process

Chopped strand mat consists of fibers that are chopped into short lengths, and held together with binder that dissolves once resin is applied. It is relatively easy to work with and inexpensive, so it is popular with small shops and home enthusiasts. Photo courtesy DOW Plastics.

"Veil is sometimes used for the same texture-blocking reasons as mat when there is concern about print-through of a fabric weave."

by directing chopped strands onto an endless wire screen belt (see also pre-forms, in Chapter 9), while strong fans suck air through the back side of the screen. As fibers accumulate on the surface, the air flow is locally blocked, which helps redistribute the material toward less obstructed areas, creating an even covering. As a result of this method of manufacture, there is a practical limit to the thickness that can be built up in one go, so mat of more than about one ounce per square foot is usually made up of two or more layers of thinner material, essentially just held together by the binder. It is often possible and convenient to split these two layers apart. Mat of 1.5 ounces per square foot, for instance, can usually be separated into two thicknesses each of about 3/4 oz.

Common square weave boat cloth typically weighs 6 oz. or 8 oz. per square yard, but an enormous variety of styles is available in a range that extends from less than 1 oz./sq. yd. to more than 40. Both cloth and mat are sold on rolls of a few standard widths—38-in. and 60-in. widths are the most common—but it seems worth mentioning that while the weight of cloth is expressed in ounces per square yard, mat is sold on the basis of weight per square foot. Confusing, but it is the industry's standard way of doing things.

Surfacing Veil—There is also a product that generally resembles extremely thin mat, called *surfacing veil*, which is made by swirling one continuous, unchopped strand onto the forming screen. Veil is sometimes used for the same texture-blocking reasons as mat when there is concern about print-through of a fabric weave. Because veil has comparatively little fiber per unit of area, it produces a layer that is rich in resin and so it is also sometimes used as the final layer of a laminate, rather than the first, to improve both surface appearance and resistance to weathering. Veils are available 0.010-in. or 0.020-in. thick. Beware: some veils have a finish which is not compatible with epoxy resins. ∎

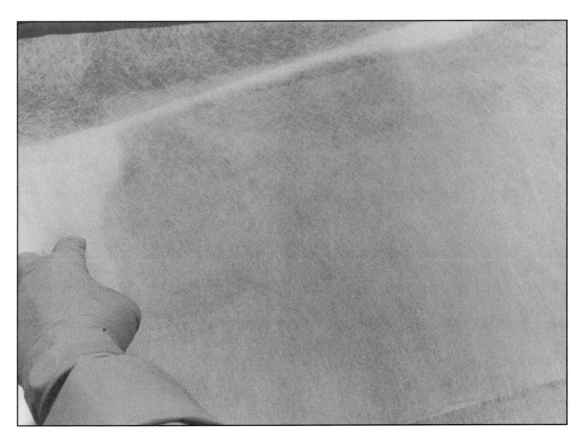

Surfacing veil looks like very thin mat. It is sometimes used as a cover to prevent print-through of fabric weave. Photo courtesy DOW Plastics.

RESINS

3

The strong fiber materials we have discussed in the previous chapter are useless by themselves, except perhaps for ropes. Likewise, fabrics woven from these fibers, while enormously strong, have no inherent shape. To encapsulate the fibers and provide the shape, we need a matrix–a solid surrounding of some kind.

Almost anything that can exist both as a liquid and as a solid can form a matrix for strong fibers, and there are many different matrix materials used in modern engineering, including concrete, ceramics, and metals. The most versatile and easily worked matrix materials, though, are *thermoset plastic resins*. "Thermoset" means they change permanently from liquid to solid as a result of a chemical reaction, and cannot be re-melted, unlike the more familiar thermoplastics, like nylon or PVC, which soften when heated and harden when cooled. The thermosets used in composites work are *polyesters, epoxies, and vinylesters; phenolic* resins are also used in some specialized applications, as noted below.

At its simplest, the making of a composite part amounts to saturating some reinforcement with resin, placing it into or onto a mold surface that defines the shape, then waiting for the resin to get hard. The magic part is the transformation of the resin from liquid to solid. The chemistry of thermoset-

The most versatile and easily worked matrix materials are thermoset plastic resins, which include polyesters, epoxies and vinylesters. The epoxies are most critical as to the mixing proportions, so some sort of metered dispensing system is desirable. Photo courtesy Gougeon Brothers.

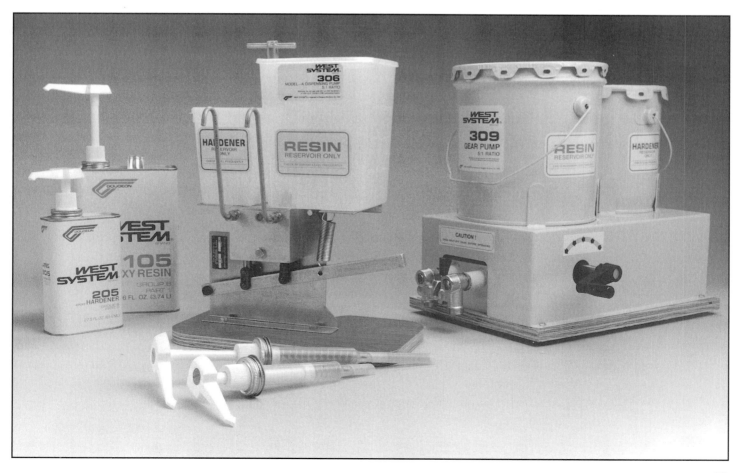

23

Resin and catalyst can co-exist peacefully for months side-by-side. But mix them together, and a chemical reaction takes place that causes the resin to cure, or turn it into a solid. Polyester (shown above) or vinylester resins don't require critical measurements, unlike epoxy, which must be mixed with its hardener in exact proportions. Photo by Michael Lutfy.

ting plastics is incomprehensible to most non-chemists. Fortunately, that doesn't matter, because the stuff works just fine if you follow the instructions. Nevertheless, it is useful to have a picture in your mind of what is going on: first so that all the Dos and Don'ts make sense; second so you can anticipate how you might need to change materials or procedures when you tackle a new job for the first time, and finally to help troubleshoot problems. We take a good crack at describing this phenomenon in the adjacent sidebar, but here's how it works in practice.

RESIN SYSTEMS

All these thermosetting plastic resin systems have two components—the resin and a *catalyst* or *hardener.* Separately, they can be stored for months or years. When the two are mixed together in the right proportions, however, a chemical reaction takes place that begins to *cure* the resin—to turn it into a solid. During the cure, the mixture passes through several distinct stages on its way to becoming a hard solid. The cure cycle always follows the same sequence, with all thermoset resins designed to cure at room temperature, even though the chemistries of polyesters and epoxies are completely different, and even though the material added to the resin is called a *catalyst* when the resin is polyester or vinylester, but is called a *hardener* or *curing agent* when the resin is epoxy.

How Resins Cure

At first, nothing seems to happen. Then, after a time that might be a matter of seconds or of hours, depending on the particular combination of materials and the temperature, the liquid will begin to give off heat. This *exotherm* can be dramatic and destructive if a large amount of material is all curing at once. As noted in the sidebar, the chemical reaction that causes the solidification is both propelled by heat and creates heat itself, so you can get into a sort of spiral where everything goes faster and faster and eventually burns the shop down. This only occurs if someone goofs seriously, of course, but the relevant point is that the rate of the reaction at any moment depends on how hot the material is, and that depends on the quantity of stuff reacting in relation to its exposed area, so a cupful of resin will cure faster in the cup than it will if the same amount of resin is spread out over a large area.

A GUIDE TO THE "COLD CURE"

The polyester resins used for FRP work are, by themselves, either solids at room temperature, or at best very thick, sticky liquids. To dilute the polyester enough to permit easy wetting-out of a reinforcing fabric, it is usually supplied mixed with somewhere between 30% and 50% of another plastic called *styrene monomer*, a watery thin, clear liquid with a strong odor—the familiar fiberglass shop smell. Depending on the temperature it is stored at, this syrupy liquid mixture would gradually harden into a solid, as the two plastics become cross linked.

You can imagine each liquid as made up of long, thin molecules, like strands of cooked spaghetti. Because the strands get tangled up with each other, the liquid is viscous. The cross links are like rungs on a ladder—they connect one strand to another, turning a viscous liquid into a hard solid. At a temperature just above freezing, this process might take years; in a poorly ventilated, tin-roofed shed in tropical heat, it will happen in a few days or weeks. To prevent this premature hardening, an inhibitor is added by the manufacturer, giving a useful shelf life of several months at room temperature.

What actually drives this cross linking is heat, but the process is greatly speeded up, at any temperature, by the addition of a catalyst—usually a material called MEKP (methyl ethyl ketone peroxide). Adding less than 2% of MEKP to such an inhibited resin would cause it to gel in just a few hours at room temperature. A few hours, though, is still too long for practical use. Quite apart from shop space and molds being tied up for an unacceptably long time, the resin would have plenty of time to flow downhill to the lowest point in the mold, draining away from inclined surfaces and leaving areas of dry reinforcement behind. What is clearly needed is more heat. Heated molds are one solution; use of an accelerator is another.

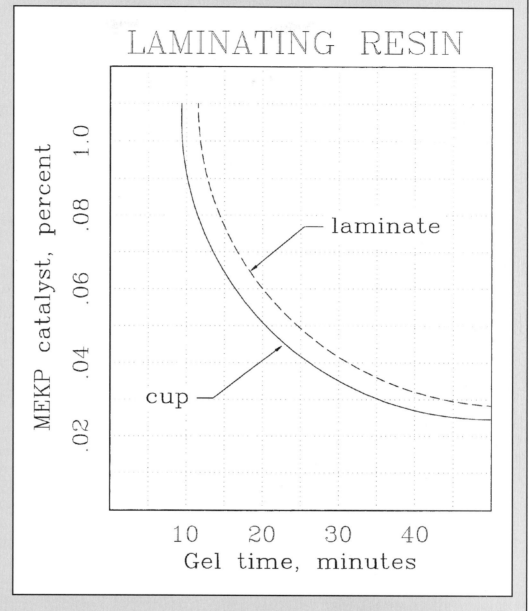

LAMINATING RESIN

MEKP catalyst, percent

Gel time, minutes

A GUIDE TO THE "COLD CURE" (continued)

When certain combinations of chemicals are mixed together, they react violently and give off energy in the form of heat. If MEKP catalyst, for instance, is mixed with something called cobalt naphthenate (or CoNap, for short), the result is ferocious—if there is more than just a little of each, there will be an explosion! So, if we mix just a little CoNap into the polyester/styrene blend (0.01% is typical), then add a small amount of MEKP catalyst, the reaction between it and the CoNap will create a substantial amount of heat. Now, the cross-linking itself produces heat, and both the rate of cross-linking and the effectiveness of the catalyst also increase as the temperature rises, so the resin mix will very rapidly harden or cure. A typical general purpose polyester resin with 0.01% CoNap and 2% MEKP will begin to gel in just a few minutes—just slowly enough to permit a worker to fully wet-out the reinforcement, yet fast enough to prevent resin drain-out. This combination of an accelerator like cobalt naphthenate and a catalyst like MEKP is what makes the room-temperature or cold curing process possible. The slightly purplish hue of general purpose polyester resin is evidence of the presence of CoNap. You may occasionally encounter the use of dimethyl aniline (DMA) as the accelerator and benzoyl peroxide (BP) as the catalyst; for some reason, this combination seems to be used in polyester-based body fillers—the BP is the yellow stuff in the squeeze tube.

A final possibility for curing styrenated resins, like polyester and vinylester, is by the use of ultraviolet (UV) light. Photo-initiated resins, as they are also called, have been around for a long time; in fact, the very first room temperature cure process for polyesters depended on UV for curing, though using a now obsolete chemistry. UV curatives are available blended into resins from some manufacturers (you can't buy the magic ingredient by itself), and these offer some striking advantages. Provided the dispensing and lay-up is done entirely under a "safe" light, the working time for the resin (pot life) is unlimited—it won't even begin to cure until it sees ultraviolet light, which permits low stress working. The exotherm of such resins when they do cure is also notably lower than conventional MEKP cures, which allows the build up of very thick sections without concern about excessive heat. On the downside, the resins are up to a half more expensive, and all of the resin has to be exposed to UV in order to cure—areas lurking in shadow will not set up hard, and any kind of core or insert that shades resin beneath will prevent that area from ever curing. Pigmented gel coats are obviously not candidates for this process.

While the above strictly pertains only to polyester resins, vinylesters are chemically quite similar to polyesters. And even though the chemistry of epoxies is entirely different, the principles remain similar, except it is worth bearing in mind that styrenated polyesters and vinylesters are "trying" to cure from the moment they are brewed—they require an inhibitor to give them a decent shelf life. With epoxies, on the other hand, no hint of a cure will occur in the absence of a hardener. This has ramifications for shelf life (epoxies will last a very long time in storage), and helps explain why thorough mixing is vital for satisfactory results with epoxy.

The effect of the heat outpaces the gradual solidification at first, so the viscosity of the resin drops for a short time. (This can be significant in practice, because the resin may now be inclined to flow, under the effect of gravity, toward the lowest point in the mold, leaving areas on vertical surfaces that are starved of resin.) Then, while the exotherm is still building, the resin thickens to the point where it will no longer flow; this is called the *gel* stage. Especially with polyester resins, the increase in viscosity that occurs before gelation can vary considerably in nature. Some brands just gradually thicken and become increasingly sticky and "stringy"; others remain workable right up to the bitter end, then go off with a bang, so to speak. These latter are much more pleasant to work with.

Soon after, the resin takes on a kind of crumbly consistency, like cheese, and the temperature begins to decline. A piece of reinforcement saturated with resin that has reached this stage has a leathery texture, and will cut cleanly with a sharp knife. It is often possible to take advantage of this *green cure* to trim the edges of a part, rather than face the hard work and flying dust involved in sawing through the same material once it has fully hardened. This, too, is the stage when body fillers based on polyester resin, though too soft and gummy for sanding, can be easily shaped and carved. Epoxy is rarely used in this way, but the same effect occurs. This is also the ideal time to add extra layers of reinforcement—the exotherm from the previous layers has died down, so the new material will not be kicked into overactivity by heat, but the chemical crosslinking (see sidebar p. 25) is not yet complete, so a true chemical bond can develop between the new resin and the old.

After this brief period of green cure, the resin grows noticeably harder—a coin tapped on the surface will ring. A part that has reached this stage can usually be pulled from the mold and handled without risk of distortion. Nevertheless, the hardening continues for some time, and it may take days or weeks before the measured hardness of the resin surface stops rising.

Polyester

Polyester is not the great grand-daddy of thermoset resins, phenolic is. But polyester was the first one that could be persuaded to cure at room temperature, which made it possible to build really big objects with a low capital investment. That led to the postwar boom in fiberglass boat building, which is most of the reason why polyester resins and woven glass fiber fabric are so thoroughly developed, so widely available, and so cheap.

Although other resin systems are starting to make inroads, especially for high performance applications, the overwhelming majority of FRP work (surely more than ninety percent) is based on polyester. Epoxies usually produce stronger laminates than polyester, and absolutely must be used with aramid reinforcement—the surface of Kevlar just doesn't seem to connect well with polyester.

Advantages—Beyond the fact that they are cheaper than epoxies by half or more, polyesters remain predominant for the very good reason that they are easy to work with. First, they are low in viscosity, which means that they can be poured, pumped, and mixed easily, and they more readily wet-out reinforcement than do the more viscous epoxies. (This also makes them easier to spray, but that is a secondary consideration, because the spraying of epoxy is to be avoided anyway, in view of the very severe health hazards.) Second, the cure rate of polyester can be adjusted over a wide range by varying the amount of catalyst added, which is absolutely not the case with epoxy. Finally, polyester is arguably less hazardous to work with than epoxy.

Drawbacks—Polyester has some drawbacks, however. The results with glass, as

> *"Beyond the fact that they are cheaper than epoxies by half or more, polyesters remain predominant for the very good reason that they are easy to work with."*

The many advantages of working with polyester resins make them practical and popular with the boat building industry. There are, however, several drawbacks as well. Chief among them is the fact that the styrene monomer in polyester resin, which is a VOC (volatile organic compound), is becoming increasingly regulated. This is creating a nightmare for some large boat builders in California, where such emissions are strictly regulated. Photo by Michael Lutfy.

noted, are generally inferior in strength and impact resistance to similar laminates made with epoxy. I believe that this is at least partly because of shrinkage. Polyester reduces in volume as much as 7% when it changes from a liquid to a solid, which corresponds to a linear shrinkage of about 2%. Of course, a part made in a ten-foot-long mold does not end up nearly three inches short, because the shrinkage of the resin is fought by the reinforcement. As the resin tries to shrink, the fibers oppose it, and they lie almost entirely in planes along and across the part. As a result, the length and width contract only slightly, but the thickness is reduced rather a lot. Also as a result, the resin is *pre-stressed*, which occupies a useful fraction of its strength. (This is also why polyester makes a poor adhesive—the joint is very nearly broken already by the locked in stresses caused by the shrinkage that occurs on curing.)

Polyester is also generally unsuitable for use in combination with advanced reinforce-ments like carbon and Kevlar; it does not have the same temperature tolerance as epoxy, particularly post-cured epoxy (see Chapter 8); and it does not form good secondary bonds. To explain this last point, there are times when it is impossible or inadvisable to produce a lay-up all in one go—a very thick lay-up, for instance, where too much exothermic heat would be built up if it were all made at once. But if the first lay-up is thoroughly cured when the next is added, there can be no actual chemical bond between the new and the old sections, so the connection between the two will be purely mechanical—they are simply glued together. The poor adhesive qualities noted above make polyester distinctly inferior for this task. Finally, polyester smells terribly.

Styrene Monomer—Actually, it is the styrene monomer that stinks (see sidebar p. 25)—that's most of what you're actually smelling when you sniff fiberglass. This can cause grief with neighbors and landlords; it can cause distress at home when you return from work reeking of styrene; perhaps worse, it can cause trouble with the government. Styrene monomer is a *Volatile Organic Compound* (VOC), and as such it is subject to increasingly stringent regulations, both from the point of view of the level of exposure for workers inside the shop and from the perspective of the total emissions from the plant into the atmosphere. This is becoming a nightmare for some large boat shops in California, where the regulations are most strict.

Apart from changing to a completely different resin system, there are a number of possible approaches to reducing the amount of styrene introduced into the atmosphere. First is the reduction or elimination of spraying polyester of any sort; roller coaters and fabric impregnators (see Chapter 5) are, to some extent, replacing spray guns. Then there are substitutes for styrene; resin manufacturers talk about such things as vinyl toluene and paramethyl styrene as alternative monomers that will cross link with polyester. Another approach is the use of styrene reduced polyester; instead of the usual 40%-45% of styrene, the proportion is reduced to below 35%. This yields a more viscous, stickier resin, which makes it more difficult to wet out the reinforcement.

Styrene Suppressed Resins—Finally, there are styrene suppressed resins. If you have read or heard anything about FRP work, you will probably have encountered a distinction made between *laminating* resin and *surfacing* resin. A feature of conventional polyester blends is that their cure is inhibited by exposure to the oxygen in the atmosphere. What that means is that, while the bulk of the resin will cure solid, a very thin layer on the surface will remain tacky. This helps subsequent layers to bond to one another, so this laminating resin is used wherever additional plies are to be added. If laminating resin is used for the last ply, however, the sticky surface is a nuisance. To eliminate this uncured layer, a *surfacing* or

waxed resin is available. As the latter name implies, it contains wax, which gets driven to the surface as the resin cures, forming a film that excludes the air and allows the cure to go to completion. This barrier between the resin surface and the air also reduces the evaporation of styrene into the atmosphere, and is the basis for many styrene suppressed resins. Of course, a surface covered with wax is not one that you want to apply additional layers of laminate to; if a resin containing wax is used for laminating, either the whole lay-up has to be done at once, or else the wax has to be removed from the last cured layer before adding more. (To simplify the inventory, it is quite practical to purchase only de-waxed laminating resin and add a little *wax solution*—simply wax dis-

Building big projects requires mass quantities of resin. Hallett Performance Boats buys their polyester resin by the 55-gallon drum. However, employees only use small quantities at a time, for obvious reasons having to do with cure time. Photo by Michael Lutfy.

"On the other hand, epoxies are distinctly trickier to handle than polyester, introduce some specific health risks, and both they and their curing agents are significantly more expensive."

solved in styrene monomer—to the final batch used for the last layer of a multi-plied laminate. If you can't find wax solution, you can make your own—see Chapter 4.)

Types of Polyester

Polyesters can be formulated to cure with different characteristics, from extremely hard and brittle to something more like hard rubber. For most automotive work, the appropriate resins are those used for boat building, which lie somewhere in between, trading off hardness for a degree of flexibility that helps reduce cracking. These formulations will almost always be pre-accelerated (see sidebar p. 25)—CoNap and/or DMA will be mixed in the resin as supplied. Finally, we should note that there are two kinds of polyester resin—*orthophthalic* or "ortho," and *isophthalic* or "iso." The difference between them is chemistry and price; iso is slightly more expensive, and better.

Epoxy

Laminates made using epoxy generally have greater strength and better chemical resistance than those using polyester, especially at higher temperatures. Epoxy also shrinks less than polyester—40%-50% less, depending on the curing agent(s) used. As well, some fibers like Kevlar and carbon are incompatible with polyester. On the other hand, epoxies are distinctly trickier to handle than polyester, introduce some specific health risks (see Chapter 6), and both they and their curing agents are significantly more expensive.

Handling Epoxy—The handling difficulties stem, first, from the fact that the epoxy resins used in composite fabrication are more viscous and sticky than polyesters. This makes it more difficult both to ensure complete mixing of the resin and hardener, and to wet out the reinforcement, adding to labor and increasing the risk of areas of incompletely saturated reinforcement. It is worth emphasizing here the necessity for

complete and thorough mixing of epoxies. To ensure that all of the resin is mixed with all of the hardener, some suppliers urge that you change containers twice during the mixing. Here's one way: pour the hardener from cup "A," into the resin in cup "B," scraping the sides of the container to get as much as possible out, and mix thoroughly; then pour this mixture back into cup "A," again scraping the container, and continue to mix; the mixture is then poured into a third cup, "C," and mixed again. This sounds a bit obsessive, but there is little doubt that most problems with epoxy result either from an incorrect resin-to-hardener ratio, or from inadequate mixing.

Thinners—Thinners (sometimes called *diluents* are available to reduce the viscosity of epoxy resins. Although these are *reactive* diluents—they cross link with the resin in much the same way that styrene does with polyester—they should be employed with caution. Diluents may reduce the strength and chemical resistance of the finished product, and certainly will if added in sufficient quantity to make the resin as easily worked as polyester. And some are particularly toxic (again, see Chapter 6).

Mixing—The second problem is that, with one exception, the hardeners used with epoxies must be mixed with the resin in a specific proportion, and some require very accurate measurement indeed. Miss by more than a smidgen and the result can be anything from an incomplete cure, leaving a weak part, to no cure at all. What is more, this intolerance of variation in the hardener-to-resin ratio means that the cure rate of epoxy systems generally cannot be adjusted by varying the amount of hardener—if you want to speed up the cure, you have to either pick a different curing agent or increase the temperature of the workspace, or the mold.

RTC Curing Agents

The very strongest laminates are produced with epoxy systems (the combination of resin and hardener) that cure at elevated temperatures—from somewhat over 100F to more than 350F. There are, however, room temperature curing (RTC) systems, though even most of these will benefit from a post-cure heating cycle, especially in terms of their chemical resistance and retention of strength at higher temperatures. This is discussed further in Chapter 8. Unlike polyesters, where the cobalt naphthenate accelerator/MEKP catalyst curing system is almost universal for room temperature work, there are many completely different curing agents for epoxy.

Polyamides—Perhaps the safest RTC curing agents are polyamides, sometimes called *nylon hardeners* (nylon is a polyamide). These are very viscous liquids with a distinct odor of ammonia that are usually mixed with the resin in a ratio of somewhere between 1-to-1 and two parts resin to one part hardener. Polyamides are, in fact, the only epoxy hardeners that permit this sort of wide range in resin-to-hardener ratio. Varying the proportions won't much affect the cure rate, though; what it does is vary the resulting cured solid from flexible and damage tolerant through hard and brittle. The more polyamide hardener, the more flexibility and the less hardness the cured epoxy exhibits.

The very high viscosity of polyamides (somewhere between corn syrup and ketchup) adds to the difficulties created by the resin, itself usually inconveniently thick. Adding diluent to the maximum proportion recommended by the supplier may achieve a manageable viscosity, though it will still be very thick compared to polyester. Polyamides also produce a very sluggish cure—in warm weather you can figure on waiting a day before it is safe to pull a part from the mold; if the shop is cold. . . well, you may as well take this week off. Never mind, as long as it doesn't freeze, it will get there eventually.

Amine Hardeners—Much faster acting

are the *amine* hardeners. What are called unmodified amines, such as diethylenetriamine (DETA) and triethylenetetramine (TETA), are somewhat dangerous to handle, but you are not likely to encounter them—few packagers supply them for use in hand lay-up operations. Modified amine curatives (curative is yet another term for hardeners) are, we are assured, much less hazardous, though you surely wouldn't want to use them for mouthwash.

All these amine curing agents are highly active—they are commonly used in concentrations below twenty-five percent, and sometimes as little as eight percent, and will cure at room temperature, at least to the point where the part can be handled, in as little as a couple of hours. Of course, the pot life drops correspondingly—you will have to use up the mixed batch within a few minutes. Their viscosity is also low, but they are generally used in such small proportions that this does not really help much in reducing the viscosity of the mixture.

Although most curatives for RTC epoxies fall into one of the above families, there are dozens of suppliers offering literally hundreds of different hardeners, and there are also catalysts available to speed up the curing process when used in combination with certain hardeners; to sort the whole lot out by yourself, you would need a Ph.D. in organic chemistry. Alternatively, you could recognize that, while there are dozens (perhaps hundreds) of formulators and packagers, there are very few companies that actually make the base epoxy resins (Shell, DOW, CIBA Geigy, Reichold and there may be one other), and get specific recommendations from one of them. Even though they may not sell the materials directly to you, their technical representatives are unfailingly helpful and informative. Another approach is to buy materials as a package—resin, curative, diluent, parting (mold release) agent—from one of the many suppliers that cater to the home-built aircraft

"Polyamides also produce a very sluggish cure— in warm weather you can figure on waiting a day before it is safe to pull a part from the mold; if the shop is cold . . . well, you may as well take this week off."

> "The only interest phenolic has for us here, then, is its use in pre-pregs, in which case it is (like the epoxies also used in pre-pregs) partially cured, and most of the inconvenient by-products have already been removed."

and boat kit market.

Vinylester

Vinylester resins were first developed about twenty years ago, for application in corrosive environments, such as linings for pipes and tanks full of nasty chemicals. While perhaps not strictly correct, it is approximately true to describe the vinylester molecule as like epoxy at one end and like polyester at the other, and laminates made with vinylester come close to those of epoxy in strength and other mechanical properties. Kevlar can be used with vinylester.

Yet vinylesters are about as easy to use as polyester, and use the same accelerators and curing agents. (Some vinylesters are supplied without an accelerator; the user has to add CoNap and/or DMA just prior to mixing in the MEKP catalyst.) Like polyester, they contain large amounts of styrene. Their price falls between those of polyester and epoxy. I am not aware of any vinylester-based gel coats (see Chapter 4), but its compatibility with polyester should mean that a vinylester laminate can be laid up against a polyester gel coat.

Phenolic

It is true that room temperature (cold) curing thermosets date from after World War II, but it would be a mistake to think that this was the beginning of thermosetting resins in general. In fact, Dr. Baekeland developed phenolic resin around the turn of the century, and patented it as "Bakelite" in 1907. Phenolic has some interesting and valuable properties, especially as electrical insulation, but it liberates by-products as it cures—which requires high pressure to oppose, and it cures only at an elevated temperature—which usually demands heated metal molds. The only interest phenolic has for us here, then, is its use in pre-pregs, in which case it is (like the epoxies also used in pre-pregs) partially cured, and most of the inconvenient by-products have already been removed.

In a number of cases, phenolic pre-pregs have replaced those based on epoxy in aircraft interiors as a response to recent aviation regulations that attempt to reduce fire hazards in the cabin. They are harder to ignite, and when they do burn they do so less vigorously, producing less heat and less smoke (which is also less harmful) than the epoxy-based materials they replace.

In other respects, though, they seem to offer no advantage: they are more expensive; they have less *surface tack*—which complicates the lay-up of complex, multilayer laminates, and give off more gas when curing—which demands greater attention during the cure cycle. ■

GEL COATS

4

To produce parts with a smooth, shiny surface comparable to painted metal, something needs to be done about the "shredded wheat" appearance of raw fiberglass. For such parts—like automotive bodywork—a coating of pure plastic resin containing no glass or other fiber is usually applied to the mold surface and permitted to cure before any glass is applied. This *gel coat* can be self-colored, which avoids the need for painting. Apart from providing a cosmetically attractive surface to the finished part, the gel coat also protects the glass from the effects of weathering, by preventing moisture from *wicking* along exposed fibers into the body of the laminate. These are good and sufficient reasons for the use of gel coat, but another purpose, seldom mentioned but arguably just as important, is to protect the mold from damage.

During the hand lay-up molding process, the wet laminate needs to be worked over with a ribbed roller (see Chapter 7—*Wet Lay-Up Technique*), to consolidate the laminate and ensure that there are no air bubbles trapped in the work. Without a gel coat, the shuffling of the wet laminate against the mold surface that results from the rolling may tear or dislodge the parting film, allowing the liquid resin to contact the mold surface. If that should happen, there is a real risk of adhesion between the mold and the part. The gel coat, then, also shields the mold from the risk of such damage.

This boat is at the gel coat application stage. The gel coat here is applied in a variety of colors and layers. Stripes have been masked off, with each set of stripes receiving a different color. A color is sprayed on, the tape is peeled off, then another color is sprayed. The gel coat is sprayed in a professional paint booth with downdraft air system and professional spray equipment. Photo by Michael Lutfy.

As mentioned on the previous page, the stripes are taped on the mold prior to applying gel coat. The base coat is applied first, then a strip of tape is removed, and that color is applied. This is how Hallett Performance Boats works, because customers choose their own colors. All boats are made to order. Photo by Michael Lutfy.

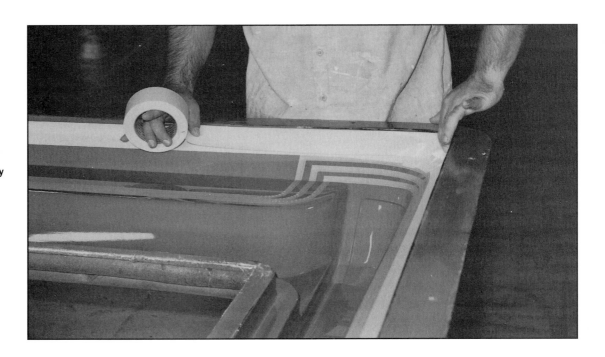

INGREDIENTS

Conventional gel coat is nothing more than polyester resin, with a few added ingredients. To prevent runs and sags when the gel coat is applied to a vertical surface, a *thixotropic agent*—usually silica gel—is blended in, to add body and so resist flowing under the effect of gravity. An inert filler such as *kaolin* (china-clay) or silicon dioxide may also be included, which adds a degree of impact resistance, and helps to reduce cracking during normal wear and tear. Such fillers also serve as *extenders* to help reduce costs. Though clear gel coats are available, a pigment is also usually added, both to impart color and to shield the finished laminate from ultraviolet light. Depending on the end use of the part, the basic polyester formulation may be modified to give greater hardness, at the expense of flexibility, or may be flexiblized, to reduce the tendency to cracking. The harder, more brittle formulations are usually sold as

This is the same boat from the previous page. The last layer of gel coat to go on is black. Although this color does not show through, it is applied to make it easier to see when doing the lay-up. This helps reduce the possibility of missing any spots. Photo by Michael Lutfy.

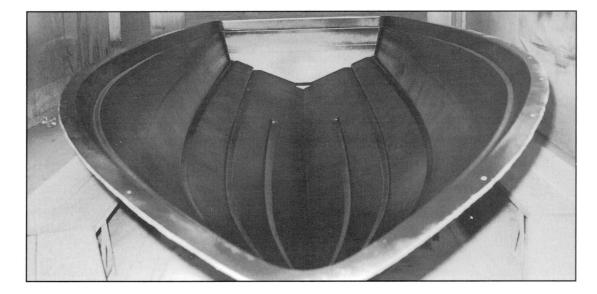

tooling or sanitary gel coats and are suitable for molds and for products, such as bath tubs or counter tops, which will be contacted by people or by food. More flexible GP (general purpose) gel coats, less hard and scratch resistant than tooling formulations, are intended for boats, automotive bodywork, and similar applications where constant vibration would tend to crack a harder plastic. Finally, because the first layer of laminate has to bond to the gel coat, the resin in gel coat contains no wax, so as to retain its *air inhibited* nature and leave a tacky, incompletely cured surface.

APPLICATION TECHNIQUES

Though it is usually intended for application by spraying, some suppliers offer a brushable gel coat. One difference between the two is the amount of styrene monomer included—additional styrene is blended into sprayable gel coat to make up for the amount that evaporates into the air during spraying. If the same amount were present in a brushed coat, the extra, unevaporated styrene would increase the brittleness of the cured coating. If you insist on brushing gel coat, purchase a formulation made specifically for brushing, use a very soft natural bristle brush, and apply the material with long, sweeping strokes. Move continuously and systematically across the surface, always working up against and toward a wet edge; do not brush back and forth as you might when applying paint. You will have to spot and correct thin areas immediately—if additional gel coat is applied over material that has gelled but not cured, the styrene will attack the incompletely cured previous coat, causing it to wrinkle (see *alligatoring*, p. 39).

Spraying Polyester Gel Coat

In truth, it is very difficult to successfully apply gel coat with a brush, no matter what

Although gel coat can be applied by brush, the practice is not recommended. Photo courtesy DOW Plastics.

the styrene content, and most of the trouble that novices experience with gel coat can be attributed to this factor. The use of a lambs wool roller is also sometimes suggested for applying gel coat. Certainly, different individuals have different styles of working and different preferences for tools, but this writer has never had any luck at all with this technique, and doesn't know anyone who has. While one of the major attractions of FRP work is the simplicity and low cost of the equipment required, and while almost every other aspect of the work can (and in many cases should) be done by hand, applying gel coat is one place where investing in some machinery is earnestly recommended. Proper spray equipment will quickly repay itself in superior results, reduced scrap, and saved time.

Spray Guns—Various spray guns suitable for gel coat application are described in Chapter 5, but it is worth spending a moment here to urge against succumbing to the temptation to use ordinary paint spraying gear. There are three problems with this approach. First, the fluid passages and orifices in ordinary paint guns are too small to deal with a dense, viscous liquid like gel coat. To make the operation possible at all, it

"If you insist on brushing gel coat, purchase a formulation made specifically for brushing, use a very soft natural bristle brush, and apply the material with long, sweeping strokes."

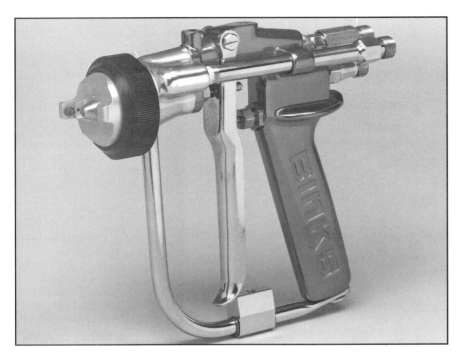

It is highly recommended that you use a spray gun specifically made for spraying gel coat, such as this one from Binks. Photo courtesy Binks Manufacturing Co.

"Miss by a few minutes and your cheap spray gun just became an expensive paper weight."

is necessary to thin the gel coat with a solvent of some sort. Acetone or paint thinners will reduce the viscosity of gel coat sufficiently to allow it to be sprayed with a conventional paint gun, but some of the solvent—perhaps a lot of it—will remain trapped in the plastic as it cures, leaving an inferior, soft coating. Dilution with styrene is better, as the styrene will cross-link with the polyester (see Chapter 3—*Resins*) but, as noted above, excess styrene will cause the opposite problem—a brittle gel coat. About 5% should be regarded as the practical limit.

The second problem is that the gel coat obviously needs to be catalyzed in order to cure. But if the catalyst is included in the plastic being sprayed, it becomes essential to completely dismantle the gun for cleaning after each use, before the gel coat has cured. Miss by a few minutes and your cheap spray gun just became an expensive paper weight. Finally, most inexpensive general purpose paint guns are made from materials that are not resistant to some of the components in gel coat. The MEKP catalyst is particularly corrosive, but the inert fillers, too, can cause rapid erosion of the metering needle and orifice. In all, the only smart move is to buy a

proper gel coat gun and pressure pot. The pressure pot is necessary because a viscous fluid like undiluted gel coat cannot be siphoned out of a container the way paint can.

Setting Catalyst Mixture—Assuming the use of an external mix gun that introduces an atomized spray of catalyst into the main spray pattern of uncatalyzed resin, it is best to calibrate the gel coat gun when first purchased, to ensure a correct proportion of catalyst. Use a small triangular file to mark the "12:00 o'clock" position on the flow control knobs when they are fully closed. After settling on a suitable working pressure for the pressure pot, set the resin flow control at some reasonable arbitrary position (two turns open is usually about right), and establish the amount of gel coat per minute that flows through the gun at that pressure and setting, and record the result. The atomizing air should be shut off during this operation; the un-atomized stream of gel coat can be squirted into a clean, empty container and re-used.

Then shut off or disconnect the resin flow, fill the catalyst container with water, and adjust the flow until the quantity per minute coming from the catalyst side of the gun gives the ratio suggested by the supplier, in relation to the previously measured resin flow. (Water is close enough in density and viscosity to MEKP to give useful information without introducing the hazard of spraying raw catalyst into the air, but dry the gun thoroughly before it is put into service.) The ratio by weight should be between 1% and 2.5%, if the catalyst is supplied as a 60% concentration of MEKP in dimethyl phthalate, which is typical. (Pure MEKP is dangerously unstable stuff, so it is always supplied dissolved in a *buffering* fluid.)

Finally, do a few test runs at your "standard" setting, shooting a working thickness (12-15 mils, i.e. 0.012-0.015 inch) of real gel coat and real catalyst at a piece of cardboard or other scrap surface, and confirm that a cure to the "squeak" stage (see

Chapter 7) is achieved in a reasonable time, say one to two hours. Once appropriate settings are established for pot pressure and resin and catalyst flow, you can return to this "standard" setting at any time; with a little experience, minor adjustments to take account of changes in shop temperature, planned gel coat thickness, etc., can then be judged "by eyeball."

It is very important to keep the proportion of catalyst within the range specified by the supplier, typically 1%-2.5%. Insufficient catalyst will slow the cure of the gel coat, requiring a long wait before it is ready to be laminated on. Apart from the hold up in production, this also allows more time for the surface to become contaminated with dust or airborne moisture. At its worst, inadequate catalyst will result in an incomplete cure—the resin gels and begins to cure, but does not progress beyond that point. While the surface may appear sound, it never gets fully hard. This is a particular problem during hot weather when the proportion of catalyst is cut back to allow increased working time and to avoid excessive exotherm. It is worth mentioning here that, while you can hasten the cure of any thermosetting resin with heat, you should be careful not to overdo it. Room temperature curing materials should not be heated above, say, 120F. And on no account blow hot air directly on the surface of any curing polyester, including gel coat, and especially tooling gel coat—this will cause excess styrene evaporation, resulting in a soft, rubbery surface.

On the other hand, excess catalyst may hasten the cure so much that the gel coat shrinks excessively, pulling away from the mold and leaving sinks in the surface of the finished part. Too much catalyst may also cause pinholes in the gel coat, because there was insufficient time for escape of air entrained in the spray as it passed from gun to mold. An extreme surplus of catalyst will cause overheating and blistering that will make the part useless, and may damage the

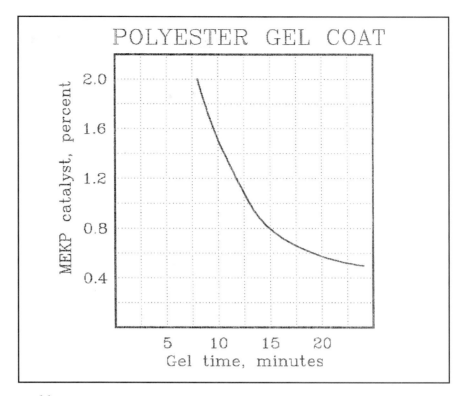

Chart indicating the relationship between gel time and percentage of MEKP catalyst.

mold.

Number of Coats—Unlike paint, gel coat should be sprayed in a few thick, heavy coats, rather then several thin ones. As noted in Chapter 5, some external mix resin/catalyst guns will only ensure thorough intermixing of the resin and catalyst when the resin fan pattern is vertically oriented. To ensure uniform coverage, though, it is nevertheless important to make at least a couple of passes in the "wrong" direction. One solution to this dilemma is to rotate the mold through 90 degrees, rather than rotating the air cap on the gun. Be very, very careful doing this, however—any rough handling will overcome the thixotropy of the gel coat, causing it to slump. If the mold is too big and heavy to tilt, about the only recourse is to ensure that at least the first and last passes with the gun are the "right" way up—i.e. with the spray pattern forming a vertical ellipse.

Excess Gel Coat Problems—When split molds are used, a problem can arise from excessive gel coat on the flanges that meet when two sections are connected. If a stan-

"Room temperature curing materials should not be heated above, say, 120F."

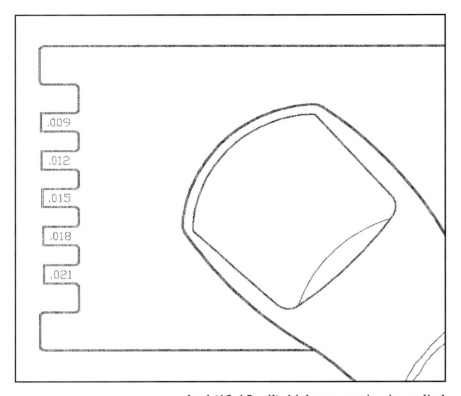

.009

.012

.015

.018

.021

A simple, plastic tool similar to this illustration allows you to measure the gel coat film thickness. The "feet" contact the mold surface; the thickness of the film is indicated by the longest "finger" to be wetted by the resin.

dard (12-15 mil) thickness coating is applied to each of these flanges, then when the mold sections are clamped together all that gel coat will get squeezed out in two directions—towards the free edges of the flanges, and toward the working surface of the mold. Gel coat that dribbles out the free edges of the flanges, or through the bolt holes used for joining the two sections, can effectively cement the two together (OOPS!). On the inside of the mold, the excess resin will form a thick ridge that effectively produces two very sharp inside radii, virtually guaranteeing that there will be a narrow band of trapped air and/or excess laminating resin. In any event, it amounts to a severe local variation in the thickness of the gel coat.

To avoid this, the mating flanges should be masked just barely outboard of where they meet the working surface. Where practical, it is helpful to design and trim the flanges so they are just a little (say 1/8 inch) wider than standard 2" wide masking tape. This masking must, of course, be removed before the two mold sections are assembled. If the

mold is designed to produce a part with narrow, turned under edges, such as for attaching race car bodywork to a tube frame, the additional sections attached to the mold flanges may consist simply of narrow strips of material. In this case, there is a nifty little trick that eliminates half of this masking and makes the gel coating process a little more convenient. If the placement of the bolt holes securing these edge pieces to the mold flanges is carefully thought out, it will be possible to arrange the edge pieces upside down on the mold flanges (temporarily located with just a couple of bolts) so that all the surfaces can be sprayed in one pass, while the edge pieces serve as the masking for the flanges on the mold itself.

REPAIRS

With the proper equipment, good work habits, and a little practice, a satisfactory gel coat can be counted on almost every time. Nevertheless, Murphy's Law can strike at any time, and there will be occasions when an otherwise usable or salable part will be spoiled by *alligatored* or severely *pinholed* gel coat. While it is not always practical, porous or bubbled gel coat and most cases of alligatoring can be salvaged.

Sadly, the repair will almost never exactly match the color of the original, and the mismatch will be especially noticeable with pale colors. Still, because the range of colors available for gel coat is not nearly as wide as the rainbow of hues that paint comes in, it is not uncommon for a part to be painted. In that case, it is usual to select a gel coat that is merely close to the paint color, to provide a degree of camouflage for minor chips and scratches. And in that case, you can use a repaired gel coat without risking embarrassment. Of course, if the part is going to be painted and color is not an issue at all, ordinary automotive polyester body filler can be used in place of the home-made filler described below.

The tools of the gel coat sprayer's trade. This bench in the gel coat spray booth of a boat builder has obviously seen some heavy use. Note the "volcano" of gel coat growing in the back. Photo by Michael Lutfy.

"While it is not always practical, porous or bubbled gel coat and most cases of alligatoring can be salvaged."

Alligatoring

These are areas with a rippled texture, like alligator skin, and it is a particularly depressing fault in a finished part. It may take the form of worm-like rills, or may extend over a large area. The cause is an incompletely cured gel-coat having been attacked by the styrene in the first layer of laminate. The fix is simple: be certain that the gel-coat has cured, which means applying a sufficiently thick, uniform, adequately catalyzed coat; make sure that the shop is warm enough; and give the gel-coat enough time to cure.

Large areas of alligatoring are often too costly to repair, but if you are determined to give it a try, sand out the damaged area, preferably with a power grinder, clean thoroughly and wipe with acetone, mask the surrounding area, then spray on a mixture of catalyzed gel coat with about 2% by weight of filler and not more than 10% by weight of acetone added. Use lots of catalyst (say 2%), be sure to stand back far enough that the acetone will *flash off*, and build up the repair in comparatively thin coats. After curing, sand and polish.

For small, localized areas of gel coat damage, there is a variation on this repair technique which is worth describing. After cleaning out and sanding the blemish and a small surrounding area, apply strips of masking tape just outboard of the edges of the repair, catalyze some gel coat (neither filler nor wax is needed, using this procedure), and paint or dribble it into place. Then tightly stretch plastic food wrap over the surface and tape it down on three edges. Using a plastic spatula or similar tool, gently squeegee surplus gel coat toward the open edge, checking for trapped air bubbles. Tape down the free edge of the plastic film, and wait for the cure. The plastic film serves the same purpose as the wax—it excludes air from the surface and so allows the surface of the gel coat to cure, while the masking tape defines both the area being fixed and the height (about 6 mils) that the patch stands above the original surface, reducing both the area and the depth of sanding that has to be done.

Pinholes

Not much can be done about small pinholes, but if they are large enough, they can be filled with a putty made by adding 3%-5% filler and about 2% wax solution to some of the original gel coat. Clean the affected area free of all wax and parting

"It is usual to select a gel coat that is merely close to the paint color, to provide a degree of camouflage for minor chips and scratches. And in that case, you can use a repaired gel coat without risking embarrassment."

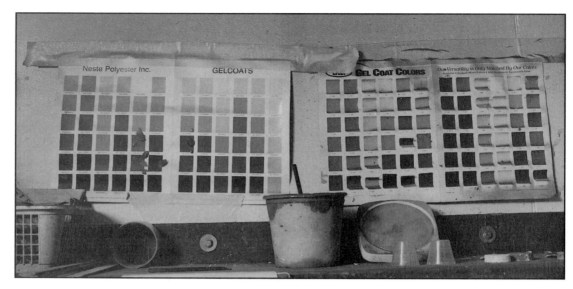

Gel coat is available in a wide variety of colors, as shown by this color chart by Neste Polyester, Inc. Photo by Michael Lutfy.

agent, catalyze the paste, and apply it with a putty knife. The same approach can be used to repair blisters, localized alligatoring, and other similar problems. Blisters should be cut open and any loose debris cleaned out; alligatoring should be attacked with a small grinding wheel or cutter in a power drill, to give the patch something to get a bite on, and then filled with putty. In each case, sand after curing with very fine wet-and-dry sandpaper until smooth, and polish with rubbing compound.

Fillers

Many resin suppliers can provide both the wax solution and a filler material. "Cabosil" and "Aerosil" are familiar brand names, but there are some home-made substitutes that can be used in a pinch. Talcum (baby) powder can be used as filler, but be sure to get a premium brand—cheap talcum powder contains not just ground up talc but also lots of corn starch! To add wax to resin (including gel coat) when no wax solution is available, get some ordinary household paraffin wax, as used for candles or for sealing Mason jars. To wax one pint (16 ounces) of resin, cut off a lump of wax a little smaller than the size of a sugar cube (you're aiming for about

1 gram of wax), and shave it into very fine flakes. Pour about 8 ounces of resin into a clean tin can and place the can in a container partly filled with very hot water, add the flaked wax and stir until it dissolves, then add this cup of resin to a further 8 ounces of room temperature resin, and mix it all together.

GEL COAT ALTERNATIVES

As noted in Chapter 3, for high performance FRP parts, epoxy is often used as the matrix instead of polyester. An immediate problem that arises is the selection of a suitable gel coat. Now, epoxy is usually reserved for high value parts where the added strength of laminates using an epoxy matrix justifies the extra cost (and these cases will often involve a reinforcement other than glass, for the same reason). Usually, too, these parts will be painted, so the weight of a gel coat is useless baggage.

Protecting Mold Surface

Omitting the gel coat, though, raises concerns about protecting the mold surface from adhesion by the epoxy-based laminate—remember that one of the purposes of the gel coat, at least in polyester-based work, is to protect the mold surface by preventing scouring away of the parting (release) agent. Note, too, that epoxy is a much more effective adhesive than polyester. Normally, however, it does not contain any solvents like the styrene monomer in polyester, so there is usually no concern about breaking down a wax-based release agent. On the other hand, a mold surface protected only by a film-forming parting agent like PVA is at peril! The mechanical abrasion that accompanies the rolling out of the laminate can easily tear that film, and epoxy's justified reputation as an adhesive can then cement part and mold together... permanently.

Most suppliers of epoxy resins offer proprietary mold release pastes that they assure will provide ample protection and a clean release, without PVA. About the only remaining cause for concern, then, is that certain diluents or reducers added to the epoxy to reduce its viscosity may themselves be solvents capable of dissolving the mold release. It is just these sorts of concerns about interaction between products that makes it sensible either to purchase all the products—resin, hardener, diluent, mold release—as a matched package from one supplier, or else to conduct extensive tests before putting a mold at risk. (Actually, unless you have worked successfully with any specific combination of materials in the past, you should probably do both—this is a place where a belt-and-suspenders approach can save much grief!) Still, there may be some instances where it is desired to apply some sort of in-mold coating that will provide a good cosmetic finish on the exposed surface of a finished part made with epoxy. There are several possible approaches.

Epoxy Surfacing Resins

Epoxy-based *surfacing resins* are available, but these vary in viscosity from brushable liquids to thick pastes intended to be trowelled into place. A trowelled or brushed gel coat will be both uneven and needlessly thick and heavy, canceling much of the benefit of using epoxy in the first place. (However, these surfacing epoxy pastes are ideal for producing a mold surface in epoxy, as opposed to parts.) Yet *sprayable* epoxy gel coat is as rare as hen's teeth. (The problem seems to be that an epoxy of sprayable viscosity lacks enough thixotropy to resist running down vertical surfaces; compatible thixotropic agents are available, but they make the resin too thick to spray!) At that, an epoxy surface coat does not possess the gloss and luster of polyester gel coat.

Using Polyester Gel Coat

It is tempting to consider retaining a polyester gel coat, and many purchasers accustomed to gel-coated polyester parts may insist on it. Unfortunately, the interaction between the epoxy used for laminating and the air-inhibited tacky surface of a polyester gel coat is unpredictable—some formulations inhibit the cure of the epoxy, and manufacturers and formulators of both epoxy and polyester resins can generally offer no advice beyond "try it and see." When I tried it, with a fairly common polyester gel coat and an even more common epoxy laminating resin, what I saw was not a happy sight. Although both the gel coat and the epoxy were fully cured, between them—right at the plane where the two met—was a thin sticky layer of uncured something-or-other. With little effort, the gel coat just peeled off, like the shell off a boiled egg.

On a subsequent trial, a satisfactory result was obtained by allowing the gel coat to cure much longer than usual—closer to two days than two hours—at which time all trace of surface tack was gone. Obviously, this delay increases the chance of contamination of the exposed surface. Protection from dust can be achieved by starting off with a scrupulously clean shop and draping a plastic tent over the gel coated mold, although some air circulation is desirable to prevent

"The mechanical abrasion that accompanies the rolling out of the laminate can easily tear that film, and epoxy's justified reputation as an adhesive can then cement part and mold together... permanently."

41

"If you are determined to use a gel coat on an epoxy-based laminate, it is perhaps better to use a gel coat based on vinylester resin, rather than polyester."

the accumulation of evaporating styrene. About the only thing that can be done about airborne moisture, however, is to carefully pick your time—wait for a spell of weather when you can be assured of a couple of days of very low humidity.

Another technique that is claimed to have worked is to add wax to the polyester gel coat to ensure that the exposed surface is fully cured, then to sand lightly to remove the wax and roughen the surface. The sanding, though, is sure to be both laborious and nerve wracking—there is a constant risk of premature release of the gel coat from the mold. This is probably best left to natural gamblers.

Vinylester Resin

If you are determined to use a gel coat on an epoxy-based laminate, it is perhaps better to use a gel coat based on *vinylester resin*, rather than polyester. While it may not be technically quite correct, it is approximately true to describe vinylester as being made up of molecules that are polyester at one end and epoxy at the other; it is thus compatible with both of the other resin systems. While the stuff does exist, vinylester-based gel coats are not widely available. An alternative, then, is to apply a conventional air inhibited polyester gel coat, allow it to cure to the squeak stage (see Chapter 7), then to spray on a thin coat of vinylester. When it too has cured to the tacky stage, the epoxy should (repeat *should*) bond completely without grief. Once again, I urge you to conduct small-scale tests, particularly in the case of such experimental procedures.

Transfer Painting

Then there is a procedure called *transfer painting*, developed by Lotus Cars. As implemented by Lotus, a coat of polyurethane paint is sprayed into the waxed mold and allowed to fully harden, then polyester gel coat is sprayed in, and a polyester

laminate laid up after it is cured. What is fascinating here is the possibility of omitting the gel coat—why not laminate directly onto the urethane paint? Presumably, Lotus doesn't do this because of the problem of print through (see Chapter 2), but it would seem that the process is also applicable to epoxy laminates, whose reduced shrinkage would reduce or eliminate the print-through. Transfer-painting seems an elegant solution to the problem of producing epoxy laminates with a lustrous colored surface, but while it is known that the paint film applied by Lotus is, by paint standards, very thick (about 0.004 inch) and that the mold surface has to be ultra glossy and flawless, what other complications might attend its use are unknown.

A variation on the use of paint as a substitute for gel coat when using epoxy-based laminates is employed by some airframe makers. It turns out that latex paint (just like you use to paint a room in your house) interacts in a favorable way with epoxy. After allowing drying time for the paint, which is sprayed into the mold, you can just laminate directly onto it. Although the final surface finish may not be up to car show standards, a little light sanding leaves a surface that will take a coat of glossy paint; meanwhile the latex paint has kept the epoxy away from the mold.

Rigidized Acrylic

Finally, it is worth mentioning something called *rigidized acrylic*. This consists of a thin sheet of acrylic thermoplastic which is first molded to the desired shape, often by vacuum forming, then has FRP material laminated onto the hidden "back" face, to provide the necessary stiffness and heft. In a sense, the pre-formed acrylic serves as a sort of self-supporting gel coat and a mold at the same time. This technique is used for many consumer products, including washroom fixtures, recreational vehicle bodywork, and some small boats. ■

THE FRP SHOP

5

HAND TOOLS

One of the great attractions of FRP work is the simplicity of tools and materials required—little is needed, and most of that little can be picked up at the local hardware store, if not at the A&P. Nevertheless, there are a few specialized tools in the laminator's kit that merit description.

Brushes

The basic tool, of course, is a brush. Since many paints and synthetic bristles dissolve in either resin or acetone, brushes should have natural bristles, set in rubber, and should have unpainted handles. At one time, suitable brushes were available so cheaply that it made sense to buy them by the dozen and discard them after one use. Alas, their cost has now risen from pennies each to the best part of a dollar, so it is usual to clean brushes, using acetone.

Cleaning—To avoid wasting the solvent, it is worthwhile setting up a "three can" system. Start with three empty tin cans about half full of acetone. Scrape as much resin as possible off the brush, then dunk it and swill it around in can #1, removing as much resin as possible; then repeat in cans # 2 and 3. After a while, can #1 will become hopelessly contaminated, so move can #2 to the first position and #3 to the second, and pour a fresh half can of acetone for position three. Rotating in this way will save a lot of acetone. Keep the cans covered when not in use. (Rubber and plastic squeegees do not present a cleaning problem—cured resin

A professional FRP shop. Cleanliness and organization, with everything in its place, fosters a similar workplace attitude. Photo by Jack Gladback.

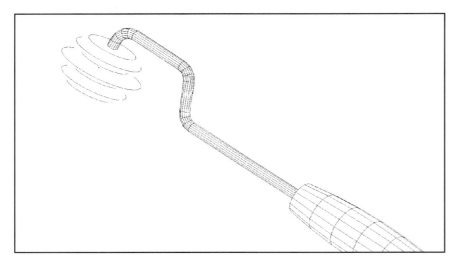

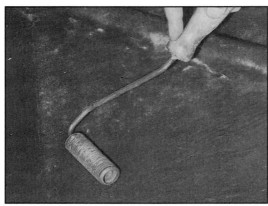

Rollers are available in various configurations. Some are straight; others are "crowned" (barrel shaped) for working curved surfaces. Special profiles are available for corners. Photo by Michael Lutfy.

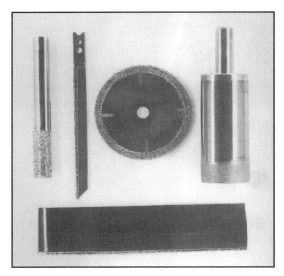

Abrasive coated cutting tools are available for trimming and other laminate cutting operations. These avoid bruising the laminate. Photo courtesy Starlite Industries Inc.

does not bond with their surfaces, so can be peeled off easily.)

The other half of the "bucket-and-brush" technique—as wet lay-up has been called—is the bucket. While it is possible to use almost any old container for the resin, disposable paper cups or tubs of a uniform size are ideal. The size is a matter of personal preference—some people favor working with a 2- or 3-inch brush and a paper tub of the size used for ice-cream sundaes; some prefer a smaller brush and a six-ounce drink cup. Either way, be sure they are hot drink containers, with a plastic coating—cold drink cups have a wax coating, and the wax will dissolve in any styrenated resin.

Rollers

The use of ribbed rollers for consolidating and compacting laminates and for busting air-bubbles is described in Chapter 7. These

rollers, made from either aluminum or plastic, are widely available, but a home-made version can be made using a paint-roller handle strung with alternating large and small flat washers. Cured resin can be easily peeled off plastic rollers (at least until their slick surface gets nicked and damaged), but metal rollers are a different story. It is often impossible to get the rollers cleaned up before the resin cures, and there is no known solvent for fully cured resin, so the only alternative to throwing them away is to burn off the hardened plastic using a propane torch. THIS MUST BE DONE OUTDOORS—apart from the obvious fire hazard, the resulting smoke is evil. The plastic will ignite after a few seconds and, depending on the amount of resin clogging the roller, will continue to burn for some time after the flame is removed. Once all the plastic is burned, the charred residue will scrub off readily with a wire brush.

Shears

While it is probably better to tear mat than to cut it (see Chapter 7), shears are needed for cutting cloth, for snipping bubbles, and for tailoring in the mold. To help in clean-

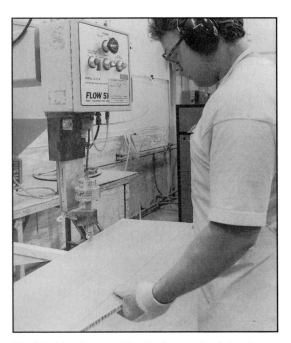

The ideal laminate cutting tool—a water jet cutter. This is the only way to cleanly cut aramid. Guy Levesque photo courtesy deHavilland, Inc.

Air-powered tools are generally preferable to electrical ones in the FRP shop. Lighter and cooler running, they also last much longer because of their self cleaning nature.

up, shears that will encounter wet resin can be waxed. Ceramic bladed shears are available for dealing with dry aramid, which is notoriously tough to cut; aramid pre-pregs, on the other hand, can be sliced fairly easily with a sharp utility knife. To ensure that it stays sharp, the kind with snap-off renewable blades is best. Much heavier shears (as used for sheet-metal) can sometimes be employed for rough trimming of cured glass laminates, but this will prove hard on the hands, as it is tough to chomp through all but the thinnest laminate. A hacksaw with a medium blade is slightly better, and a power jigsaw will work, but blades are good for only about an hour of steady work, and the entire saw will devour itself inside of a couple of weeks, especially if the reinforcement is glass. Besides, the saw-cut edge requires a lot of finishing. Also, both the jigsaw cutting itself and the finish sanding create a lot of very nasty dust.

Note, too, that any trimming action that tends to crush the cured laminate will leave a bruise of fractured resin extending any-

where from 1/8 inch to 1/2 inch from the trimmed edge, depending on the degree of violence inflicted. Accordingly, a certain margin has to be provided beyond the final edge, to allow this damaged area to be ground off using a coarse sanding disk, then finished by hand as described in Chapter 7. An air-powered cut-off tool with a small diameter abrasive wheel is by far the best tool for trimming as it inflicts minimal bruising and leaves a clean edge that needs only a little work with wet-and-dry sandpaper for a final finish, avoiding much hard work and clouds of abrasive dust in the air.

Not that such things are affordable by a small shop operator, but the very slickest way to cut finished laminates (and about the only practical way to cut an aramid laminate without leaving a fuzzy edge) is with a *water-jet cutter*—a device like a million horsepower Water Pik™.

AIR POWER

Apart from the obvious need in spraying operations, there are a number of excellent reasons for using compressed air as the basic power source in all kinds of reinforced plastic work. Not the least of these is safety.

There is an obvious shock hazard in wet-sanding with an electric sander. Worse, electrical machinery and their switches are capable of making sparks. Sparks and highly combustible vapors are the perfect combination for putting yourself and your shop into low orbit. You will have combustible vapors—lots of them if you work with styrenated resin; you need not have

"Sparks and highly combustible vapors are the perfect combination for putting yourself and your shop into low orbit."

A hefty air compressor is essential. This one at Aerodine Composites sits in a soundproof closet. Note use of remote mounted air intake filter. Photo by Jack Gladback.

"You have not known panic until you reach the moment-of-truth in an operation worth two months' pay, you need some air right now, and the compressor makes a noise like Pink Floyd. But no air."

Compressor

Now that you're sold on "canned wind," you're going to need some equipment. For starters, you need a compressor. As a general guide, anything less than a 2 hp compressor is a toy; on the other hand, 5 hp should exceed any small shop's needs. To pin it down closer, though, you should first of all establish the air requirements of all of the air-powered equipment you have (and expect to get in the future), which can be determined from manufacturer's specifications. These numbers are expressed in cubic feet per minute (cfm), but beware—many manufacturers list a figure for "typical" use, which assumes that the equipment is being used intermittently, with long breaks during which time the compressor can recuperate. You need to know the consumption during continuous use. A small air drill, for instance, may have a "typical" rating of 4 cfm, but a continuous rating of 20 cfm; one popular gel coat gun requires 7-12 cfm for continuous use, depending on the pressure it is operated at.

A larger tank can help tide the compressor over brief periods of high demand, but the compressor still has to supply the average air requirements. Compressor output is expressed in cfm of free air at a certain pressure. Pressure is not a problem—there's likely more than you will ever need, but look carefully at the cfm ratings. As with other products, there are many exaggerated claims; read the fine print, and remember that you usually get what you pay for.

Never forget that the air compressor is your friend, and you've got to take care of your friends. You have not known panic until you reach the moment-of-truth in an operation worth two months' pay, you need some air right now, and the compressor makes a noise like Pink Floyd. But no air. And it's 8:30 on a Saturday night.

Immediately, at once, trash whatever kind of cheapskate air filter the manufacturer put on your air compressor and do whatever it

sparks—almost any kind of tool that is powered by electricity is also available in air-powered form. Air driven cutters, grinders, drills, sanders and all the rest are widely available, and since you have to have compressed air for spraying (and some substances pretty much have to be sprayed), then you may as well do everything with air power.

There is the added benefit that air-driven tools are self-cleaning in their vital places—abrasive dust is constantly blown out of the moving parts. While electric drills, jigsaws, etc., will live for only a few hours in a fiberglass shop, air tools seem to last forever in the same environment, and they can't be hurt by overloading or stalling. Besides, air tools are lighter and more compact than the corresponding electric model, which makes for reduced fatigue and easier handling, as does their cool-running nature, thanks to the inherent forced draught. Compressed air is also sometimes useful to help pop parts out of their molds.

takes to fit a decent automotive-type disposable paper air filter. Drain water from the tank, check the belt tension, check the oil level and have a general look over your friend at least once a week. Change the air filter when you can't see daylight coming through the element.

Plumbing—Getting the air from the compressor to the tool requires some sort of piping. The actual layout will obviously depend on the particular arrangements in your own shop, but certain general considerations should be borne in mind in all cases.

First, remember that the compressor makes the air hot. To help it cool down, a considerable length of line should be provided after the compressor before anything else is connected up. Second, as the air cools, condensation will form in the line, so you can't just lay twenty or thirty feet of hose on the floor or the water will form puddles in the loops of hose and pass through the system in gulps, causing a horrible mess in the work. Water in lacquer or resin, and especially in gel coat, is a serious problem, causing bubbles, discoloration, and patches that just never cure or dry.

Also, there will be a drop in pressure due to the friction of the air passing through the lines. To minimize this, the plumbing should be large in diameter. One solution to both problems is to make as much as possible of this air piping hard plumbed—i.e. metal pipe instead of flexible hose. This can be of steel or copper but iron pipe tends to develop rust and scale on the inside, so copper is arguably preferable. 3/8 inch copper pipe for household plumbing is available everywhere, the sweat soldering skill needed to assemble copper plumbing is easily learned, and the conductivity of the copper will help cool the air quickly.

One common arrangement is to run a continuous loop of pipe around the shop; that way air gets supplied from two directions at once, reducing the flow—and thus the pressure drop—through both pipes. The plumb-

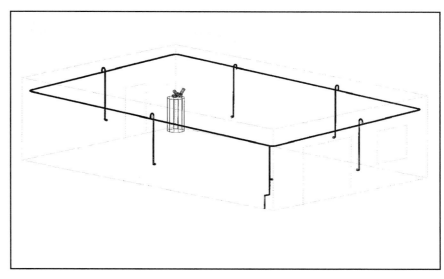

ing should be arranged high up near the ceiling, with a slight but steady downhill slope from the compressor connection to the furthest point in the loop, to ensure that any water in the piping flows to that corner. There, you should provide a branch line pointing straight down, with a tap of some sort to let you bleed off the worst of the water. To further help with control of water in the lines, every drop point from the main loop (except this intentional water drain line) should go up first, before it turns down, forming an inverted "J". Here again the wide availability of various elbows and fittings in copper makes the actual fabrication a snap.

Traps & Separators—For clean, dry air you certainly require the usual water trap and trash separator, but note that the kind of air needed by power tools is, to some extent, different from that required for spraying operations. While spraying requires air to be completely oil-free, power tools benefit from a little oil in the diet, and so could use a lubricator spliced into the line supplying them. Color code the lubricated line(s) so you don't give a spray gun an unintended grease job; better still, use two different, non-compatible brands of quick-disconnects, so it's impossible to connect a spray gun up to a lubricated line. Assemble all threaded fittings with Teflon™ (DuPont) plumber's tape, screw a lawn-mower muf-

Ring-main air plumbing–the air supply line forms a loop completely around the shop, sloped downward to the corner furthest from the compressor, where a drain line is provided to bleed off accumulated water. Note also the use of inverted "J" fittings at each drop point to reduce risk of water in the work.

"While it is usual for regulators to be permanently mounted, spraying of gel coat or resin is greatly facilitated if the entire package of spray gun, pressure pot, and the regulators for both are all portable."

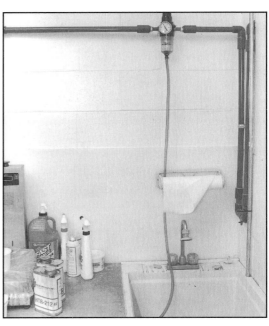

Aerodine takes no chances with dirty air. This duplex water trap removes most moisture...a second trap gets the remainder. Note drain hose into sink–water is the enemy of epoxy. Photos by Jack Gladback.

fler onto every vent to the atmosphere to cut down the blast which raises dust and rattles nerves, and provide a short piece of flexible hose at the compressor connection to help isolate vibration.

Regulators—For spraying, the full output pressure of the compressor far exceeds requirements, so one or more regulators will be needed. While it is usual for regulators to be permanently mounted, spraying of gel coat or resin is greatly facilitated if the entire package of spray gun, pressure pot, and the regulators for both are all portable. Elaborate rigs on wheels, with articulated booms and all sorts of other pricey features, can be purchased from various suppliers. For amateur or small shop use, however, something functionally similar can be made up using a cheap utility cart to carry the pressure pot, its regulator, a second regulator for the gun, a water trap and—to expedite cleaning out the gel coat gun and its fluid line—a three position valve, to isolate the pressure feed while venting the pot to the atmosphere.

Spray Guns

If you are working with polyester or vinylester, and especially if you plan on making your own plugs and molds, you will also need a minimum of three spray guns. One of these will be a rather special gun for gel coat and possibly other resins; the others are just ordinary paint guns. Of these, one should be reserved for water soluble substances, like latex paint and PVA parting compound; the other gun is for lacquer and other solvent based materials. Each gun should be fitted with a quick-release connector.

Dual Pot—Ordinary paint guns require no detailed description here, but it is worth remarking on the variety of different gun designs used for *plural component spraying*. Polyester resin with catalyst added, but without an accelerator, has a pot life measured in hours or days, and polyester containing accelerator but not catalyst will last for months. One technique, then, for spraying a catalyzed, accelerated resin without having it set up solid in the gun within minutes is to use two separate heads—one for

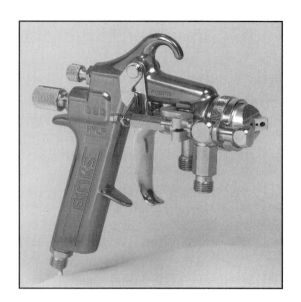

A "side injection" HVLP plural component spray gun. Catalyst spray nozzle is in foreground. Photo courtesy Binks Manufacturing Co.

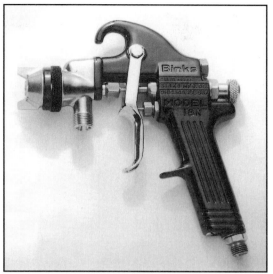

A catalyst injection type gun. The catalyst flows through the "ears" for atomizing air. Photo courtesy Binks Manufacturing Co.

"If you are working with polyester or vinylester, and especially if you plan on making your own plugs and molds, you will also need a minimum of three spray guns."

resin-plus-accelerator, the other for resin-plus-catalyst—and to arrange for the two streams to meet and intermingle outside the gun. This two-pot technique is among the first to have been used, it works quite satisfactorily, and is popular in some production applications.

External Mix—A more common arrangement is to spray accelerated resin and catalyst as two separate streams, the two again mixing a few inches in front of the gun. Sometimes the catalyst is lifted out of a separate container by the suction of the atomizing air, just like an ordinary paint gun; some-

LAnother brand of catalyst injection plural component gun. You can see the catalyst spraying from the atomizing air ports. Photo courtesy Glas-Craft, Inc.

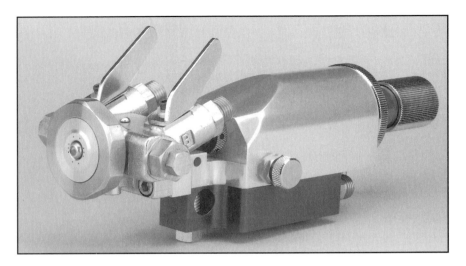

Internal mix guns require provision for flushing with solvent before the resin hardens. This valve assembly facilitates the flushing operation. Photo courtesy Binks Manufacturing Co.

"For the hobbyist and small scale business, the choice will almost certainly be limited to an external mix resin/catalyst gun."

cheap and familiar technology, but it causes a lot of overspray (resin going into the air and everywhere else except directly onto the mold) and bounce back (resin hits the mold and rebounds back into the air).

To control these effects and thus cut down on evaporative emissions, waste, and mess, the airless gun was invented. Here, the fluid stream is forced through the gun by a pump running at enormously high pressure (2000 psi is typical) and atomized in the same way that your shower head works—if the pressure is high enough, the liquid explodes out of the orifice with sufficient violence that the stream breaks up into fine droplets; no air is required. Airless guns are pleasant to use but, considered together with the pumping equipment, the whole package is shatteringly expensive—well beyond the budget and needs of a small shop.

HVLP—A more recent innovation is the High Volume Low Pressure (HVLP) gun. This does not really operate on a different principle from other air atomized guns, but by refining the details it has become possible to obtain satisfactory atomization with less than 10 psi of atomizing air pressure, so overspray and bounce back are dramatically reduced, even compared to an airless system. VOC emissions are also significantly reduced, even in comparison with airless systems.

Recommendations—For the hobbyist and small scale business, the choice will almost certainly be limited to an external mix resin/catalyst gun. Apart from the overspray problem of air-atomized setups, the greatest limitation of this type is that, while the fan pattern of the gun can be varied from a vertical to a horizontal ellipse, the catalyst spray is usually fixed in a roughly circular shape. Uneven catalyst mixing can occur if the resin fan pattern and the catalyst spray do not perfectly overlap. With care—avoiding a horizontal fan pattern when possible and, when it can't be avoided, assuring that the first and last passes with the gun are done

times it is forced through the gun by an external catalyst pump, in which case there are a couple of variations. One is the side injection style, where the atomized catalyst issues from a separate nozzle off to one side, and aimed sideways to collide with the atomized spray of resin. The other arrangement is for the catalyst to be injected into the atomizing air stream. This is ideal from the point of view of ensuring adequate mixing, and is a somewhat more elegant form of construction; on the other hand, it requires special materials for the air hose downstream of the catalyst injector.

Internal Mix—Then there are internal mix guns in which two resin streams—one catalyzed, the other accelerated—flow into the gun separately and meet in a mixing chamber. This mixing chamber is easily removed for cleaning, and easily replaced if it is not cleaned in time.

However the issue of keeping the catalyst-bearing component from the accelerator-bearing component is handled, there is a further choice between air-atomized and airless designs. Apart from the need for a pressure pot to persuade the viscous resin to flow into and through the gun, the first type functions very much the same as an ordinary paint gun—the fluid issues from the front of the gun as a stream of liquid, then is atomized by jets of air flowing through the little "ears" at either side of the nozzle. This is reliable, with a vertical fan—the drawbacks are more than made up for by simplicity and low cost.

MISCELLANEOUS TOOLS

As described in Chapter 12, *polystyrene foam* (sold by Dow as "Styrofoam") is an excellent material for the construction of plugs. And while other kinds of foamed plastic offer superior mechanical properties, Styrofoam can also be used as the filler in a structural sandwich (see Chapter 15). In both cases, the foam will have to be cut. At its simplest, this merely amounts to trimming a sheet to size; often, complex curves and profiles need to be produced.

Hot Wire Cutter

The easiest, most precise and tidiest tool for either job is a *hot wire cutter*. The principle is straightforward—a modest electrical current passing through a fine wire causes it to become hot enough to melt its way through the foam. Commercial hot wire cutters are available, but the device is so simple that it is probably easiest to make your own.

Like power tools for working any material, there are situations where it is better to take the tool to the job, and others where the job should be brought to the tool. In the first case, what is needed is a portable, hand-held apparatus; in the latter, the machine might be arranged to make either a horizontal or a vertical cut. For blanking out foam station sections (see Chapter 12– *Plugs*), a vertical cutter is most convenient, and an utterly simple device rather like a band saw with no moving parts can be built in less time than an executive lunch, and for considerably less money.

Table Requirements—First you should think about the size of table surface required. Even though you may sometimes need to pass an entire sheet lengthwise past the wire, the actual working surface can be kept conveniently small, with extra temporary surfaces placed around the cutter to

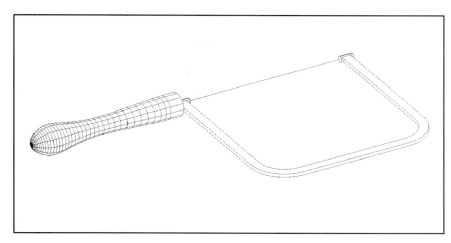

A portable hand-held hot wire cutter can be made from a fret saw frame.

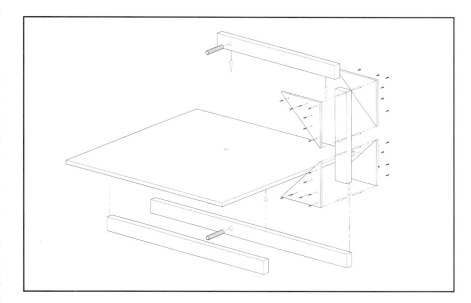

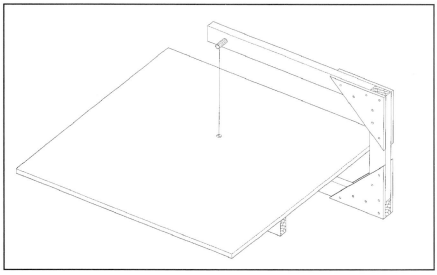

You can make a simple vertical wire hot wire cutter yourself.

51

> *"Essentially, fabric impregnators are nothing more than a bath of catalyzed resin through which the fabric is drawn, and a pair of pinch rollers to wring out the surplus resin. The technology is no more complex than the wringer on an old-fashioned washing machine."*

help support such oversize jobs. Also, since a sheet can be tackled form either side, the maximum reach required by the cutter need be no more than half a sheet width—about two feet. A working surface four feet square with a wire running through its middle has been found suitable.

For many other jobs, the wire is best oriented horizontally. To reduce the thickness of a sheet, for instance, the wire can be held above and parallel to the table surface by simple spacer blocks; to produce a "flat" curve (a curve in one plane), the wire can be strung across a bow which is free to swivel about a horizontal axis. With suitable templates secured to the edges of the foam using nails or double-sided carpet tape, the wire, guided by the templates, will rise and fall as the sheet is pushed across the table surface. Many builders of home-built aircraft cut the foam blanks for wing sections this way. Of course, the templates (and anything else contacted by the hot wire) must be heat resistant. Aluminum or other sheet metal works fine (you may be able to get off-cuts of vinyl coated aluminum from a contractor who installs aluminum siding on houses); surprisingly, so does tempered Masonite™. Plywood is less satisfactory, as it is difficult to produce an edge smooth enough to avoid snagging the wire.

For the working table top, particle board with a thin coating of melamine applied to its surface (widely available as *melamine board*—a building material for kitchen cabinets) is perhaps best. The slick plastic surface allows the foam to slide easily, and the particle board base is hefty enough to be free-standing. A variety of different materials can be used for the wire itself. Ni-Chrome wire, as used for electric heater elements, is often found on commercial machines, but stainless steel lock-wire (*safety wire*) works well, and even ordinary soft iron wire will do, though it will rust rapidly.

Voltage—To supply the "juice" for the wire it is usual to use a transformer to cut the voltage from 110 to something safer. While suitable transformers can be bought at an electrical supply house, you probably already have one—a battery charger! While it is theoretically pretty rough on the charger, it works. To adjust the current in the wire—and thus its temperature—some sort of variable resistance is needed. This can be a rheostat or simply an extra length of stainless wire wrapped around something heat resistant and non-conducting—a concrete block is dandy. By tapping off this resistance coil at various points using an alligator clip, the current can be adjusted for various jobs.

The wire can actually be run directly on household 110 volt electricity, and while it would be irresponsible to recommend the practice in view of the electric shock hazard, you're likely going to avoid touching the wire whatever its voltage, since it is hot enough to produce a nasty burn anyway. If using 0.020 inch stainless lock-wire, a total of twenty feet of wire will produce sufficient resistance to pass about two amps at 110 volts—enough to get the wire glowing visibly in a darkened room. Whatever isn't needed for the working length of the wire can be wound around the concrete block resistor. Bear in mind that the wire will expand in length when heated, and shorten again when cool. Some of the stretch will also become permanent, so some sort of tensioning spring will be needed. Depending on its design, the bow may take care of this more or less automatically.

Fabric Impregnators

Although usually thought of as a mass production tool, a fabric impregnator can quickly earn back its purchase price in labor savings; the improvement in laminate quality they permit—by virtue of uniform resin distribution and the ability to use tightly woven fabrics—is a bonus. Essentially, fabric impregnators are nothing more than a bath of catalyzed resin through which the fabric is drawn, and a pair of pinch rollers to

A simple hand-powered fabric impregnator. Photo courtesy Gougeon Brothers.

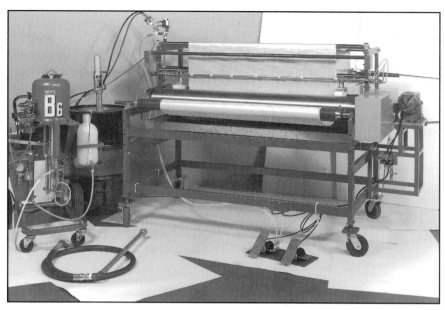

wring out the surplus resin. The technology is no more complex than the wringer on an old-fashioned washing machine.

Elaborate air or electrically powered machines with features ensuring automatic replenishment of the resin and catalyst metering pumps are available, at considerable cost. Simpler and less expensive units are also sold, that use a hand crank for the transport of the fabric, and require that the resin be manually mixed and poured into the trough. Or you could make one yourself; the only tricky part is to ensure that the rollers don't spring apart near the middle of the swath of cloth passing through.

SHOP LAYOUT

Reinforced plastic work makes a mess. If you don't keep the mess under control from the very first, you'll soon be tripping around in a lumpy, hairy, hopelessly dusty fire-trap. Not nice.

If you start off with a concrete floor, patch up any cracks and holes as much as feasible, clean it furiously, then crank up the fan, slip on your mask and gloves, and lay on an epoxy paint job. After it's fully cured (read the label!), rent an industrial floor polisher and wax it thoroughly several times. Now you've got a floor you can clean.

Work Areas

Ideally, mold preparation and spraying operations, fabric cutting and laminating, and trimming operations would occupy three separate areas. You certainly should not have both trimming and laminating going on in the same space at the same time—the inevitable dust from trimming will get into the work. In particular, if you get dust on the exposed surface of a gel coat before you laminate, you're in trouble. Trimming areas should be swept up frequently, using a sweeping compound to keep down the dust, and vacuumed thoroughly a couple of times a week. Hardened lumps of resin will have to be attacked with a scraper on the end of a short broom-handle before sweeping. Despite the wax job, some little puddles of resin may prove absolutely stubborn and eventually, when it's time to re-wax the floor, you will just have to wax right over the top of some of them.

Room Temperature

Shop heat can be problematic. First, the shop must be maintained above 65F, and preferably 70F, any time work is going on or plastic is curing. What's more, the need for constant ventilation to keep vapor concen-

A fabric impregnator is another useful production tool, but this complex machine featuring automatic catalyst metering and resin replenishment is perhaps more than a small shop needs. Photo courtesy Binks Manufacturing, Co.

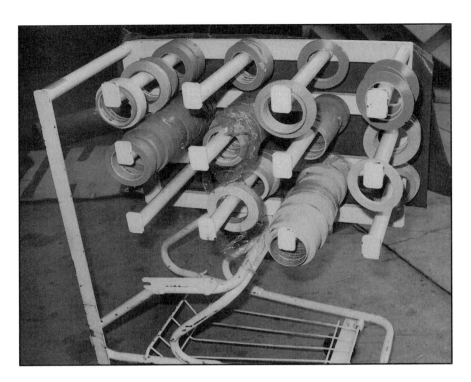

A wide assortment of masking tape is essential for masking molds. Photo by Michael Lutfy.

a particular problem with filled resins, gel coat and putties. Discarding this is both wasteful and harmful to the environment. A rubber spatula, as sold for scraping mixing bowls in the kitchen, is the tidiest tool for scraping this excess material from the sides of cans. Get the real rubber kind with a wooden handle—the semi-clear plastic type dissolves in styrene!

The glue on ordinary masking tape and "Scotch" tape (TM 3M Co.) also tends to dissolve when exposed to polyester, or more precisely to styrene. "Invisible" mending tape—the sort you can write on—seems impervious, though, and this is the best stuff to use to secure masking, etc. For the masking itself, ordinary masking paper is fine for paint, but any kind of paper may become saturated if drenched in resin. Aluminum foil is preferable here. ∎

trations under control will require a lot more heat during cold weather, especially in the northern parts of the continent, than in a space where the air can safely be recirculated. (Note, too, that in some rented industrial spaces the heat is turned down at night.) Second, the source of heat should not present a fire hazard, so open gas flames, etc., are out of the question. We can only envy people who work in sun belt areas where these problem seldom arise.

Handy Odds & Ends

A clock with a large face, legible numbers, and a sweep second hand should be hung somewhere so it is visible to both whoever is doing the laminating and whoever is preparing batches of resin; more than one may be required. (If there are three or more people working, it often makes sense to designate one as "gaffer," to mix batches of resin, clean up tools on the run, and make sure supplies are available to the laminators.) Likewise, one or more large thermometers should be within sight.

A substantial amount of resin will remain stuck to the sides and bottom of containers,

Keep your supplies organized in such a way that they are readily at hand. Photo by Jack Gladback.

HEALTH & SAFETY

6

I know that you are probably all excited to start making parts out of FRP material; you've got the tools, materials and the desire. But before we get into lay-up technique, which is the focus of the next chapter, we still have some more preparation to do concerning safety.

Reinforced plastics can be, to put it bluntly, miserable to work with. They stink and itch, and if you ever get any in your hair, you're definitely up for a new hair-style. Oh well, it grows back! And that's the good part—there are also some fairly serious potential health and safety hazards to be encountered when slopping around with these materials. These include fire and/or explosion risks, and the unhealthy effects of various fumes, dusts and liquids.

MSDS

Those who manufacture and market these goods are required by law to provide a Material Safety Data Sheet for each product, identifying its known health and safety hazards, and providing instructions on its safe handling and use. You should insist on an MSDS for every chemical product you purchase. READ IT, AND HEED IT.

Polyester and Vinylester Resins

Polyester and vinylester, as purchased, usually contain various other materials.

Styrene—Styrene monomer, which both serves as a diluting solvent and also reacts with the resin during the curing process, accounts for about 40% of the mix, and for

FRP work can be a very messy operation indeed! As you can see, the particles spewing forth from this chopper gun can work their way into your lungs. Proper precautions must be taken when working with any FRP materials. Photo courtesy FRP Supply Division, Ashland Chemical Co.

> *"Because styrene is fat-soluble, the liquid effectively de-greases the skin on contact, which causes symptoms ranging from mild local irritation to severe dermatitis, including blistering. Liquid styrene is readily absorbed by the skin."*

most of the familiar fiberglass shop smell. Styrene—also known as vinyl benzene—is a clear, colorless, highly flammable liquid, with a very distinct and pervasive odor which can be detected at a concentration of less than one part-per-million (ppm). Because styrene is fat-soluble, the liquid effectively de-greases the skin on contact, which causes symptoms ranging from mild local irritation to severe dermatitis, including blistering. Liquid styrene is readily absorbed by the skin.

Styrene is volatile, and ten to fifteen percent of the styrene in the resin can evaporate into the work place air during manual lay-up. These vapors are irritants to the eyes and upper respiratory tract. Prolonged inhalation at 15 ppm and higher can cause burning eyes, sneezing and coughing, and can have narcotic effects (headache, dizziness, drowsiness, vomiting); 50 ppm and higher can cause central nervous system depression. Exposure even to levels below 50 ppm over months or years—such as a full-time worker in the industry may experience—can lead to chronic health effects including liver and kidney damage. A re-examination of the long-term effects of styrene by a division of the World Health Organization has also increased concerns about its potential as a human carcinogen. Its strong odor and irritating effects help to discourage extended exposure, however.

Not only is liquid styrene highly flammable, its vapors form an explosive mixture in air at concentrations of 1.5%—6.7% by volume. To put this into perspective, however, 1.5% corresponds to 15,000 ppm, so the critical limit is human exposure rather than the formation of an explosive mixture.

Vinylester Resins—Vinylester resins, introduced to the market about twenty years ago, resemble polyester in their ease of handling, yet yield mechanical properties near to those of epoxy. Vinylesters, like polyesters (and for the same reasons), include large amounts of styrene in the can as

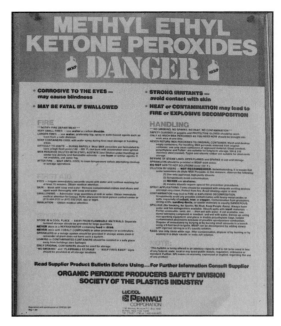

Check the MSDA (Material Safety Data Sheet) of every product before you work with it. Manufacturers must provide them by law. Photo by Michael Lutfy.

bought. They also generally use the same catalysts and accelerators as polyesters, with the exception that in some formulations the accelerator is not pre-mixed into the resin, but rather must be added by the end user, prior to catalyzing.

Catalysts & Accelerators For Vinylester & Polyester

To transform the liquid resin into a solid, a catalyst is mixed in immediately before use. This catalyst is usually methyl ethyl ketone peroxide (MEKP) or benzoyl peroxide (BPO).

MEKP—MEKP is a clear, colorless liquid. It is explosively unstable in its pure form and so is supplied as a diluted solution in an inert liquid *buffer*. While it is not itself highly flammable, it is a powerful oxidizer which may cause some readily flammable substances—like paper, rags or sawdust—to ignite spontaneously if it comes in contact with them. It is also quite corrosive, and prolonged contact will cause skin burns. MEKP splashed in the eyes can cause serious, permanent eye damage. The vapors may cause headaches and intoxication, and corrosive damage to nose, throat and lungs.

BPO—BPO is not usually used as a catalyst in curing polyester and vinylester laminating resins, but it is the most common catalyst for polyester-based auto body filler. It is usually supplied as a paste, dispersed in some stabilizing medium; otherwise, this powerful organic peroxide can be regarded as similar to MEKP.

DMA—Dimethyl aniline (DMA) and/or cobalt naphthenate (CoNap) are usually present in store-bought polyester resin as accelerators, or promoters, to speed up the curing process.

DMA is a liquid solution, ranging from water clear to light-yellow to brownish. It is strongly alkaline and so can cause skin burns. Both liquid and vapor may be absorbed through the skin and act as a central nervous system depressant. DMA vapors are both flammable and an irritant, and inhalation of the vapors may be fatal, as may swallowing of the liquid. Chronic health effects of exposure include liver and kidney damage.

CoNap—Cobalt naphthenate solution is a combustible red-violet liquid, with an odor of mineral spirits. As either liquid or vapor, it is irritating to the eyes and skin, and may be absorbed through the skin. Breathing of concentrated vapors may cause headache and loss of coordination. It is especially harmful if swallowed, symptoms including gastrointestinal irritation, vomiting and depression.

Epoxy Resins

Epoxy resins have better mechanical performance than polyester, but are significantly more expensive and rather trickier to handle. They also have different health hazards associated with them.

Epoxies, as used in wet lay-up fabrication, are moderately viscous liquids, varying in color from water clear to brown. Skin contact with either the liquid or vapors of some

Some modern epoxy formulations have very low odor. This permits work without a respirator–though we cannot in conscience recommend this. Gloves, however, are absolutely required when working with uncured epoxies. Photo by Jack Gladback.

formulations can cause moderate to severe irritation, and inhalation of their vapors can cause irritation of the nose, throat and lungs. Ingestion of even the smallest amounts can lead to an overall allergic response. (Although the most basic kind of common sense would seem to exclude the notion of actually swallowing substances such as epoxy resins, an effective way to ingest them is to eat lunch or smoke a cigarette with incompletely scoured hands.)

Lower viscosity resins theoretically have a greater hazard potential than more viscous ones. This observation is of only academic interest, however, as individual formulations can yield, on the one hand, highly viscous yet highly irritating products or, on the other hand, something like the popular "safety" epoxies, which combine low viscosity with very low irritation potential. These differences to some extent depend on which of various glycidil ethers are present in the resin.

Glycidil Ethers—Glycidil ethers serve as a reactive diluent for epoxy resin—they both reduce the viscosity of the base resin and react with it during the cure, analogous to the role played by styrene monomer added to a base polyester or vinylester resin. Glycidil ethers are colorless liquids of low viscosity and slightly sweet odor. They vary from negligible to severe in potential for irritation, and some are suspected carcinogens. Major resin makers and formulators assure

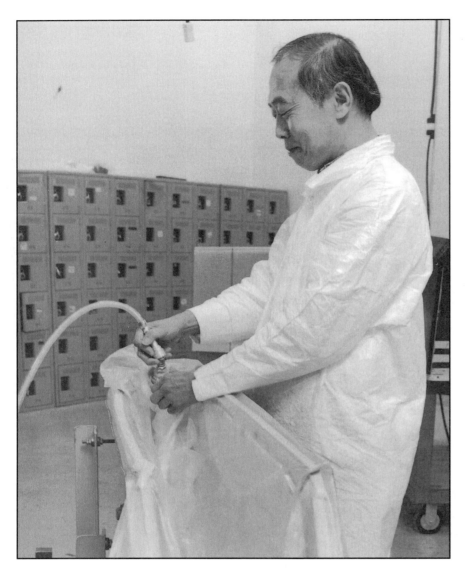

Use of pre-preg material eliminates messy resin and encourages a healthy workshop atmosphere. Note cleanliness and neatness in deHavilland's composites shop. Guy Levesque photo courtesy deHavilland Inc.

kind of sensitization can occur with glycidil ethers; moreover, a cross-sensitization can occur between epoxies and glycidil ethers, and vice versa.

Epoxy Curing Agents

Unlike polyester and vinylester, the cure rate of epoxy systems cannot be varied by adjusting the amount of catalyst. For any given combination of resin and hardener there is a very narrow range of hardener-to-resin proportions which will yield a proper cure, so if a faster or slower cure is needed, a different curing agent must be used. (Some degree of adjustment of the cure rate can be achieved by varying the shop or mold temperature). Common hardeners for room-temperature cures are aliphatic amines, modified amines, and polyamides.

Aliphatic Amines—Epoxy curing agents of the aliphatic or "unmodified" amine type, such as "TETA" and "DETA," are seldom seen in the amateur field. They are corrosive substances of high irritation potential, can cause dermatitis, severe burns, and may have other serious long-term health effects. Amines in direct contact with the eyes will produce severe damage.

Modified Amines—Modified amine curing agents are now available which have very much reduced potential for both irritation and sensitization. Nevertheless, prolonged contact with either liquid or fumes may cause both effects in some individuals. To compound the irony of sensitization, some people exhibit cross-sensitivity among epoxies and glycidil ethers and amine curing agents.

Polyamides—Polyamides (sometimes called nylon hardeners—nylon is a polyamide) are viscous liquids with a distinct odor of ammonia. They are probably safer than any of the amine curatives, but are awkwardly thick unless diluted. While a mixture of epoxy resin and polyamide hardener can be thinned to a workable viscosity by diluting with a large amount of reactive

that no responsible supplier markets any products containing the nastier glycidil ethers to amateurs, but the message may not have reached some small re-packaging retailers—beware when purchasing epoxy diluent of anything labeled phenyl glycidil ether or butyl glycidil ether.

As many workers have discovered to their dismay, a sensitization can occur with epoxy systems. If an allergic reaction is ever triggered—whether by a single severe exposure to a particularly irritating resin, or by long-term exposure to low doses of a relatively innocuous one—subsequent exposure to small doses of even the most benign epoxy can cause a recurrence. Ironically, the same diluent, the hazards of the diluent may defeat the purpose and may also result in a structurally inferior end-product.

Acetone

Once cured, none of the three types of resin can be dissolved, in any usual sense of the word. Until fully cured, however, they are all at least partially soluble in solvents such as acetone, which is thus widely used for general clean-up purposes.

Acetone is a clear colorless liquid with a strong solvent odor. It is highly flammable. Exposure to liquid acetone can cause dermatitis due to its fat-solvent properties. Liquid acetone may be absorbed by skin, though the vapor probably is not. As it is very commonly used for clean-up purposes, its vapors—which are irritating to the eyes and upper respiratory tract—are likely to be present in large concentrations in the shop. Prolonged exposure to acetone vapor at 310 ppm or more can cause loss of coordination and central nervous system disturbances.

Reinforcing Fibers & Finished Laminates

Although virtually everything will burn under the right circumstances, cured thermoset resins (polyesters, vinylesters and epoxies) do not represent a particularly severe fire hazard. Yes, when they do catch they can be tough to put out, and meanwhile make lots of very nasty smoke. But you cannot just walk up to a fully cured laminate and light it with your lighter; you have to work at it to ignite a cured reinforced plastic laminate. The reinforcing fibers themselves—at least glass and carbon—are completely benign, from the point of view of fire. Aramid fiber is inherently fire resistant, but it chars above 800 degrees F. and will burn if an ignition source is maintained. Its products of combustion have been compared by the manufacturer to those of wool.

A fully cured resin is quite harmless, but how do you know it is fully cured? Especially with hand-measured and hand-mixed epoxy resins, there is a good chance that some small fraction of the resin remains

"Prolonged exposure to acetone vapor at 310 ppm and greater can cause loss of coordination and central nervous system disturbances."

Contrast mess in this jobbing shop where a chopper gun is used with surgical cleanliness attainable when less messy fabrication methods are employed. Photo courtesy Composites Fabricators Association.

"Skin contact with a solvent which has been contaminated with resin, such as from cleaning tools, should NEVER, EVER, be allowed—this is a spectacularly efficient way of driving the resin deep into the lower layers of the skin."

unreacted, so contact of unprotected skin with apparently cured laminates should be undertaken with caution. This is a particular problem when grinding or trimming the cured material, since the resulting tiny dust fragments have an enormous surface area, and thus a proportionately increased potential for irritation.

Also, the dust from grinding/sawing/sanding operations usually includes things other than cured resin. While the dust of some materials, like asbestos, is known to cause cancer, finely divided particles of anything are bad for your respiratory system. Otherwise innocuous substances like wood, flour, and stone can cause grief if inhaled as a dust. Partly this seems to be a function of particle size and shape. Glass or carbon fibers have a very small diameter, and when such fibers are fractured into short lengths, they lodge in the lungs with distressing tenacity if inhaled. They may also irritate the outer layers of the skin, and thus greatly increase the irritant effects of resins, hardeners, and solvents.

THE PRECAUTIONS

By now you have the bad news—almost all of the materials referred to above have at least some potential for adverse health effects, one way or another. Now the good news—given common-sense precautions, which includes adequate ventilation, protecting eyes and skin with appropriate clothing, and the use of a respirator mask, the health risks are minimal. If these simple acts of self-preservation are observed, probably the greatest real hazard is fire.

Flammable Items

Flammable solvents and resins should be kept in their original containers, stored in a well-ventilated cool place, away from any source of heat or ignition. Only as much as is needed for a single work session should be brought into the shop, in suitable closed

vessels. Obviously, smoking and any sort of open flame must be banned from the work area, and a big dry-chemical fire extinguisher and a bucket of sand should be on hand, just in case. Water does not do a very good job of extinguishing a plastic fire.

Solvents

Solvents are to clean uncured resin off tools, not people. Apart from the horrible prospect of a worker half-drenched in acetone suddenly becoming a human torch, the solvents serve as vehicles to drive nasty chemicals further into the skin. Skin contact with a solvent which has been contaminated with resin, such as from cleaning tools, should NEVER, EVER, be allowed—this is a spectacularly efficient way of driving the resin deep into the lower layers of the skin.

Catalysts & Accelerators

Catalysts and accelerators for polyester and vinylester also require cool storage, but particular precautions must be taken to avoid these two classes of material from ever coming in undiluted contact with one another, because of the risk of fire and explosion. It is sound practice to keep accelerators in a locked metal cabinet, with the key always on your person.

Because of their potential to cause spontaneous combustion, peroxide catalyst spills of any consequence should be soaked up with sand (never sawdust, rags, or paper towel), and any residue thoroughly washed down with water.

Ventilation

Satisfactory ventilation is a must. Air should flow from behind the worker, across the work, and away. (Actually, there is no "away." Check your local codes for possible trouble with the law; also, consider your neighbors downwind.) If, as is likely, you are using a fan to draw air out of the shop, situate it so it is aiming downwind under typical prevailing wind conditions. The

ideal, of course, is a vertical exhaust stack—it never points upwind, so an occasional strong gust will not reverse the air flow and give you a big shot of gel coat in your face.

Since most of the troublesome vapors are heavier than air, exhaust fan inlets should be located close to the floor, with fresh make-up air supplied close to the worker, higher up. Similarly, fumes will tend to accumulate in high concentrations in any sort of hollow depression—such as, say, a monocoque tub being worked on open-side up. Portable fans can be placed to dissipate such local pockets of vapor, but care must be taken to avoid inundating other unprotected workers.

Respirators & Masks

With good ventilation, there are some jobs you can do without a respirator. These include admiring yesterday's work, waxing molds, and taking coffee breaks. Some loonies will laminate without a mask. These people have—or soon will have—brain pans filled with yogurt. You really must wear a mask anytime you have plastic brew-

ing. Certainly any spraying, sanding, or grinding operation, cutting or tearing mat or cloth, cleaning anything with acetone or methylene chloride, plural component foaming, hot-wire foam cutting, and all resin mixing and laminating absolutely require a good mask.

A good mask is definitely not the pathetic little rag that the local paint dealer hands out free with a quart of lacquer. That may keep out the big lumps, but not dust and tiny fiber fragments, and it does absolutely nothing about fumes and vapors that can zap your liver and/or brain, so that you can no longer tie your shoelaces without blinding pain and a perplexing inability to find your hands. The mask you need is the authentic Darth Vader model, with a honker out both sides, each with a reactive cartridge. To save the cartridges from getting clogged up with dust, there is usually a mechanical particle filter upstream of the reactive cartridge. These felt-like strainers should be changed at least weekly—if you're working steadily—and the reactive cartridges should be

Grinding of incompletely cured epoxies produces particularly hazardous dust. Note use here of dust collection hood which connects with the giant vacuum machine. Photo by Jack Gladback.

"Some form of eye protection is mandatory, if only to guard against splashes. Catalysts, curing agents and accelerators, especially, can cause severe and almost instant damage to the eyes."

The best ventilation is provided by this OSHA-approved downdraft bench, yet note operator's dust mask—this wise worker takes no chances. Photo by Jack Gladback.

replaced as soon as you start to smell what you're working on.

Eye Protection

Some form of eye protection is mandatory, if only to guard against splashes. Catalysts, curing agents and accelerators, especially, can cause severe and almost instant damage to the eyes. In view of the eye irritation characteristic of many of the above substances, there is a case to be made for a more elaborate respirator device that incorporates a partial face shield—rather like a combination respirator and snorkeling mask. On the other hand, with an effective respirator, itchy, scratchy eyes are the sole remaining cue that vapor concentrations are becoming excessive, perhaps indicating a change in wind direction, or a failure in the ventilation system. This argues for conventional safety goggles, which provide protection against splashes, but do not exclude fumes from the eyes. For any kind of grinding, sawing, cutting, or sanding operation you absolutely and definitely need shatter-proof eye protection.

Gloves

Also, you will want protective gloves. The disposable vinyl plastic kind are hopelessly clumsy and keep falling off; pure latex surgical gloves are far too flimsy, are impossible to get on or off, and are not effective barriers against the various resins and solvents. On the other hand, anything heftier than the ordinary household type at the supermarket is too thick and clunky. Butyl, nitrile, and neoprene rubbers are effective barriers to epoxy and related compounds; latex is not. Conventional domestic rubber gloves—as for dishwashing—are mostly latex. Theoretically, these do not provide an adequate barrier to epoxies and some others of the above nasty fluids; they also are not strongly resistant to solvents. In practice, many workers find them adequate if frequently replaced, and so cheap and widely available that there is no excuse for not doing so.

Barrier Creams—Whatever you settle for, you may want to also use a barrier cream, which is applied to the skin prior to the work session, then washed off afterwards. Claims are made that some of these

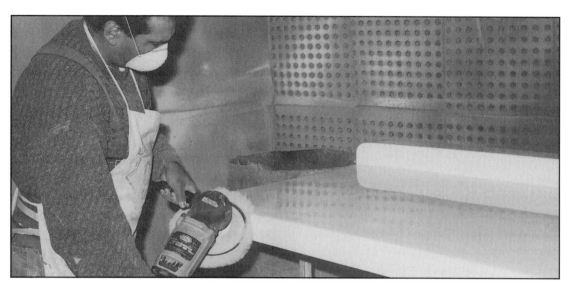

This shop worker almost gets an "A" for his protective gear. He's got the mask, an apron (gloves aren't really necessary here) but he's missing eye protection. Photo by Michael Lutfy.

creams provide adequate protection all by themselves, though if you have ever suffered through an episode of epoxy rash, you may wonder just who volunteered to test that claim! Certainly barrier creams can be a useful back-up to gloves, especially if you opt for thinner, more flexible gloves, which are more permeable and more prone to accidental tears.

With all gloves, mop the worst of the gunk off the outside, leave them turned inside-out after you remove them, to let the sweat evaporate, sprinkle a bunch of talcum powder on the inside before re-use, and throw them away if they become torn or if the inside becomes contaminated with resin. If you are working with latex (i.e. dishwashing) gloves, they should be replaced at least once a week. Gloves should be worn outside cuffs.

Clothing

Most resins work best at temperatures rather higher than most people work best, and all common thermosetting resins undergo an exothermic cure—they put out heat when they cure. Also, some reinforced plastic operations involve physically hard work. Put this lot together and you just know

you're going to sweat some, and you're going to want to work in shorts and a T-shirt. Boy, are you a sucker. If you work fiberglass with a bare belly, one of two things will happen—either you will never, ever touch it again, or you will work well-covered ever after.

Well-covered means lightweight coveralls with sleeves rolled all the way down. By far the best arrangement is disposable coveralls with an integral hood that makes you look like Commander Hygiene. Made of a paper-like material called "Tyvek" (a registered trademark of E.I. DuPont de Nemours, Inc), these are widely available (try an autobody shop supply outfit), sturdy enough for umpteen days of light duty, and—all things considered—dirt cheap. For really filthy operations like cutting and grinding, the hood is a godsend, but may prove hot and uncomfortable at other times. Nevertheless, you'd better cover your head—if you splash plastic in your hair, you can get it out later, with scissors; there is no other way. A painter's hat works fine, but you'll want to amputate most of the peak with scissors and/or wear it back-to-front, to prevent bumping into your work when peering closely at an air bubble. You should snap up

"Well-covered means lightweight coveralls with sleeves rolled all the way down. By far the best arrangement is disposable coveralls with an integral hood that makes you look like Commander Hygiene."

"If you breathe enough glass fiber dust from grinding, you'll get itchy lungs and cough blood. Later, you may die. If you think that's fun, try breathing two-part polyurethane foam while it's reacting: you'll turn green, curl up like a worm, and lose control of your bowels. Ditto fumes from hot-wire cutting of polystyrene foam. And you do not want to know what happens if you get a good snoot full of certain industrial strength epoxy hardeners."

several such outfits and toss out each one after a week or so of use.

Also, you will get an astonishing number of dribbles on your shoes. You will want leather shoes, so you can wax the bejeezus out of them before you ever wear them (loafers are best, since there are no laces to get glued shut), and from then on you can watch as, over the months, they turn into a work of spontaneous sculpture. Extremely silly looking disposable Tyvek "booties" are available to defeat this effect.

Cleanliness

Good housekeeping should obviously be practiced in the shop. Dust should be vacuumed up, not blasted away with an air hose. Resin dribbles should be cleaned off all surfaces. Disposable paper coverings for mixing tables and elsewhere are an excellent way to keep things clean and to avoid incidental contact with uncured resin. Waste of all types should be disposed of responsibly. Probably the most environmentally responsible way to dispose of waste resins and/or hardeners is to react them, leaving an inert solid. Beware, however, that a container of reacting resin generates much more exothermic heat than the same quantity of material spread over the large area of a laminate, and may represent an unrecognized fire risk. To avoid this, the container full of reacting resin can be floated in a bucket of water.

On top of all this, you should have a locker on the upstream side of the air-flow where you can keep your street clothes and your supply of clean Commander Hygiene outfits. If at all possible, you should arrange for a shower adjacent to the workshop. This may seem like a flagrant luxury; you will soon learn otherwise. This is pretty messy work at the best of times, and gritty and grim and awful the rest of the time. At the very least, there must be a hand-basin and plenty of hot water and soap. A well-known formu-

lator of epoxy systems suggests the use of a waterless hand cleaner to remove inadvertent splashes of resin from the skin, followed by soap and hot water. There seems to be no high-tech substitute for plain old hot suds as a medium for cleaning-up people. Besides, what are you doing with that stuff on your skin?

If this personal hygiene business sounds like a lot of work, you'll find it's worth it. If you breathe enough glass fiber dust from grinding, you'll get itchy lungs and cough blood. Later, you may die. If you think that's fun, try breathing two-part polyurethane foam while it's reacting: you'll turn green, curl up like a worm, and lose control of your bowels. Ditto fumes from hot-wire cutting of polystyrene foam. And you do not want to know what happens if you get a good snoot full of certain industrial strength epoxy hardeners. So you wear a mask, right? But you're pretty tough, so you'll skip on the gloves. Besides, they're clumsy and you work better without them. Sure. Now, figure out how you're going to answer the phone. Or the call of nature. Besides, while you might get away with it working with polyester or vinylester, if you get certain epoxy agents on you often enough, you will get a horrible sensation like you just sand-papered yourself and feel compelled to tear your skin off. Either that, or it will fall off all by itself.

Don't kid yourself, you're still going to get itchy and sticky from time to time. Sensible precautions, however, will vastly improve your sense of humor, your chances of staying healthy, and the quality of your work—it's hard to concentrate and be patient when you're desperately uncomfortable. So: fan cranked up; non-porous shoes; clean Commander Hygiene outfit; idiotic pink rubber gloves; Darth Vader mask. You look lovely! Now, FOLLOW THE DIRECTIONS ON THE CAN! ∎

WET LAY-UP TECHNIQUE

7

While many mass-produced FRP goods are manufactured by a variety of mechanized processes (see Chapter 9), most large and/or custom products—like boats, race car bodywork, and lightly stressed covers and fairings for light aircraft—are still produced by wet lay-up. The wet lay-up process appears simple—just put some reinforcement into the mold, slobber it with catalyzed resin, and wait a while. Indeed, reduced to its fundamentals, that's all there is to it, and given just those simple instructions, a complete novice might manage to produce some sort of finished part, though it would probably look amateurish and would surely be unacceptably heavy and weak. It is more likely, however, that our rookie would simply waste his time turning valuable materials into a waste disposal problem and, worse, there is a definite possibility that he would damage or ruin the mold. Like doing anything worthwhile, consistently producing light, strong, attractive goods requires a degree of skill and care.

The care is mostly a matter of taking personal pride in what you do. The skill, on the other hand, is something that only develops with practice, over time. If my experience is anything to go by, the practice is usually gained by working first in an existing mold. Then, after getting the basics down, sufficient confidence is gained to explore the art of mold making, using an existing part (say, an automobile hood or fender) as the master shape from which the mold is made.

Although it may seem like putting the cart before the horse, you should practice your technique before you make any molds. Hone your lay-up skills with existing molds, striving for surface perfection. Any flaws on molds will show up in every part, so it is best to learn on existing ones first. Photo by Michael Lutfy.

"PVA is not only unnecessary in a well made, aged mold, it is undesirable, since the PVA leaves a slightly pebbly, orange peel texture on the surface of the finished part that has to be polished out. For a green (new) mold, though, PVA is vital insurance."

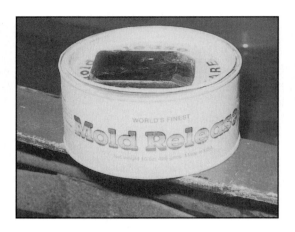 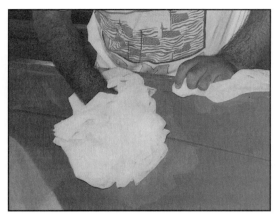

Waxing the mold is the first step. Although you may be all right with ordinary carnauba-based wax, it's best to get specially designed "mold release wax." Apply three separate coats (wax/buff, wax/buff, etc.) to the mold just to be sure. Photos by Michael Lutfy.

As we shall see in Chapter 11, the procedures for making an FRP mold are very similar to those for making a part in that mold. Nevertheless, molds are usually somewhat more complex in shape than the part they produce. They almost always involve more material, and they certainly are more critical—slight flaws that might be insignificant in an individual piece can turn into a nightmare when they are built into the mold. Beginners, then, are urged to start by producing a simple part in a mold that is known to be OK; the experience can later be applied to making molds.

MOLD PREPARATION

Assuming that a suitable mold already exists, and that we are working with polyester, the procedure generally goes something like this. First, if the mold is not well aged (that is, if several pieces have not already been produced in it), a parting agent is applied to prevent the part from sticking to the mold. The most common parting agent is a wax based on carnauba—a natural wax scraped from the leaves of the carnauba plant, *Copernica prunifera*. Sometimes you will get away with using ordinary household floor wax, but sometimes you won't; unless you can afford to risk throwing away both the part and the mold, buy a specially for-

mulated mold release wax. Even thoroughly aged molds need an occasional waxing, but new ones need extra protection, until the heat generated during the cure of the first couple or three parts helps complete the post-cure hardening of the plastic in the mold surface.

PVA

With a new mold, you first wax and thoroughly buff several times—at least three. (You don't need that much wax, but you might have missed a few spots the first time.) Terry-cloth toweling seems to work well for the waxing and buffing. Next, you apply a coat of polyvinyl alcohol (PVA), which dries to form a thin barrier film that provides a second line of defense against the nightmare of a part firmly stuck in the mold. PVA is not only unnecessary in a well made, aged mold, it is undesirable, since the PVA leaves a slightly pebbly, orange peel texture on the surface of the finished part that has to be polished out. For a green (new) mold, though, PVA is vital insurance.

Applying PVA—It is possible to apply PVA without a spray gun (a small piece of old T-shirt seems to work better as an applicator than a brush), but spraying is definitely preferable. The PVA should be sprayed in stages, starting with a very light misting, and finishing with several heavier coats.

Obtaining a uniform and, above all, a continuous film of PVA is much easier if the mold has a color that contrasts well with the PVA, which is green. The film should be thick enough that it will peel off the mold in one piece without tearing. Once the PVA has dried, a process that can be speeded up with a hair drier, the next step is the gel coat.

GEL COAT

In Chapter 4 we strongly urged that gel coat be sprayed, rather than applied with a brush or roller. Even with the right equipment, though, gel coat can cause problems. Some of these can result from contamination of the gel coat surface by dust, handprints, etc. Pinholes, small bubbles and general porosity of the gel coat may be caused by an excess of catalyst, by trapped solvents (which shouldn't be there anyway), or by water in the air lines (see Chapter 5). Soft, incompletely cured areas can result from a mis-aimed catalyst stream, in the case of external-mix gel guns (again, see Chapter 5). And there is always the nightmare of alligatoring, caused by the gel coat being attacked by the styrene in either added gel coat or in the first layer of reinforcement.

Thickness

As explained in Chapter 3, polyester does not "dry," in the way that, say, lacquer paint does; it hardens by a chemical reaction, and that reaction depends, among other things, on the volume of plastic that is reacting. Thin coats cure more slowly than thick ones. Also, since a thin coat has more area for a given volume of resin, a thin coat will lose proportionally more styrene into the air, and the inhibited surface layer will account for a larger proportion of the total thickness of the film. If the coat is too thin, alligatoring will inevitably result. Generally, the gel coat should be about 15 mils (0.015 inch) thick. 12 mils (0.012 inch) is the minimum; anything thicker than 20 mils will be prone to

cracking unless the laminate is unusually stiff, and anyway represents unnecessary weight and expense. (We're talking about a piece part here; the gel coat on a mold surface is usually somewhat thicker than this, as noted in Chapter 11.) The thickness of a wet film of gel coat can be measured with a simple tool which is often given away free by resin suppliers; slightly more elaborate ones can be bought.

Gel Coat Curing Time

The gel coat should be allowed enough curing time to prevent alligatoring, but not so long that the surface becomes contaminated by dust or by reaction with humidity in the shop air. Uncured polyester will react with moisture in the air, forming a microscopically thin layer of polystyrene, sometimes visible as a whitish blush on the surface, that interferes with proper adhesion of the layers of laminate that follow. There are a couple of trade tricks to judge when a gel coat has cured sufficiently to start laminating. One is the "fingerprint" test—a fingertip pressed on a properly cured gel coat should leave a distinct print, but none should stick to the finger. Goop on your finger? Wait a while. No visible print? You've waited too long! You're aiming for the time

Apply gel coat no thicker than 20 mils, but no thinner than 12 mils. Wait until it has sufficiently cured before proceeding. Use the "fingerprint" and "squeak" tests to determine if it is dry. Photo by Michael Lutfy.

"*If cloth or woven roving is used for this first layer, the slight shrink-age of the resin which occurs on curing tends to create a cosmetic problem called* print-through—*the texture of the weave gets telegraphed through the gel coat and is visible on the surface of the finished part.*"

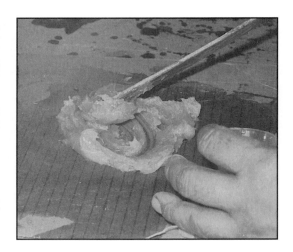
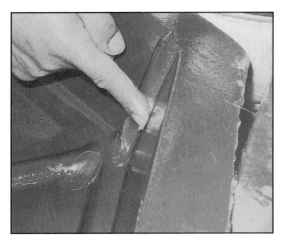

Sharp corners should be filled with filler, or a strand of roving can be set into the space. Here, resin has been mixed with Cabosil to fill in the brace seams of this patio umbrella. Photos by Michael Lutfy.

bracket between these extremes. The other technique is the "squeak" test—a finger drawn across the surface should produce a light squeaking sound. Once the gel coat has cured to this stage, it is almost time to start laminating. Remember that you can speed up the cure, if necessary, by applying a moderate amount of heat, but heat the back of the mold, not the exposed uncured gel coat, to avoid boiling off too much styrene.

Sharp Corners

Although it is generally bad practice to design anything for production in FRP that has sharp corners, there are times and places where this is unavoidable. Before placing any reinforcement onto the gel coated surface, it will be necessary to deal first with any sharp inside corners, as the reinforcement will not conform to a tight radius, bridging over it instead and leaving a pocket of unsupported gel coat. As noted in Chapter 11, the sharp corner can be rounded using filler, or a strand of roving can be laid in the corner, to the same effect.

Some of the technical issues behind the choice of reinforcement (glass or some other fiber, in the form of mat, cloth or roving) are discussed in Chapter 2, but even if it has been decided to use woven goods in the laminate, it is customary to apply mat for the

first layer of reinforcement in contact with the gel coat. If cloth or woven roving is used for this first layer, the slight shrinkage of the resin which occurs on curing tends to create a cosmetic problem called *print-through*—the texture of the weave gets telegraphed through the gel coat and is visible on the surface of the finished part. It is tempting to omit the mat in the interest of saving weight, and for the very lightest parts a little print-through might be acceptable; it is also possible to sand it off. Generally, though, it is wise to use a cushioning layer of mat.

APPLYING RESIN & MAT

There are two schools of thought about the next step. Dry mat can be applied to the exposed gel coat, and then saturated with catalyzed resin, or a coat of catalyzed resin can be brushed or sprayed onto the gel coat first before setting the mat in place. Since it takes about the same amount of time either way, it is probably best to use the second technique to avoid the risk of leaving a few hidden dry fibers right next to the gel coat.

Any spray gun suitable for gel coat can be used to apply laminating resin but, as explained in connection with gel coat (see Chapter 4), more styrene will be lost into the air if the resin is sprayed rather than brushed, and the stickiness of the remaining polyester can not only make life difficult for the laminator but also cure to a more rubbery, less hard solid. Additional styrene may be added to make up for this evaporative loss, but consult with the resin supplier and/or conduct some experiments on this point to establish the amount. Unless the job is really large, though, it will generally prove less trouble to apply the laminating resin by brush than to clean all the gel coat out of the gun, pressure pot and fluid lines, and to reset the gun for the less viscous laminating resin. Take care, however, to disturb the gel coat as little as possible if applying the fresh resin by brush—scrub too much and you'll have alligatored gel coat.

In any case, all the reinforcement should be tailored to shape in advance. Both mat and cloth cut readily with sharp shears (though they won't stay sharp for long!), but mat is probably better torn rather than cut, as the fuzzy edges prove helpful in smoothing the transition from one piece to the next. It is not wise to attempt to work with very large pieces of mat, especially in a mold with a complex shape. Tear off pieces about the size of a small magazine page, and apply them with their frayed edges overlapped, working systematically from one end of the mold toward the other. After you get the hang of it, you may choose to work with larger pieces. During this "shingling" operation, you should try to keep the thickness uniform. Since the amount of material overlapped will vary at the seams between shingles, you need to fiddle about with the tip of the brush, coaxing fiber away from the thick areas and toward the thin ones.

When the glass is wetted by the resin, its opaque white color disappears and it becomes transparent. As soon as this happens, deal with any visible air bubbles by nudging them with the brush to the free edge of the piece of mat. After completing an area of a couple of square feet in this way, work vigorously over the area with a ribbed roller,

pressing firmly to compact the laminate and drive out any remaining air bubbles. Try to avoid breaking big bubbles into multiple smaller ones, which are even tougher to remove. This operation will also help to level out differences in thickness. Keep at it until you're sure all the mat is wetted and all the air is gone.

Once a piece of mat has been set onto the resin-wetted gel coat, do not attempt to pick it up again, or to slide it across the gel coat

We suggest it is better to tear mat than to cut it, but for large numbers of identical pieces, many layers of mat can be stacked and cut together. In the top photo, boat kits are being prepared. At bottom, shears are used to cut lengths of mat. Top photo courtesy FRP Supply Division, Ashland Chemical Co. Bottom Photo: Michael Lutfy.

Resin

The resin used at this stage should be a *laminating resin*. Like gel coat, laminating resin contains no wax, so the uppermost surface in contact with the air has its cure inhibited—it remains sticky, permitting a sound bond to subsequent layers. To avoid a tacky surface on the inside of the finished part, a surfacing resin containing wax is used for the last layer. The dissolved wax rises to the surface of the resin, excluding air and allowing a full cure.

Mixing—Mix up the resin in small batches; whatever you don't use within a few minutes of adding the catalyst will turn to stone. While polyester is tolerant of fairly wide variations in the catalyst-to-resin ratio, you should still develop some scheme for measuring both components. For small (battery box) to medium (bathtub) sized jobs, a six ounce hot drink cup about two-thirds full is a convenient amount of resin to work with. If the catalyst is the usual 60% MEKP and the shop temperature is moderate (say 65 to 75 degrees F), a medicine dropper filled about half-way provides a roughly suitable amount of catalyst. Mix in the catalyst thoroughly (wooden popsicle sticks work well), but don't stir violently or use any power tool for this mixing—you'll get air bubbles trapped in the resin. Both the cup and the stick should be discarded after one use. Don't engage in petty economies here; even traces of partially cured resin will mess up the gel time of the fresh resin.

Mat Layers

What happens next depends on the size of the job, the rate of cure (determined mostly by catalyst ratio and shop temperature), how many workers are on the job, and how well you have planned. Certainly, the first layer of mat should be completed in one pass, each section being laid in place, saturated, and rolled out, before the adjacent piece has gelled. It would also be ideal if each layer of laminate is begun before the previous one

When applying more resin, use a paint brush but don't "brush," like shown above. Use a poking or "stippling" motion to coat the mat. Photo by Michael Lutfy.

Thorough and vigorous working of laminate with a ribbed roller is essential to ensure uniform resin distribution and to exclude air and consolidate the laminate. Note dry areas which appear white; glass becomes completely transparent when thoroughly wetted by resin. Photo courtesy DOW Plastics.

surface—this is guaranteed to scour away some of the gel coat, leading to alligatoring. If you encounter a particularly persistent air bubble, or a place where the mat bridges across a hollow, just snip the mat with the shears and fill any resulting gap with another little shred of mat. Using a small (1" or 2") paintbrush, apply more resin, and work the mat firmly onto the gel coat with a poking or *stippling* action, rather than a painting motion. The binder that holds the mat together dissolves almost instantly in the resin, liberating the individual fibers, so brushing across the mat simply drags fibers loose and rapidly turns the brush into a fur-ball-on-a-stick.

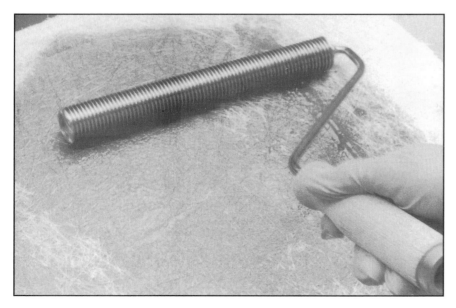

has cured. This is not always possible; one reason is because it is already long past quitting time. Also, for very thick sections, as used in boat construction, a problem arises because of the tremendous amount of heat created when a large quantity of plastic "kicks" all at once. About six to ten ounces of plastic per square foot is the practical limit. For lighter parts, this is not an issue.

If the part is small, or if there are extra hands available, it should be possible to get the second layer of reinforcement in place before the first has begun to gel. In that case, you need not be overly concerned about excess resin in the first layer of mat—the surplus will be soaked up by the next. If you are working alone, or the part is large, or you goofed on the catalyst and the plastic is gelling too fast, be sure to use the brush to sop up excess resin while it is still liquid, scraping it off the brush on the edge of a container. DO NOT USE THIS SCRAP RESIN—it is full of air! A slight surplus of resin is probably preferable to dry areas, but puddles of resin are unacceptable. It is quite correct that the strength-to-weight ratio of composite laminates falls steadily with increasing resin content, for reasons that are discussed in later chapters, but all this really means is that the strength remains more or less constant, while increasing resin content just adds weight—up to a point. When the degree of excess resin reaches the point where any appreciable thickness of neat (i.e. unreinforced) resin exists on the surface, though, any severe flexing will cause the resin to crack, and that crack will act as a stress concentration that will reduce the overall strength of the laminate.

If you are forced to work one layer at a time, wait until the previous layer has gone through its peak exotherm before continuing. The heat would otherwise speed up the cure of the fresh resin, demanding frenzied work to stay ahead of the plastic. Be sure you have used de-waxed resin, and don't wait too long—as with gel coat, the air-

When multiple layers of reinforcement are being used, material can be set down dry on previous wet layer. Photo by Jack Gladback.

inhibited surface of the resin is easily contaminated, jeopardizing the adhesion of the following layer.

Secondary Bonds

Applying more laminations to a fully cured surface is asking for trouble; even sanding or grinding all over and etching the surface with a quick scour with acetone does not alter the fact that any subsequent adhesion between layers is purely mechanical—the new resin does not chemically bond to the old. Boats, which often have to be made in stages for the reasons noted above, sometimes experience *de-lamination*—peeling apart of layers—for this reason. Try to organize the job to avoid these secondary bonds if at all possible.

Peel Ply—When secondary bonds are unavoidable, the grinding of the cured previous layer can be avoided, along with the risk of incorporating some of the grinding dust, by use of peel ply—a layer of fabric treated so it does not readily adhere to cured resin. It is applied as the last step in making the first part of the laminate. When it is time to add new material on top of fully cured old, the peel ply is torn off, leaving a surface which, though still not chemically active, is at least textured and clean.

Either way, the second layer is now applied. You should use larger pieces of reinforcement at this stage even if mat is being used for the whole job, and especially

"About six to ten ounces of plastic per square foot is the practical limit. For lighter parts, this is not an issue."

Additional resin to ensure complete saturation can then be applied by brush. Photo by Jack Gladback.

Reinforcement can be urged into place with a gloved hand. Photo by Jack Gladback.

stretched into and onto quite tight curves, cloth, you will discover, does not stretch! Depending on the weave, this limits the amount of three-dimensional curvature that can be handled before the cloth forms wrinkles around the edges and refuses to lay flat. To avoid bridging over depressions and inside corners, set the material down first in the middle of the hollow and work out toward the edges, urging it into place with brush and gloved hand. Where it rumples, snip pie-shaped pieces out of the creases with the shears.

Remove Surplus Resin & Air—Once a reasonable area is covered—say, as much as you can reach with one hand without moving your feet, work over the zone with the ribbed roller, to compact the laminate and ensure that all the air is out. Special rollers are available for corners, in various radii. The surplus resin that the rolling operation will bring to the surface should be sopped up with the brush and discarded. Another useful tool for working air and surplus resin out of cloth is a plastic or rubber squeegee. Special rubber squeegees made specifically for this job are available; the cheap plastic spatulas

if you have switched to cloth or woven roving. If the first layer is still wet, just plop the fresh reinforcement down, and let the surplus resin wick up into it; if working over a cured first layer, more resin should be painted on first. Add more resin where it seems to be needed; sop up and discard any surplus. Try to be neat, and keep the overlaps fairly uniform—a couple of inches is all you need. While mat, once wetted, can be fiddled and

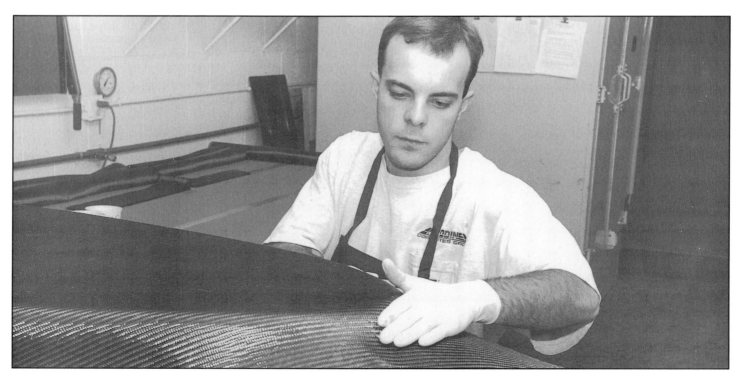

Especially when mat is used, each layer of laminate must again be consolidated by rolling. Photo courtesy FRP Supply Division, Ashland Chemical Co.

sold for applying body filler also work fine.

Positioning the Mold—Since it is always easier to work on a surface which is approximately horizontal, you will usually find it necessary to tilt the mold around to various attitudes as you work across or along a piece. Often you will end up in a situation where what was "down" just became "up," and the still wet section you just finished carefully rolling out begins to sag and droop away from the mold. To avoid this, clip the edges to the mold with spring type clothespins. Unless you want clothes-pin-reinforced-plastic, protect their ends with food wrap. While this problem usually only occurs at free edges, occasionally the edge of a piece of reinforcement in the middle of a laminate will begin to flop loose. For cloth, at least, aluminum bandage clips can be used to snag the loose piece.

Also, be careful not to bang the mold around too much when handling it—a severe jolt can cause premature separation of the gel coat and/or laminate. One hidden danger here is that the laminate loses weight as the styrene evaporates, so the center of gravity of the whole thing might move. An unattended mold, jury rigged into an apparently stable position, can suddenly tumble over all by itself. It is seriously depressing to return from lunch to find your work has disappeared from the saw-horses you had the mold on, and is now on the floor, incomplete

but partly released from the mold! This doesn't do the mold a world of good either.

Repeat the laminating operations with each subsequent layer, rolling each thoroughly and sopping up surplus resin as you go, until the desired thickness is reached. For the final layer of laminate, surfacing resin containing wax should be used, to avoid a tacky finish. If you don't have any waxed resin (or you thought you did but just ran out!), you can make some up by adding wax to laminating resin, as described in Chapter 4. If you can't even get that organized, don't panic. The surface will soon lose its tack if you cover it with plastic food wrap after the resin has kicked.

A plastic or rubber squeegee is often preferred for working resin through woven reinforcements. Photo by Jack Gladback.

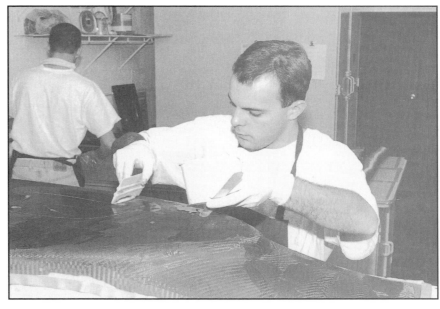

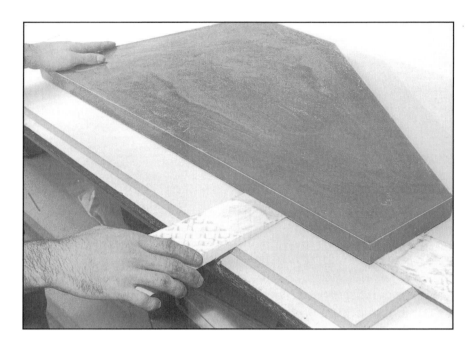

Nylon wedges sometimes aid separation of mold and part. If this doesn't work, more drastic measures will have to be taken. Photo by Jack Gladback.

"The next day, at the earliest, you get the real reward."

Removing the Part

At this point you can clean up and take a well-earned breather. You may be tempted, especially on your first project or two, to get the part out of the mold as quickly as possible to see how it turned out. DON'T! Under ordinary circumstances, the part should be left in the mold overnight, at least. While the part may be quite hard to the touch, the resin continues to cure for a long time, and a part removed from the mold too early may become distorted. Also, the forces involved in getting the part out of the mold can be substantial, especially with the first few parts pulled from a new mold. A green part may not be able to take it!

The next day, at the earliest, you get the real reward. If everything worked out right, you should soon be popping a shiny, perfect piece of your own handiwork out of the mold. First, check for edges that have wrapped onto the outside of the mold and may be attached there, and clip or saw free any such inadvertent adhesions. While you're at it, think about where you are going to grab hold of the part in your efforts to free it—sometimes a flap of hardened laminate extending outboard from the mold makes a good hand grip; sometimes it makes savage, deep, painful cuts in your hands. Now the real fun begins.

Twisting—Once in a while, with a mature, well-seasoned mold having adequate draft, the part will virtually fall out if you look at it hard. Usually, it's not quite that easy... and sometimes it just won't budge! Before you make recourse to explosives, try the following. First, get some help, arrange things so gravity is helping your efforts, and try to twist the mold. Reverse the direction of twist and try again. When the part does release, and especially if PVA has been used, there will usually be a terrifying cracking noise that sounds for all the world like fiberglass breaking. This takes a bit of getting used to! Also, mind your toes—sometimes parts will resist parting for half an hour, then suddenly drop out on your feet.

The Hammer—No luck? Next try to work a free edge loose manually, without using any kind of tool. Once you've got an edge free, you've usually got it beaten. If that fails, firmly but gently rap all over the outside of the mold with a rubber mallet. Go easy here—many molds have been ruined by needless violence with a rubber hammer; the symptoms are spider web cracks in the gel coat, usually in the middle of large flat areas. Again, the startling bang is the cue that the part has started to release (whump, whump, whump, CRAAACK!).

Still no joy? If there are enough spare hands, try swatting with the rubber hammer and twisting at the same time. Next try carefully driving wedges into an exposed edge, but be very careful here as you obviously risk doing some damage to the mold. Those same plastic body filler applicators that you might be using for squeegees have a tapered edge, and are soft enough you're not likely to hurt the mold. Cedar shingles are perhaps better wedges, but they're also more likely to score the mold surface. The nylon wedges used for log splitting work well on thicker, stiffer parts.

Ironically, PVA makes the job tougher. It is a terrific parting agent, from the point of view of protecting the mold, but it also is an effective adhesive. Fortunately, it is water soluble, so if you have been able to work edges loose without much trouble, but the bulk of the part is still stuck somewhere deep inside the mold, pour water (preferably warm) down the gaps opened up by the wedges, and resume twisting and socking gently with the rubber hammer. If all of this fails—you are just going to have to decide which to try to salvage, the mold or the part. Actually, if things are this bad, when you break the thoroughly stuck piece out of the mold you are going to discover some spots that are well and truly fused to the mold surface. Look on the bright side—this almost never happens except with a brand-new mold, and then only if you decide to gamble and do without PVA. 'Nuff said.

Trimming

Once the part is out, all you need to do then is trim the ragged edges, rinse the PVA off with warm water, and allow the good feelings to wash over you. The rough trimming can be done with a hacksaw or sabre saw, but an air powered cut-off tool is much quicker, tidier and easier, and it produces much less nasty, itchy dust. Saw-trimmed edges are quite ragged and can inflict really nasty cuts; even edges trimmed with a cut-off wheel need further smoothing. Ordinary sandpaper works fine; start with a coarse grit, and work finer. Wet-and-dry paper, used wet, eliminates the dust, but saw cut edges need a coarser grade of paper than is generally available with wet-and-dry— another good argument for a cut-off wheel.

While it's probably too much to expect on your first try, you will eventually be able to judge and anticipate well enough that you can save a lot of unpleasant work later by trimming the part in the mold before it has thoroughly cured. As explained in Chapter 3, the resin goes through several distinct

With careful timing, and luck, laminates at a *green cure* stage can be trimmed in or on the mold. This saves much difficult and messy cutting of fully-cured laminate. Photo by Jack Gladback.

stages as it cures. At one of those stages, the edges of a partially cured laminate can be cut cleanly and easily with a sharp utility knife.

As with the rest of life, practice helps. In the meantime, you can cut down the grief by following a few simple rules. Begin working with small, simple parts; pre-cut all reinforcement and do a "dry run," checking the fit and drape of the reinforcement in the mold and rehearsing which direction you're going to work in; don't use an excess of catalyst to make up for a cold shop; don't mix up too much resin at once. Above all, protect yourself from the unpleasant and unhealthy effects of resins, catalysts, solvents and particles of glass fibers (see Chapter 6). ■

"As with the rest of life, practice helps. In the meantime, you can cut down the grief by following a few simple rules."

8

ADVANCED FRP TECHNIQUES

While fiber reinforced plastics have been around in one form or another since the 1930's, early applications involved the use of resins such as phenolics, which required high temperatures to cure. At the same time, the curing of these resins involved the liberation of a substantial amount of by-products. To prevent these from affecting the finished product, the process had to be conducted under considerable external pressure. Since the combination of heat and pressure also demanded metal molds, this technology was limited to the production of parts having a simple shape, and produced in large enough numbers to justify the elaborate facilities—"Bakelite" electrical parts, for example.

The real breakthrough came in the late 1940's with the introduction of polyester resins that cured at room temperature, without liberating any by-products and thus not requiring high pressure processing. It was this development that made possible the open mold, hand lay-up process, which in turn allowed the economical production of small numbers of parts having a complex shape, and of almost unlimited size. Ironically, quite apart from the appearance of stronger reinforcing fibers, such as carbon and aramid, the quest for reinforced plastics having greater strength and stiffness than traditional contact molded glass/polyester laminates has led to materials and processes that require elevated temperatures and pressures. At the state-of-the-art level, these processing requirements take reinforced plas-

Heat speeds curing of all thermoset resins. Here radiant heaters hasten cure of Indycar bodywork in Aerodine Composites' shop. Photo by Jack Gladback.

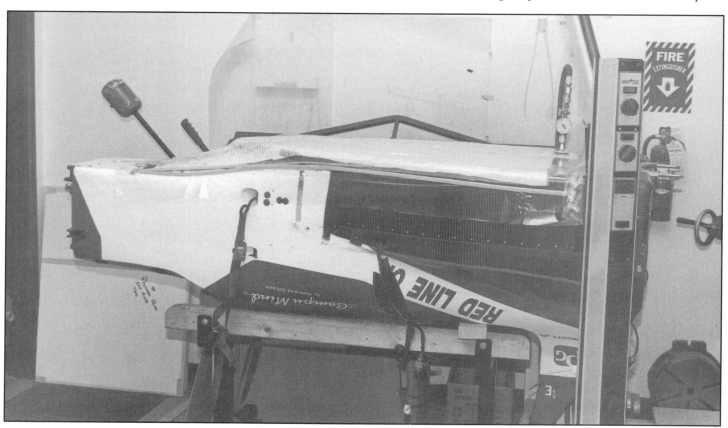

tics completely out of reach of the small workshop and into the aerospace factories. Fortunately, there is some middle ground.

POST CURING OF EPOXIES

As noted in Chapter 3, epoxy resins, and thus laminates made with them, often gain improved mechanical properties from a post-cure heating cycle. Here, a laminate made with a room temperature curing (RTC) resin system is allowed to gel at room temperature, then is subjected to a specific heating cycle, which ramps the temperature up in a series of steps over the course of several hours. The greatest benefits from post curing, generally speaking, are seen in improved retention of strength at higher temperatures, but even when measured at room temperature, the results can be dramatic. Depending on the particular combination of resin and hardener, increases in hardness and toughness up to 20% can be realized, with comparable improvements in laminate strength.

Print-Through

Another benefit of post curing in many applications is the reduction or elimination of *print-through* of the texture of the fabric weave onto the outer surface. To explain, first understand that a surface exposed to the sun on a hot day—especially a dark colored surface—can reach 160 degrees F, or more. Second, remember that even after they have gelled, typical structural resins (polyesters, vinylesters and epoxies) continue to cure and harden for a considerable time. During this long post-gel cure cycle, epoxies in particular become very soft if their temperature is raised to as little as 120-130 degrees; at the same time, they slightly expand. The bond between the resin and the reinforcement, though, was established earlier, when the resin gelled. The softening and expansion of the gelled but incompletely cured resin that occurs when the temperature gets

For the close temperature control demanded by HTC resins, ovens with complex temperature controls are required. Guy Levesque photo courtesy deHavilland Inc.

up to that critical figure, combined with the mechanical restraint of the resin/fiber bond, "telegraphs" the texture of the weave through the resin, causing the print-through phenomenon. The solutions are to wait however long it takes for the cure to become fully mature (which might be a very long time indeed—perhaps months in a cool climate) before exposing the finished part to the real world, or to post cure, which pretty much guarantees that any print-through

Knowing the temperature of the oven is insufficient; to keep track of the temperature of laminate itself, thermocouples are embedded in the laminate. Plug permits connecting thermocouple to oven controller/ recorder. Guy Levesque photo courtesy deHavilland Inc.

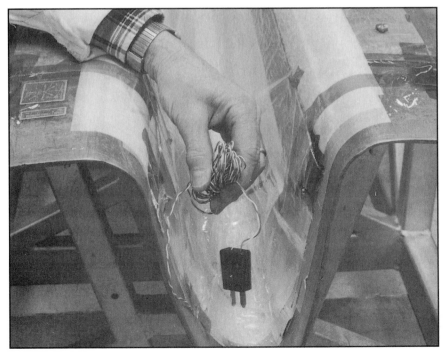

Post-cure ovens for ETC epoxies can be bought, or you can make your own, like this example in Gougeon Brothers' shop. Photo courtesy Gougeon Brothers Inc.

"Of course, for parts where cosmetics are not critical, the whole issue can be ignored."

apparent at the time the part is de-molded can be sanded off with the assurance that it will not return. Of course, for parts where cosmetics are not critical, the whole issue can be ignored.

Drawbacks

There are two points to note, though. First, while it seems to always help reduce print-through and to improve mechanical properties at moderately elevated temperatures, some epoxy formulations do not seem to gain any room temperature strength or toughness at all from post curing. Second, the whole operation only works if it is controlled. Too little heat, or too little time at temperature and you may as well not bother; too much heat, or ramping up the temperature too rapidly can produce a completely junk part. Epoxy manufacturers and formulators can provide details on the effectiveness of post curing their products, and on the time/temperature relationships needed to realize optimum properties. The recommendation of one supplier of kit-planes to paint the structure black and leave it (well supported) out in the sun is surely a little too slap-dash.

Heating Advantages

Heat speeds up the curing of all ther-

mosetting resins, and most workers sooner or later find themselves forced to improvise some sort of supplementary heating for parts that are taking too long to harden. These makeshift arrangements often take the form of portable heaters inside a tent made from plastic sheeting that surrounds the job. To increase the effectiveness of the heaters and cut heating costs, the tent can be insulated in some way; some builders use bubble pack made from metallized, silver colored *Mylar,* which insulates better than ordinary plastic sheeting. Whatever the materials, such stop-gap measures are often adequate for post curing.

Another advantage to using heat (within reason) to accelerate the achievement of a full cure is that it reduces the exposure time of the incompletely cured laminate, which minimizes the risk of the surface becoming contaminated with dirt, moisture, hand prints, etc. And this is true of all resin systems, not just epoxies. Of course, reducing the length of time a part has to spend sitting in the mold before it can be removed without risking distortion also frees the mold up for the next job.

ELEVATED TEMPERATURE CURING EPOXIES

For applications where minimum weight and maximum strength are important, higher performance resins may be selected, and that often means epoxy resin systems designed to cure at higher than room temperatures. For a true high temperature cure (HTC), the temperatures required with some resin systems are so high (up to 400 degrees F) and the demand for close control of the heating so strict that simple tents and other ad-libbed arrangements are inadequate. The only solution is a purpose-built oven, fitted with precision timers and automatic temperature controls. Large and expensive industrial ovens are available for this purpose.

Between RTC and HTC resin systems,

though, there are some that offer better properties than purely room temperature systems, without absolutely demanding a sizable additional investment in equipment. While there are no firm dividing lines, a distinction is often made between HTC's and elevated temperature curing (ETC) systems, depending on the actual temperatures called for. Indeed, some manufacturers list resin systems that call for a room temperature cure, followed by an elevated temperature post cure. These differ from post-cured RTC's only in that the post cure is mandatory. (Note that we say "resin systems," rather than simply "resins"; very often the same resin is used for room and ET and HT cures—it is the curing agent that differs.) While the cost of a commercial oven obviously cannot be justified for one-time or occasional use, the temperatures called for by many such ETC systems are achievable with much less elaborate arrangements.

Heating Methods

In this connection, never forget that an oven is simply an insulated box with a heat source inside; in some cases it may be quite practical to make your own. It is not prohibitively expensive to construct a frame for a simple shed-like structure, with sheet-rock walls and ceiling, heavily insulated on the back side with rock-wool or fiberglass batts. (Forget about foam insulation; apart from increased fire risk, insulating foams may soften at the temperatures involved.)

Cautions—While undiluted epoxies do not include flammable, low boiling point solvents, like the styrene in polyester and vinylester resins, these materials are nevertheless flammable, and extreme care must be taken to avoid fire. That pretty much limits the possible heat sources to electricity, steam and hot water, though the use of water is obviously limited to temperatures below its boiling point of 212 F.

Heating the Mold—An alternative to heating the space surrounding the laminate/mold assembly is to heat the mold itself. Electric resistance heaters are available for this purpose; some are in the form of blankets to be applied to the outside surface of the mold, others are flexible tapes that can be incorporated right into the laminations that make up the mold. Again, insulation will increase the effectiveness of the heaters, and cut energy costs.

Other means to heat the mold could be used. On one occasion, I considered building heating tubes of either aluminum or soft copper into a mold, to serve both as closely spaced mold stiffeners and as conduits for hot water from a domestic water heater. There were several attractions to this scheme. First, electric heating tapes are not cheap; in order to use them, control of the temperature at the mold would require a fairly complex and expensive collection of thermocouples and controllers. Second, the shop already had a huge spare electric hot water heater, with a built-in, adjustable thermostat. This scheme was never tried, for a variety of non-technical reasons, but the idea remains intriguing if only because of its low-buck, "made-it-myself" appeal. Therefore, I'm going to mention some of the problems I had anticipated while planning it out, just in case you decide to build one.

First is the hassle of draining, filling and bleeding the system whenever the lines are hooked up or disconnected. Another is the potential hazard of scalding hot water spilling out if a line or connection ever springs a leak. Also, to avoid using outrageous amounts of water and electricity (or gas), the system would have to be a closed loop type, with water circulating from the heater to the mold, then back to the heater. A circulating pump would also be necessary; thermo-siphon might do the job, but the heater would have to be located well below the mold and the plumbing runs made short and large in diameter. But if the system were truly closed, a leak, even a slight one, would cause an unattended heater to boil dry, thus

> *"While undiluted epoxies do not include flammable, low boiling point solvents, like the styrene in polyester and vinylester resins, these materials are nevertheless flammable, and extreme care must be taken to avoid fire."*

"Another factor to bear in mind whenever exposing a laminate and mold assembly to elevated temperatures is the issue of compatibility of the mold and laminate materials."

Plastic sheeting surrounding mold and laminate provides a sealed space which can be evacuated. Atmospheric pressure of about 15 psi then squeezes laminate firmly against mold, improving resin-to-reinforcement ratio and so laminate strength. Guy Levesque photo courtesy deHavilland Inc.

A complete "bag" is not essential. As here, film can be secured to edges of mold outboard of laminate using double-sided tape. Guy Levesque photo courtesy deHavilland Inc.

certainly trashing the part undergoing the cure cycle and possibly also the heater. Also, the pressure in the system would be essentially uncontrolled. To deal with these concerns, it was intended to provide the plumbing with a vent stack open to the atmosphere, and a replenishment arrangement using a float and check valve, as in an ordinary toilet tank. (We also had a spare toilet tank!)

Expansion—Another factor to bear in mind whenever exposing a laminate and mold assembly to elevated temperatures is the issue of compatibility of the mold and laminate materials. For one thing, their comparative thermal expansion has to be considered, especially if the dimensions of the part are critical. For example, some carbon fibers exhibit *negative* thermal expansion—they get *smaller* as they heat up; other forms of carbon fiber do have a positive thermal expansion coefficient, but they grow much less with heat than most other FRP materials. For this reason, the molds for carbon fiber reinforced race car and aircraft components using ETC resin systems are themselves usually made from the same CF as the

part, to ensure that the mold and laminate shrink and grow in sync. Then there's the problem of any thermoplastic foam incorporated into either the mold or the part. While various plastic foams make excellent core material for sandwich construction parts (see Chapter 15–*Sandwich Contsruction*), and while it is often convenient to use foam cores in the construction of mold stiffeners, the plastics used for these foams soften and become useless at high temperatures. (Just how high is "high" depends on the foam; the range is from about 150-175 degrees for ordinary urethane and styrene foams to as much as 350-400 for some epoxy based foams.) And note that wood dries out, shrinks and splits when it is heated, so balsa as a core has its temperature limits, too.

PRESSURE MOLDING

Traditional hand lay-up is a highly flexible and versatile process, and has the great advantage that virtually no facilities or equipment are required; it can even be done outdoors, if the weather is favorable. This obviously excludes the use of ETC resin systems, thus entailing a modest reduction in mechanical properties, but a more serious problem is that the strength and stiffness of parts produced in this way are restricted by the low reinforcement-to-resin ratio, because the only force available to compact the laminate is gravity. This inevitably means there is more resin in the product, and thus more weight, than is necessary to carry the load from one fiber to another, which is a drawback in any performance application, even for parts whose job is mostly cosmetic.

Matched Molds

A substantial improvement in the ratio of reinforcement-to-resin can be achieved by increasing the force compacting the laminate, squeezing the fibers closer together, driving out air and excess resin, and thus yielding a denser, stronger product. In mass production of some FRP goods this is achieved by using matched male and female molds—usually made from metal—squeezed together in a press. This process is generally limited to parts with a comparatively simple shape having no undercuts, such as cafeteria trays, institutional furniture, and some auto body parts. Apart from this drawback, and the requirement for double the number of molds and a press, the matched mold process cannot easily accommodate the local increases in thickness that occur at overlaps between individually tailored pieces of reinforcement. Accordingly, such goods usually involve *sheet molding compound* (SMC) or *pre-forms* (see Chapter 9), whose inferior mechanical properties frequently offset the potential advantage of the higher molding pressures.

Vacuum Bagging

A comparatively simple way to increase the pressure on the laminate during the cure cycle, without accepting the shape limitations and cost of matched molds, is to fit the entire assembly of laminate and mold into a flexible bag, then to suck all the air out of

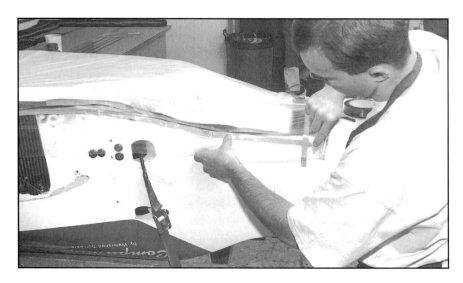

the bag with a vacuum pump. This exposes the outer surfaces to atmospheric pressure—a bit less than 15 psi. While the amount of pressure is modest, properly made vacuum-bagged goods will show better strength and stiffness than contact moldings, for the same weight. As an added bonus, the inside surface of the laminate—the one in contact with the bag—ends up with a smoother texture than with contact molding.

Two points are worth noting. First, it is not actually necessary for the bag to completely surround the mold—only the laminate surface needs to be covered, with the flexible bag secured to flanges at the edges of the mold surface. Of course, the mold itself must be air-tight. This is not a problem with FRP or metal molds, but it can be if the mold is plaster, wood, or another porous material. Second, either way, the forces on the mold are balanced, so it does not need to be any more sturdily constructed than a mold for contact lamination. Indeed, it is often practical to convert a contact lay-up process to vacuum bagging, provided that the mold has been built with a sufficiently wide flange around all its edges.

Bag Material—The requirements for the bag material are few in number, but stringent. It must resist attack by the resin system used; it must not interfere with the cure; it must tolerate the temperatures experienced

Though this bag material is claimed to be self-sealing, workers at Aerodine Composites take no chances; note use of sealing tape. Photo by Jack Gladback.

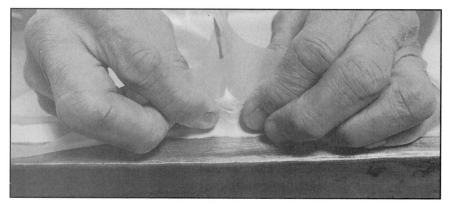

To deal with inevitable excess of material at edges, "tucks" are formed. Guy Levesque photo courtesy deHavilland Inc.

Tucks can be a source of vacuum leaks; sides of tuck must be stuck together with sealing dough. Photo by Jack Gladback.

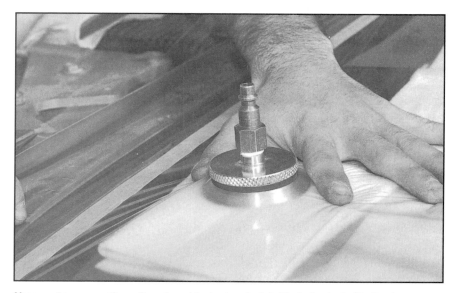

Vacuum taps pass through and seal to bag material. Photo by Jack Gladback.

during the cure; it must part cleanly from the cured laminate; and it must be flexible enough to faithfully follow the contours of the exposed laminate face. In the earliest days, the preferred material was rubber, but this had several drawbacks. To protect the rubber from attack by the resin, a second protective film such as cellophane had to be interposed between the wet laminate surface and the bag; the heat of curing shortened the life of the bag; also, it was not possible to see the laminate once the bag was in place. Now, several different clear plastic films are available (usually PVC or a nylon-like material) which address those problems. While bags are often cut and pieced together to conform to the contours of the laminate surface, this is not absolutely essential— wrinkles are not necessarily a problem.

Sealing—There is a bit more to vacuum bagging than the basic description given above. First, there is the problem of sealing the bag to the edges of the mold. Double-sided adhesive tape works well in many cases, provided air leaks are not introduced by wrinkles at the edges of the bag material. If the part being made has significant three-dimensional curvature, then a simple flat, un-tailored bag obviously has to be much larger than the part, to permit the bag to reach into recesses. That naturally leaves excess material at the edges. To deal with that, "tucks" are formed at intervals, and the two sides of each tuck sealed together with more tape. Nevertheless, the intersection of the sealed tuck and the mold flange can be problematic. A dough-like sealing material is now available that helps solve this problem; depending on the resin used, ordinary caulking compound can work, too.

Vacuum Lines—Depending on the shape and size of the part, the vacuum lines can terminate under the edges of the bag, at the mold flanges, or they can be connected to a number of through-fittings distributed over the bag surface. In either case, to prevent catalyzed resin from being drawn into the

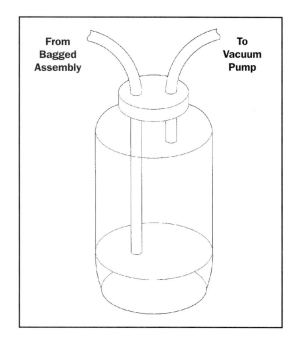

If a large quantity of surplus resin is expected, a simple resin trap can be used to prevent resin entering vacuum lines.

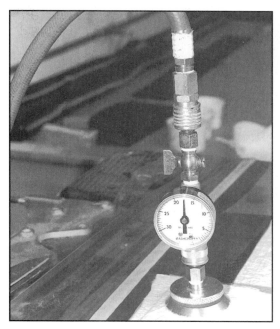

After vacuum is drawn, the tap, visible immediately above gauge, can be closed. Any drop in gauge reading indicates a leak in the bag. Photo by Jack Gladback.

"Alas, other kinds of rein-forcement, such as aramid and carbon, do not exhibit this white-when-dry, clear-when-wet effect; they are a lot trickier to judge by eye."

vacuum lines and solidifying there, it is common to provide resin traps just outboard of the ports.

Vacuum Bagging Procedure

In the simplest application, the component is laid up by hand, taking the usual care with tailoring of reinforcement, smoothing out wrinkles, and rolling to consolidate the laminate, but without becoming obsessively concerned about resin content, provided of course that there is enough! (It's best to weigh out the materials in advance, allowing a modest surplus of resin). As soon as the lay-up is completed, and before the resin gels, the bag is laid over the exposed laminate surface, tucked and pleated as needed, and sealed to the mold flanges at the edges. The vacuum lines are then hooked up and a vacuum drawn and held while the laminator carefully squeegees over the surface of the bag, urging excess resin toward the suction point(s). Depending on the number and location of vacuum ports, it is possible for

too much resin to be drawn out of the laminate, leaving dry areas. In the case of laminates using glass reinforcement, these dry areas can be identified by pressing a finger onto the surface, which will produce a white spot visible through the bag that doesn't turn transparent again when the finger pressure is released. Backing off on the vacuum will usually allow some resin to drain back into the laminate. (Alas, other kinds of reinforcement, such as aramid and carbon, do not exhibit this white-when-dry, clear-when-wet effect; they are a lot trickier to judge by eye.)

Resins for Vacuum Bagging

While the process as described deals with the problem of a high *average* ratio of resin to reinforcement, a problem that may arise is a tendency for too much resin to be sucked away from some areas, while others remain resin rich. To improve the uniformity of resin distribution, the laminate may first be covered with a material called *breather film*, which is a plastic film punctured by zillions

Vacuum draws resin through holes in breather film, while worker carefully squeegees surface—instant polka dots! Photo by Jack Gladback.

um over the surface of the part, while the bleeder ply soaks up the excess resin. Extra thicknesses of bleeder ply are set in place directly below the vacuum ports to help prevent resin being sucked into the vacuum system.

Resin Types—Room temperature curing (RTC) resins can be used for vacuum bagged parts, but because of the additional time and effort involved in vacuum bagging, the process is usually reserved for parts where minimum weight and maximum strength are required, which usually suggests the use of ETC resins. The same reasoning also works the other way around. You can use ETC epoxies to produce parts by contact molding, but to gain maximum benefit from the more expensive resins and the investment in ovens or other heating arrangements, laminates made with such resin systems are frequently vacuum bagged. In short, ETC or HTC epoxy systems and vacuum bagging tend to go together, presumably on the principle of "in for a penny, in for a pound."

Laminate is first covered with breather film... then bleeder ply laid on top of that. Photo by Jack Gladback.

of tiny holes, though each is small enough that the overall porosity of the film is around two percent. Usually when breather film is used, a layer of absorbent material called a *bleeder ply* is laid over it. (The stuff used as the filling for quilts or sleeping bags works, and is widely available at dry-goods stores.) Together, these help to distribute the vacu-

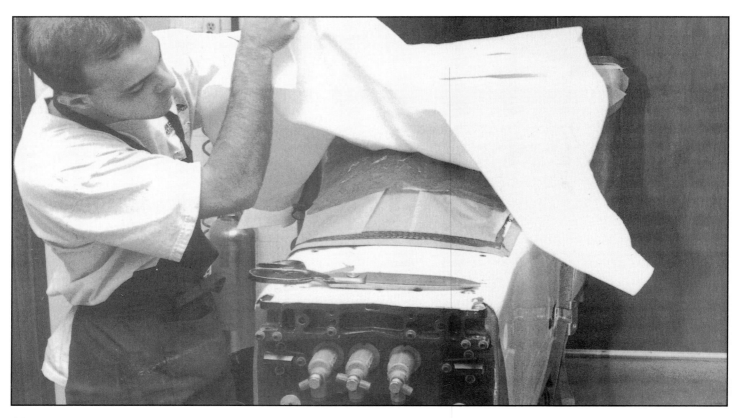

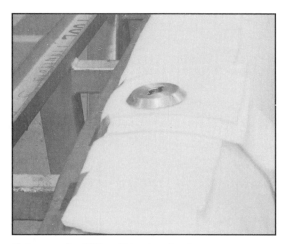

For multiple jobs, or insurance against pump failure, Aerodine Composites shop has several electrically driven vacuum pumps. Here are two of them. Note sound absorbing material in this compressor/pump closet. Photo by Jack Gladback.

Note use of additional bleeder ply at vacuum connections to prevent resin entering vacuum system. Guy Levesque photo courtesy deHavilland Inc.

Vacuum Devices

The suction can be provided by a purpose-built commercial vacuum pump but, again, there are homemade substitutes. With a little modification, almost any air compressor can be used as a vacuum pump, and there are also stories of people using a vacuum cleaner for this purpose. (Without adequate airflow through it, though, the motor is bound to overheat.) Though it will not develop the same amount of vacuum as electrically driven pumps, there is an ingeniously simple device available from Gougeon Brothers Inc. that uses a combination of the shop compressed air system and the venturi principle to turn "blow" into "suck." And I once discovered the world's cheapest vacuum pump—another venturi-like device bought at the local hardware store for about two bucks that was intended to be hooked up to a running water tap to siphon water out of an old wringer-type washing machine. It worked, after a fashion, though its effectiveness was limited. The worst problem was that it quit working altogether when anyone in the building flushed a toilet!

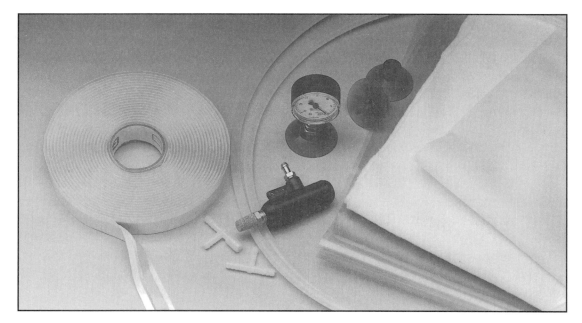

Ingenious vacuum pump using shop compressed air and venturi principle (black object in center) is part of assortment of vacuum bagging supplies available from Gougeon Brothers. Photo courtesy Gougeon Brothers Inc.

Awesome force developed on autoclave door is suggested by battleship construction of locking mechanism. This autoclave can operate up to 90 psi at over 500 degrees F. Guy Levesque photo courtesy deHavilland Inc.

AUTOCLAVING

If even denser, more compact laminates having a correspondingly higher ratio of reinforcement to resin are sought, then more contact pressure is needed than the fourteen psi or so available from a vacuum bag. The only solution is to place the mold/laminate/bag assembly into a pressure vessel. Because of the logical linkage between high performance techniques and high performance materials, these pressure vessels are almost always provided with controlled heating, to allow the use of ETC resin systems. This appliance providing a combination of pressure and heat is called an *autoclave*.

The use of autoclaves is limited to enterprises with very deep pockets. Apart from the cost of a certified pressure vessel

the size of a city bus (though, obviously, there are some small ones), an elaborate automatic temperature monitoring and control system is required. And the door on the end through which the parts are loaded has to be built like a safe, to resist the huge forces involved (100 psi acting on a five foot diameter door produces a force of 140 tons!).

Apart from the aerospace field, autoclaves are essential equipment for the makers of Indycar and Formula One chassis. The Williams F1 team, for example, has two of them. The big one is 6 feet in diameter by 15 feet long, and operates at up to 400 degrees F and 100 psi pressure; the other is 3 feet 7 inches by 8 feet, and works at up to 480 degrees and 150 psi. Some aerospace firms have autoclaves you could drive a transport truck into.

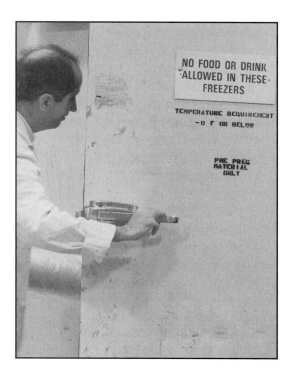

Pre-pregs produce the best composites, but this performance is obtained at a hefty price. Beyond the cost of the materials, there is the problem of refrigerated shipping and storage. Guy Levesque photo courtesy deHavilland Inc.

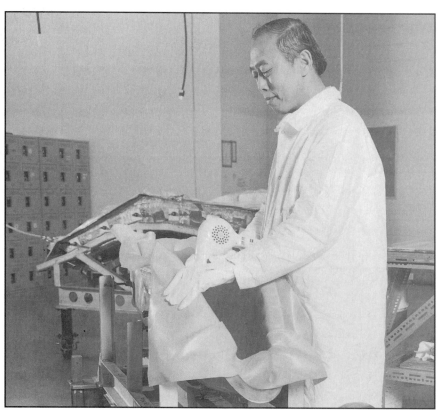

Satin weave aramid pre-preg can be made to conform to extreme changes in curvature, aided by softening stiff "B-staged" epoxy resin with a heat gun. Guy Levesque photo courtesy deHavilland Inc.

PRE-PREGS

Care and vacuum bagging can increase the ratio of reinforcement to resin, and improve the uniformity of parts, and ETC resin systems can offer improved properties over RTC systems, but the very strongest and stiffest laminates—the state of the art—are obtained from pre-pregs.

These are sheets or ribbons of reinforcement, uniformly machine-impregnated with resin. The resins used for pre-pregs are usually epoxies, for the simple reason that epoxies can be formulated that cure extremely slowly at low temperatures, so a resin mixed with its curing agent can be applied and the curing process arrested, or at least slowed to a near standstill, by refrigeration. This state of cure is called the B-stage, and in this condition, they will remain usable for several months, until the end user laminates the pre-pregs into a finished product and completes the cure by the application of heat. Unfortunately, pre-pregs are expensive, partly because the HTC epoxies are themselves costly, partly because the demand for them is limited, and partly because of the need for refrigerated shipment. On the other hand, the reduction in wasted resin and the almost complete absence of mess and odor is surely worth some premium. Whatever the economics, their physical properties are unsurpassed.

Pre-Preg Types

A wide variety of reinforcement materials and styles is available, though the emphasis is, naturally, on high performance fibers like aramid, S2-glass and carbon. Also, since there is no need for open weaves to facilitate wetting out, pre-pregs using woven reinforcement usually have very tight weaves with lots of fiber and not much space between the interwoven yarns. As with wet lay-up, though, the best mechanical properties come from unidirectional reinforce-

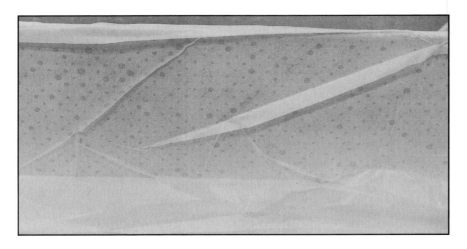

Minimum resin content of pre-preg means less resin flows into bleeder ply. Note few and small polka dots on this pre-preg laminate just removed from autoclave. Guy Levesque photo courtesy deHavilland Inc.

ment, in which the fibers are packed closely side-by-side. The close packing and the unidirectional alignment of the fibers yields the greatest strength and stiffness possible. Where multi-axial properties are needed, successive layers of pre-preg can be applied at an angle to one another.

Although the dryness of commercial B-staged epoxy pre-pregs is a virtue, it also means that there is no surplus resin to help glue adjoining layers together. To ensure that multiple layers act together as an integrated laminate, vacuum bagging or autoclaving is essential. Depending on the resin

Simple, hand-cranked fabric impregnator from Gougeon Brothers. Photo courtesy Gougeon Brothers Inc.

formulation used in the pre-preg, there may or may not be sufficient adhesive strength to ensure a satisfactory bond to the next layer; if not, a layer of film adhesive has to be interposed between plies. As mentioned, the very nature of B-staged pre-pregs also means that an elevated temperature cure is required, so an oven (or cobbled-up equivalent) or a heated mold are also essential for their use.

Fabric Impregnator

There is also a method of working that involves something like a homemade pre-preg, using a machine called a *fabric impregnator*. This apparatus mechanically draws woven or unidirectional goods through a bath of resin and then passes it through a set of pinch rollers, yielding more uniform resin distribution and a higher reinforcement-to-resin ratio than is usually possible with hand work. At the same time, labor is reduced. Virtually any liquid resin system can be used in this process, but unless the material is going to be used almost immediately it is obviously an advantage if the resin either cures very slowly at room temperature or can have its cure postponed in some way. Epoxy based systems which can be arrested at the B-stage are well suited to this technique, and this is, in fact, the way commercial pre-pregs are made. There is also the possibility of using ultra-violet curing polyester or vinylester resins. If the dipping were done under a "safe" light, the impregnated fabric could be re-wound onto a roll, using a sheet of polyethylene to prevent layers from sticking together, and would store indefinitely until exposed to UV light, such as by being taken outdoors. The cost of fabric impregnating equipment generally limits its use to those who either need large quantities of material or who are working with weight and strength-critical goods, or both. Pre-pregs can also be produced by *filament winding*, as mentioned in the next chapter. ∎

MASS-PRODUCTION TECHNIQUES

9

FRP materials are used in a tremendous number of products, ranging from everyday household items to those for the military. Obviously, when dealing with numbers in the thousands, hand lay-up techniques are impractical. What follows is an overview of the techniques used by industry to mass produce FRP products.

SPRAY UP

Much of industrial FRP production is by the spray up process—a technique which is economical but which produces relatively weak and heavy parts. In this process, a continuous strand of fibrous glass looking rather like heavy twine is drawn from a supply reel into an air-powered chopper mechanism attached to a spray gun. There, it is cut up into short lengths (3/4 to 2 inch) and carried onto the surface of the mold, together with the liquid resin issuing from the gun.

Drawbacks

Continuous roving is the least expensive form of reinforcement, and a chopper gun is capable of laying down material very rapidly, so spray up is an economical method of production. Against this must be counted some significant drawbacks, however. From an economic standpoint, we must first discount a little of the apparent labor saving,

Producing a truck cap by spray up of glass fiber and polyester resin. Photo courtesy FRP Supply Division, Ashland Chemical Co.

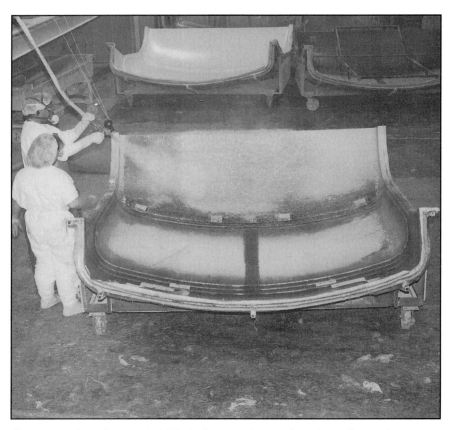

Chopper gun lays down material fast. Gun operator can keep two other workers occupied in rolling out the laminate. Photo courtesy Composites Fabricators Association

limitation is the shortness of the chopped fibers, which limits the strength of the finished part. Also, control of the thickness of the laminate depends very much on the skill of the operator. (To assist the worker in applying a uniform layer of chop, a fine colored thread, often red, is incorporated into the roving; the distribution of this colored *tracer* across the surface aids in visualizing thin and thick areas.) Most important, though, is the excessive amount of resin required in relation to the quantity of glass; 30-35% reinforcement is typical for sprayed up goods. Remember that the strength and stiffness of a part increases directly with the proportion of fibers in the mix.

In these respects, sprayed up goods are physically comparable to parts made by hand lay-up using mat. Lighter, stronger parts can be produced by the wet lay-up process, especially if woven cloth or other continuous strand reinforcement is used. Nevertheless, even when woven reinforcement has been chosen for the majority of the laminate, it is desirable to have a layer of randomly oriented fiber applied between the gel coat and the first layer of fabric to avoid print-through. This cushioning layer can often be achieved cheaper and faster with a quick pass of the chopper gun than by the use of mat. Likewise, if woven roving has been chosen for the main structure of the laminate, it is prudent and customary to introduce a coupling layer between successive plies of roving, both to provide some fibers connecting the two layers and to improve the overall reinforcement-to-resin ratio by avoiding the resin-rich zone that would otherwise exist between the layers of roving, on account of their coarse weave. Again, chop may be preferable to mat for this purpose.

Carbon Fiber—While it has been reported that some people have run carbon fiber reinforcement through a chopper gun, this seems a wasteful way to use such an expensive material. If CFs properties are sought

since the process leaves a poorly consolidated deposit which includes a considerable amount of entrained air, so rather more time and effort than usual has to be spent in working over the surface with a ribbed roller, to compact it and to drive out the air. Also, since the chopper gun can lay down material far faster than one man can work over it with a roller, there can be problems with making good use of manpower—either the chopper gun operator must pause frequently to allow the individual doing the rolling to catch up, in which case he will spend a lot of time idle, or else several laminators have to be working simultaneously, while the "trigger man" moves from one area to another. This last method will obviously only work if the component being made is large, such as a boat hull.

From the structural point of view, another

for reasons of strength and stiffness, then a sprayed up laminate is surely not the way to maximize its benefits. Aramid fiber (DuPont "Kevlar") is too tough to chop satisfactorily.

Pre-Forms

Another use for a chopper gun is in the production of *pre-forms*—essentially a custom-shaped piece of glass mat. First, wire screen is formed into the desired three-dimensional shape and secured to a perimeter frame. A powerful fan is then arranged to suck air through the screen. Using a chopper gun (though dedicated, purpose-built chopper/blowers are often used instead), glass roving or possibly some other reinforcement is chopped and sprayed onto the form, together with a small amount of resin-soluble binder, which temporarily holds the fibers in place. As the chopped fibers build up on the surface of the screen they locally obstruct airflow, thereby increasing the flow through unfilled areas. This draws more chop to bare areas, thus achieving a reasonably uniform thickness. After a suitable interval to allow the binder to dry (usually accelerated by heating), the pre-form can be stripped from the screen and is ready for use.

Pre-Form Benefits—As an alternative to conventional spray up, pre-forms offer better control of laminate thickness, plus the opportunity to separate the mess and noise of the spraying from the laminating operation. (While much of FRP work is unpleasant, it at least has the merit of being quiet work. A chopper gun, though, howls like a siren.) Conversely, for situations where mat would otherwise be used, pre-forms eliminate the need to shape and fit individual pieces of mat, and eliminate wasted off-cuts. The economic merits of pre-forms depend on the cost saved by the use of roving versus mat, and the reduction or elimination of mat tailoring, compared with modest tooling requirements (for the screen or screens) and the labor involved in making the pre-forms. These factors, in turn, depend on the number

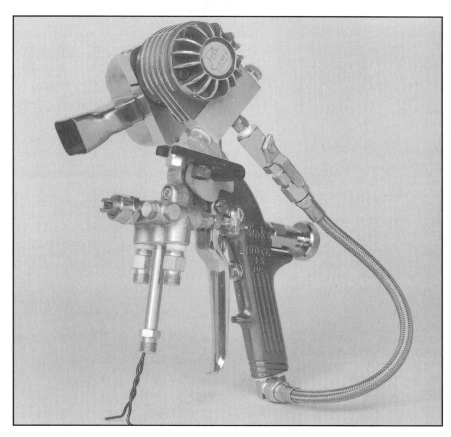

Air-powered chopper mechanism attached to spray gun cuts continuous rovings into short lengths. Chopped strand issues from funnel and intermingles with resin from gun orifice. Photo courtesy Binks Manufacturing Co.

Shortness of chopped strands from chopper gun limits the strength of laminates produced in this way. Photo courtesy DOW Plastics.

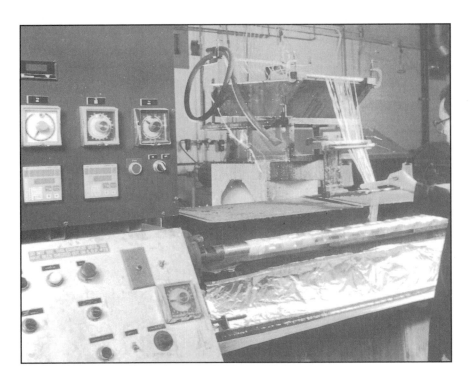

Filament winding. Note helical pattern on wind up. Photo courtesy DOW Plastics.

individual strands—a closely related process uses pre-manufactured unidirectional or woven tapes. This *tape winding* is commonly used for the manufacture of ducting and other hollow sections. It is of course possible for the mandrel to remain stationary, while the mechanism that deposits the fiber rotates and traverses, though this is more commonly seen in tape winding than in filament winding.

Applications

While the process is usually associated with cylindrical goods like piping and pressure bottles, many other shapes can be filament wound; the only requirement is that the part form a "surface of revolution," having no undercuts. In the aerospace industry, for example, filament winding is used to produce composite rotor blades for helicopters, in addition to circular shapes like rocket motor cases and spherical pressure vessels. Perhaps the most significant automotive application of filament winding to date is in the manufacture of driveshafts for certain General Motors trucks.

Procedure

At first sight it would seem that the length of a filament wound part is limited by the dimensions of the winding bed. In fact, there is an ingenious and elegant process for producing pipe continuously (miles of it!) which uses a mirror-smooth mandrel having a very slight taper, surrounded by a collar containing a sort of circular microwave oven. The radio frequency heating cures the wind up as fast as it is laid down, while the finished pipe slips continuously off the end of the mandrel. This permits the production of seamless, continuous pipe, limited in length only by the storage space available, and subsequent problems of shipping.

of pieces to be made, the rate of production, and the local costs of labor and materials.

FILAMENT WINDING

In much the same way that string is coiled onto a roll, glass or other reinforcing fibers can be wound onto a rotating mandrel. This process of filament winding is capable of producing parts with a very high proportion of reinforcement—up to 90%. Filament winding is, in fact, the only wet process that can produce parts having mechanical performance competitive with pre-pregs, and because it is an automated procedure it offers both low labor costs and exceptional consistency from one part to the next. Like a chopper gun, filament winding also uses reinforcement in its least expensive form—continuous strands.

Actually, winding individual filaments is comparatively rare; the technique might better be termed "strand winding." To increase the rate at which the reinforcement is applied, multiple guide heads may be used to deposit several strands simultaneously. For that matter, the process is not limited to

For straightforward cylindrical shapes requiring a circumferential wind (see below), simple mechanical means can be used to guide the fibers onto the mandrel

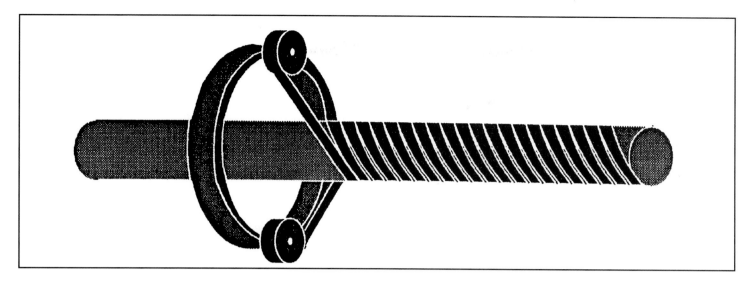

surface. For more complex surfaces of revolution, precise control over both the pattern of fiber application and the angle at which it is deposited is achieved by regulating the traversing motion of the guide head by a program on magnetic or punched paper tape, or by computer.

Wet or Dry Winding

The winding can be done dry, with resin applied to the continuously forming surface of the part, but it is more usual to lead the strand or filament through a bath of catalyzed resin on its way to the guide head. Pre-pregged yarn and strand are also available. The tension in the strand being applied to the mandrel also needs to be carefully controlled, as this controls the resin-to-fiber ratio. Too much tension, though, can be as bad as too little; tests have shown that the tension maintained during winding can leave residual stresses in the fibers after curing, which can significantly affect the strength of the finished part.

Tension vs. Geometry—One problem that arises with non-cylindrical shapes is the limited number of paths across the surface of the part which will not tend to cause the yarn or filament to slip out of position when it is tensioned. Mathematicians describe these as *geodesic* paths. On the other hand, the lay of the reinforcement determines the directional

strength and stiffness properties of the finished part, and the optimum pattern from this perspective may not correspond to a geodesic path. The amount of tension required, then, depends not just on the geometry of the part, but also on the winding pattern, and whether the winding is done dry, wet or, in the case of pre-pregged yarn, tacky. In making the choice between dry or wet winding, particularly in the case of glass, another consideration is the extreme abrasiveness of glass, which rapidly wears out the guide pins, rollers, etc., over which the strands pass, even though hard-chromed, ceramic, or ceramic-coated guide eyes and

Tape winding. Illustration courtesy Owens-Corning.

Filament winding is ideal for production of pipe. Photo courtesy Escom Advertising Group Inc.

> *"The amount of tension required, then, depends not just on the geometry of the part, but also on the winding pattern, and whether the winding is done dry, wet or, in the case of pre-pregged yarn, tacky."*

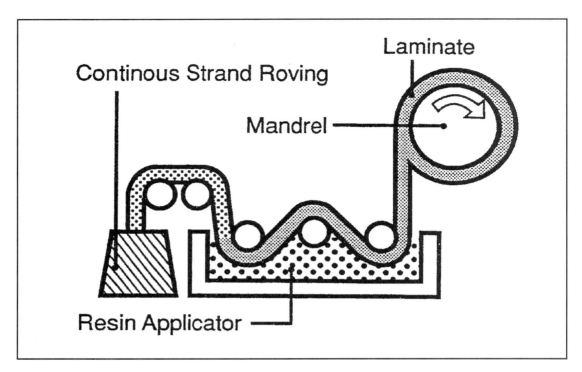

Schematic illustration of filament winding process. Illustration courtesy Owens-Corning.

pins are generally used. This abrasion also tends to damage the fibers at the surface of the strand, weakening the finished product. (For this latter reason, the radius of any rollers over which the yarn passes should be kept as large as practical; two inches has been cited as a minimum.) If the winding is done wet, the applied resin serves as a lubricant, reducing the problem, though not eliminating it.

The Mandrel

Another peculiarity of filament winding is that, with many shapes, the mandrel will obviously end up trapped inside the finished winding. In some applications, this is not a drawback. In pressure vessels, for example, it is often desirable to have some sort of continuous, impermeable membrane lining the inside, a function provided by the encapsulated mandrel, often a light metal shell. On the other hand, there are applications where the trapped mandrel is simply a necessary evil, in which case the specification of its wall thickness is a balancing act between excessive weight, on the one hand, and the risk of crushing the hollow former during the wind-up or from shrinkage of the part during the cure. (In one application involving winding over a very thin stainless steel shell, it was found necessary to pressurize the inside of the former throughout the cure, to prevent its buckling inward due to shrinkage.) Alternatively, a collapsible multi-piece mandrel can be used, which is dismantled and removed in sections after the winding has cured.

Of course, there are many cases where an open-ended product is desired, and the wrap of the winding over the ends of the mandrel simply assists in establishing and maintaining the desired pattern of reinforcement in the sides until the assembly cures. In these cases, the ends can be cut off after the resin has cured, liberating the mandrel.

Winding Patterns

A variety of winding patterns are possible. If the guide head moves slowly and gradually down the length of the part as the mandrel

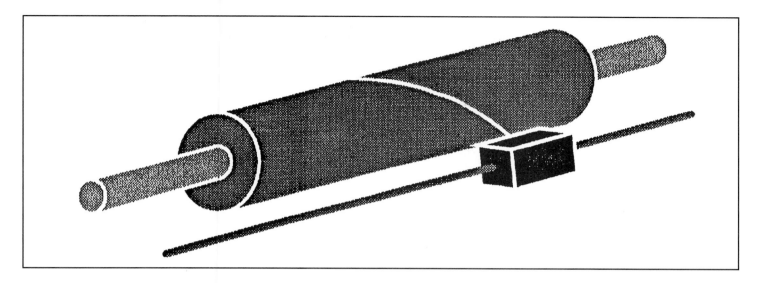

steadily rotates, a simple *circumferential* pattern results—like sewing thread on a reel. This orientation of the reinforcement gives the finished part maximum resistance to radial forces, such as the hoop stresses that try to burst a pressure vessel, but offers negligible strength in the lengthwise direction. On the other hand, if the head traverses the full length of the part during just a few degrees of rotation of the mandrel, the fibers will be arranged essentially from end-to-end, which produces the opposite effect— enormous longitudinal strength suitable for something like a pushrod, but almost none in the radial direction.

Helix Angle—The angle formed between the axis of rotation and the lay of the fibers is called the *helix angle* and, for the reasons noted above, a helix angle of fifteen degrees is typical for many applications, including pressure vessels, often with a final layer of circumferential winding. For maximum torsional strength, such as that required for driveshafts, the theoretically optimum helix angle is forty-five degrees. Such a pattern is produced by a *helical wind*, again often followed by a final circumferential layer. (Note, though, that each pass has to be slightly offset lengthwise from the previous one, to avoid producing a thick figure eight instead of a continuous cylinder.) Given suitable automatic control over the travers-

ing head, any combination of wind patterns is possible. For some applications, longitudinal fibers are hand-laid between successive layers of machine winding.

After the winding is concluded, filament wound goods are no different from laminates produced by any other "contact" method. They can be left as is, or vacuum bagged to further reduce resin content, though again the problem of crushing the former may have to be considered. If ETC

A helical wind pattern. Illustration courtesy Owens-Corning.

Filament wound fuel storage tanks for a natural gas powered commercial vehicle. Photo courtesy DOW Plastics.

Pultrusion operation. Photo courtesy FRP Supply Division, Ashland Chemical Co.

techniques. Nevertheless, the process is sufficiently simple in principle and its potential structural benefits so clear cut that it is again worth thinking about cottage industry variations on the theme. At its crudest, this might amount to arranging a simple motorized "rotisserie" that slowly rotates the mandrel/molding surface, while the reinforcement is guided into place by hand.

PULTRUSIONS

For the mass production of structural shapes such as angles, channels, "I"-beams, etc., bundles of resin-saturated fiber in the form of continuous filaments or strands are pulled through a die having the cross sectional shape of the finished product. Usually the die is also heated, which cures the laminate as it is produced. Virtually any cross section, including hollow sections, can be produced in this way. Modifications of the process even permit the manufacture of goods having one or more individual bends, or a continuous curve over their length but, as might be expected, pultrusions are usually straight lengths.

Advantages

Like other goods made up from unidirectional reinforcement, pultrusions possess exceptional strength and stiffness when measured along their longitudinal axis, but are sorely lacking when measured at ninety degrees. To improve strength properties across the section, additional reinforcement has to be applied at right angles to the long direction. This can take the form of tape laid by hand or machine or, when the cross section of the pultrusion forms a closed surface of revolution, filament winding can be used for this purpose.

resin systems are used, the finished part can be autoclaved, to gain additional structural benefits. Interestingly, filament winding has been used to custom produce unidirectional pre-pregs: a winding formed using a simple circumferential pattern is slit lengthwise and removed from the mandrel before curing.

Considering the specialized nature of this process, there are a surprisingly large number of manufacturers of filament winding machinery. Needless to say, these machines are often custom designed for one specific application, and are extremely expensive. Their cost is justified either by "cost-no-object" aerospace budgets or by the long-term returns from rapid and economical production of large numbers of identical parts. Accordingly, we have included filament winding in this chapter on mass-production

Like filament winding and spray up, pultrusion uses raw materials in the lowest cost form—continuous strands. Ladder rails, fishing rods, golf club shafts, automotive anti-intrusion door beams, and ski poles are

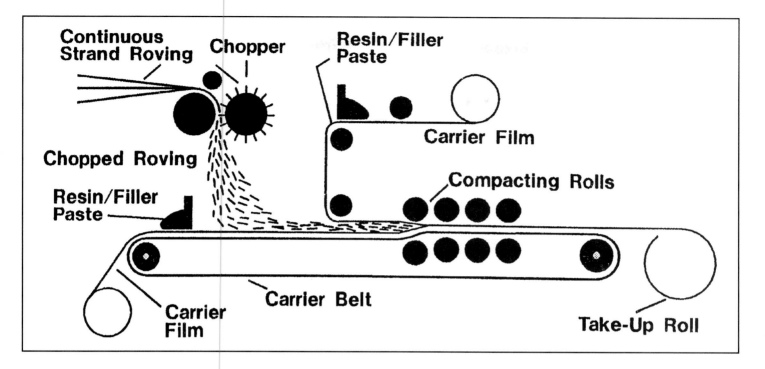

Continuous Strand Roving

Chopper

Resin/Filler Paste

Chopped Roving

Carrier Film

Resin/Filler Paste

Compacting Rolls

Carrier Belt

Carrier Film

Take-Up Roll

just a few examples of the wide variety of industrial and consumer products made by pultrusion, or a combination of pultrusion and filament winding.

SHEET MOLDING COM-POUND (SMC)

While techniques like spray up and the use of pre-forms offer some improvement in cost and rate of production over convention-al wet lay-up, these processes nevertheless remain unacceptably slow and labor inten-sive when production quantities reach into the thousands. To answer this challenge and, above all, to achieve fast turnaround time for the molds, a different approach is needed.

For goods needed in the numbers demand-ed by the automobile industry, heated, matched metal molds are commonly used, together with material suitable for high tem-perature processing. To minimize labor and ensure consistent, predictable properties, the preferred material for such items as station wagon tailgates, hoods, fenders and other bodywork is *sheet molding compound*, or SMC, which comprises resin, catalyst, rein-

forcement, fillers, and an internal mold release agent, all combined together in sheet form. The raw material is set into the heated mold cavity, the mold closed, and within as little as 90 seconds the cure has proceeded far enough to permit the part to be with-drawn.

Compound Components

The resins used are generally polyesters, combined with a catalyst system (often there are multiple catalyst components) that is more or less inert at room temperature. This provides an acceptable storage life, but it decomposes rapidly at the molding temper-ature of about 300 F. It can be appreciated that, to facilitate the flowing of the material within the mold, the reinforcing fibers have to be comparatively short—about one inch. At the same time, a substantial quantity of fillers and other additives are included in SMC to control shrinkage and to produce a smooth surface finish that needs little or no preparation prior to painting.

Low Profile SMC—Apart from the same kind of inert materials like talc and calcium carbonate that are sometimes used as fillers

How sheet molding com-pound (SMC) is made. Illustration courtesy Owens-Corning.

"The two factors of short fiber length and a low fiber fraction mean that SMC goods are structurally inferior to properly executed wet lay-ups, especially if the latter are based on woven reinforcement."

in RTC polyesters, SMC formulations usually include a hefty portion of a thermoplastic such as polyethylene, in finely divided form. The thermoplastic becomes fluid at molding temperature then solidifies on cooling, contributing substantially to surface smoothness and to the reduction of distortion caused by shrinkage around abrupt changes in section thickness. Sheet molding compound having these properties is referred to as "low profile SMC."

Pros & Cons

The two factors of short fiber length and a low fiber fraction mean that SMC goods are structurally inferior to properly executed wet lay-ups, especially if the latter are based on woven reinforcement. Nevertheless, the light weight, dent resistance, and immunity to corrosion of FRP panels makes them an attractive alternative to metal body parts. At the same time, the comparatively low cost of the molds (at least when compared to the numerous stamping dies needed to progressively form metal parts) means that styling changes can be undertaken quickly and at much lower cost.

For these reasons the use of SMC is expanding rapidly in the automotive field, and the material is constantly being improved. Recently, for instance, SMC has been developed that contains up to 60% chopped glass fiber by weight, compared with the 30-35% figure of earlier formulations, and SMC based on continuous roving is also available now. This last type, which is really a form of pre-preg (see above), understandably lacks a surface finish suitable for exterior body panels, but its structural properties permit its use for such secondary structural applications as bumper beams.

It is worth noting that most manufacturers experience difficulty in adapting parts designed around wet lay-up to production in SMC. Partly this may be because of the comparative structural inferiority of SMC,

but mostly it seems to be just a matter of a thousand and one unanticipated details. The Chevrolet Corvette, for example, was originally produced entirely by wet lay-up. As production numbers for this car grew, an attempt was made to gradually replace wet lay-up parts with those made from SMC. Eventually, the entire body was redesigned, and that styling change used as an opportunity to refine those troublesome details, permitting production of the entire body in SMC.

RESIN INJECTION

Increasingly stringent environmental and health regulations are having dramatic effects on the FRP industry. Reductions in the permissible levels of volatile organic hydrocarbon (VOH) emissions, for instance, has led to the introduction of polyesters with reduced styrene content, and a search for alternatives to styrene monomer (see Chapter 3). Another approach is to use a closed mold process—one in which the catalyzed resin is piped into the space between matched male and female molds, thus minimizing contact of the resin with the atmosphere.

In the usual arrangement, dry reinforcement—often as a pre-form—is set into the mold, the mold then closed, and the resin introduced at the bottom and forced through the reinforcement. Displaced air is vented through one or more ports at the top. As can be imagined, there is a tendency for the resin flow to displace the reinforcement. An improvement on this *resin injection molding* (RIM) that helps deal with this problem, and also speeds up the whole process, is to apply a vacuum to the mold once it is closed with the reinforcement in place. This *vacuum assisted resin injection* (VARI) helps hold the reinforcement in place, increases the speed of the upward flow of the resin and reduces entrapped air. ■

10

MOLDS

W hile there are a handful of "moldless" techniques for forming FRP goods, as discussed at the end of this chapter, by far the most common method is to use a mold. If one does not exist, it will have to be made. The mold might be made from any of several materials, including wood, plaster and metal. The only real requirements are that the mold should have the desired shape, be stiff and hard enough to keep that shape, and have a slick, glossy surface that does not affect the cure of the resin system used and is itself unaffected by the resin.

METAL MOLDS

Metal molds have a very long life and can be used with high-temperature and/or high-pressure curing systems and so are frequently used in mass-production operations. However, apart from the use of an existing metal part such as a fender or other body panel as a pattern, metal molds are far beyond the budget of the small specialty shop, and beyond the scope of this book.

WOOD MOLDS

For small objects with a simple shape,

Metal molds are extremely sturdy and long-lived, but extremely expensive. This mold for a section of the wing leading edge of the deHavilland Dash 8 aircraft is made from electrodeposited nickel. Guy Levesque photo courtesy deHavilland Inc.

Large flat areas are best avoided in FRP construction, because such shapes lack the inherent stiffness of curved panels. Photo by Jack Gladback.

"Perhaps the greatest drawback to plaster is the difficulty of repairing or re-working the surface."

ture fine detail from the master pattern it is formed in or on, and harden to form a surprisingly sturdy working surface. As with wood, the surface must be sealed before use. Lacquer (cellulose acetate) is known to work reliably; certain other, more modern coatings such as urethane and epoxy paints are more durable, but some may be incompatible with the resin. Again, conduct trials to be sure. Note, too, that the back of the plaster should be coated with whatever is used as a sealer, to avoid the possibility of water entering.

Plaster Problems

The substantial weight of plaster can be an advantage with small molds—they will be less prone to moving around while you are working than molds made from lighter weight materials. As the size of the mold increases, though, that same heft—especially combined with the weak and brittle nature of plaster—rapidly becomes a drawback. Another problem with plaster is ensuring that there are no air bubbles trapped at the mold surface; this is mostly a matter of technique, though, and can be beaten with practice (see *Plaster Transfer Molding*, p. 105).

Grinding or sanding plaster produces clouds of very fine dust that goes everywhere and seems to linger forever; fresh material added to old plaster will invariably differ in hardness when dried, making it nearly impossible to sand a smooth junction. For both these reasons, by far the best use of plaster that I have found is for producing intermediate patterns and shapes by a process I call *transfer molding*, as described later in this chapter.

wood can sometimes make a suitable mold material, especially for a male mold. Clear, straight-grained hardwood should be used, and preferably laminated rather than carved from one big chunk, to reduce warping. The laminations and the grain should preferably run in the direction the part will be pulled from the mold, though this is not always practical. The sealing of the wood surface is obviously critical. Shellac, lacquer and urethane paints, and certain epoxy varnishes work well, but experiments should be made to ensure that the surface finish is compatible with the resin system. About the worst problem with wood is its tendency to change size—especially across the grain—with changes in its moisture content. This problem can be reduced, though not eliminated, by the use of kiln dried wood and by ensuring that *all* surfaces of the wood are sealed.

PLASTER

Plaster is another material worth considering. Like FRP, but unlike wood or metal, plaster can itself be molded, and it has the further advantages of dimensional stability and absurdly low cost. It will faithfully cap-

FRP MOLDS

While all these materials have their uses, the vast majority of molds made and used by small-scale FRP fabricators are themselves made of FRP, and it is in many respects an ideal material for the job. First, it is *mold-*

able—it doesn't have to be beaten or whittled to shape; second, a well finished gel coat surface is about as slick and glossy as you can get, short of chrome plated metal; third, the light weight of the material makes even large molds manageable; finally, the materials and equipment are familiar and available.

Designing FRP Molds

The actual manufacture of an FRP mold is performed in basically the same way as subsequent parts are made in that mold, as described in Chapter 7, though there are enough differences to justify a detailed description of the entire process, which is provided in the next chapter. Whatever the mold material, however, there are a number of design issues to be considered before construction starts. First is the shape of the object, both overall and in detail. In most cases, the overall form of the part will be set by functional requirements, but the characteristics of the material have to be considered, too.

Curves—FRP works best at producing smooth, "streamlined" shapes, having curvature in all three dimensions. Apart from the fact that these eye-pleasing shapes are easier to produce in FRP than in most other materials, the curvature adds stiffness to both the part and the mold. Another reason to avoid flat areas is that they will invariably tend to warp, forming a curl with the gel coat side inward. (While both the gel coat and the laminate shrink slightly on curing, the reinforcement in the laminate "fights" the shrinkage more than the unreinforced gel coat; it is the difference in the amount of shrinkage that causes the curl. A flat mold, in other words, will not produce a flat part.) When designing in stiffness in this way, however, beware of re-entrant curves—ones that turn back on themselves. These will require a split mold, to allow the part to be removed. We will have more comments about split molds later; for now it is suffi-

cient to say that while it is better to use split molds than to produce an inefficient or ugly product, it is foolish to have more split lines than necessary.

Corners—As to detail shape, the most important thing to avoid is sharp corners, especially inside corners, because of the difficulty of getting the reinforcing fibers to conform to such tight contours; as a rule of thumb, 1/4 inch radius should be regarded as the bare minimum. Remember that what is an inside corner in a female mold becomes an outside corner on the part, and sharp outside corners are places where the gel coat is easily damaged. Beware, too, of niggling lit-

Where functional requirements demand a flat surface, stiffness can be restored through the use of sandwich construction. Here honeycomb filler is applied by Aerodine Composites workers to make the undertray for an IMSA WSC car. Photo by Jack Gladback.

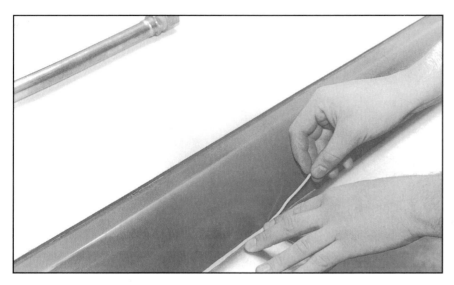

Sharp corners are also best avoided in FRP. Sometimes it is easiest to produce a plug with "square" corners, then form a radius before mold making using a fillet of wax or modeling clay. Photo by Jack Gladback.

This is the console on the top half of a split boat mold. Note the combined use of wood and FRP to produce nice rounded curves. Photo by Michael Lutfy.

tle details. While it is possible, for example, to produce louvers in FRP, it is definitely not practical to mold their holes; these will all have to be cut out by hand later.

Male or Female?

The second decision is the choice between male and female molds. The surface of the finished product that contacts the mold will have a glossy surface, while the back face will be rough, so for goods where visual appearance is important, the surface that is exposed determines which way it must be molded. Thus, a bathtub would be formed over a male mold, while a canoe would be made in a female mold.

"The Wrong Way Around"

For a quick-and-dirty one-off project, it may be practical to work "the wrong way around," then to grind and fill the rough surface to acceptable cosmetic standards. For example, you could make a replica of a car hood by simply molding directly off the hood; the copy would be larger than the original by the thickness of the material, and the "shiny side" would be "in." requiring that the visible surface be filled and smoothed, but that still might be quicker and cheaper than first making a female mold off the hood, then forming a replica hood in that mold. Then again, maybe not; the "smoothing" takes a lot of time if it is to come anywhere close to professional standards. If appearance is not critical, then the choice can be based purely on convenience.

Considerations—There are two points to note in this connection. First, the slight resin shrinkage that occurs on curing will cause a part to contract onto a male mold, making removal more difficult, while a female molded part will tend to shrink away from the mold. On the other hand, there is a limit to how small a cavity you can work in, so it is possible to produce smaller objects over a male mold than can be made in a female one—a small, deep battery box is a good example. The second point to keep in mind is that it is generally much more practical to produce a mold-quality surface finish on a male shape than on a female one—it is obviously easier to sand or paint the outside of a box than the inside. If a male mold will be needed, like our battery box example, it would ordinarily be produced in turn from a female master. That female master will require a fine finish on its interior, and that would be very tough to achieve, working from scratch. In such cases, it may make sense to produce a male master, use it to make an intermediate female piece, then to use that female intermediate to produce the

Multi-piece boat molds.
Photo by Michael Lutfy.

Multi-Piece Molds

The next decision is whether the mold will be made in one piece or several. Except for very simple shapes, a multi-piece mold will often be preferable. For one thing, while you may be able to lay up the surface in one piece, spraying gel coat into a deep, narrow cavity is impossible, and we have already expressed the view that gel coat really should be sprayed. This is especially important for something as critical as a mold. There is also the problem of getting the part out of the mold. It makes sense that a tapered shape will be easier to extract from the mold than one with parallel sides; split molds can eliminate the need for this taper or *draft*, as it is called.

Draft—For a one-piece mold (or any individual section of a split mold), the actual amount of draft required will depend on the depth of the draw, the stiffness of the finished part, and whether the mold is male or female. Small parts (say, breadbox sized) of fairly thin, flexible construction can get by with zero, if made in a female mold; a three or four-foot-long nose section for a race car

body made in a one-piece female mold will require a minimum of 5 degrees of draft, no matter how willowy the construction. Male molded parts require more draft, because of their tendency to shrink onto the mold; working with polyester, 5 degrees should be regarded as the bare minimum. It is important to realize, though, that when a female mold is being produced over a male pattern, or *plug* (see Chapter 12), the draft requirements for the mold will be the same as for a male molded part. In other words, while you might have no problem getting a part out of a mold with negligible draft, you might very well discover that you can't get the mold off the plug in the first place!

Auto Body Parts—For something like automotive bodywork, multi-piece molds are pretty much essential, for two reasons. First, a car body capable of being pulled from a one-piece mold would look a lot like a '49 Nash. Second, while openings like doors and hood and trunk lids can be cut out of a one-piece body molding, all these parts need jambs, sills, etc.; and it is much easier to make these integral than to fake them up later. The re-entrant curves formed by these features will necessitate a multi-piece mold. Even for simply shaped race car body panels, there will generally be a need for turned-

final male production mold. This is a fine example of the use of *transfer molding* (see p. 105).

"For some-thing like automotive bodywork, multi-piece molds are pretty much essential, for two reasons."

Race car body parts such as these will need multi-piece molds. Photo by Michael Lutfy.

> *"While there are drawbacks to split molds, the situation is not as grim as is sometimes suggested."*

under edges of some sort where the panels attach to the structure, and these form re-entrant curves that will lock the parts into the mold unless the mold is split. To permit aligning and securing adjacent mold sections, it is customary to provide them with bolt-together flanges at right angles to the working surface. In the case of the simple, flat inward projections, or *returns,* needed for mounting flanges, as mentioned above, the extra mold section can simply be a piece of flat stock that bolts to the flanges on the main part of the mold. (For detail on how to deal with the sharp corner created by mounting flanges formed in this way, see Chapter 11.)

Drawbacks—While there are drawbacks to split molds, the situation is not as grim as is sometimes suggested. The complications include a visible *flash line* on the outside of the finished part, the problem of ensuring exact registration of mating sections, and the labor involved in assembling and dismantling the mold every time it is used. Against this inconvenience can be counted vastly

greater freedom with respect to shape, and the reduced consequences of screwing up during the mold making—repairing the original pattern and starting over again is much less daunting if only one of, say, half a dozen mold pieces is junk, than if the entire project is scrap.

Flash Lines—The flash line problem can be minimized by masking the flanges of the mating mold sections, as described in Chapter 4; by making the flanges stiff enough to uniformly distribute the clamping load of the fasteners holding the two sections together, so they aren't just pinched at discreet points while a gap is allowed to open up between bolts; and by ensuring that the flanges are either both truly flat or else are exact mirror images of each other. (This last is pretty much automatic if each mold section is formed with the previous section still in place on the plug.)

Registration—As to the registration problem, for products to be produced by hand lay-up in small quantities the usual way to clamp two mold sections together is by means of nuts and bolts. After a while, the holes in the mold flanges become worn and sloppy. This problem can be dealt with by metal inserts at the fastener points—ordinary drill bushings, available at any machine-shop supply house, are just the ticket. To help ensure that there is no step in the mold at the seam, and thus in the surface of the finished part, any final finish sanding and polishing of the mold in the area of the joint line must be done with the adjacent sections assembled together, no matter how difficult this may be. (But see Chapter 11 regarding this business of sanding a mold surface.)

Labor Intensive—There remains the labor issue. The wrench-twirling gets really exhausting and time-consuming with large, complex molds with many sections and long joint lines, especially after the fasteners get all clogged up with resin and fibers.

Above all, of course, you have to be able to get the part out of the mold, but just how many split lines there will be, where they are to be located, and how to model the flanges will require some careful thought and planning. This should be worked out thoroughly even before you start making the plug. Wherever possible, the seams should be hidden, or made to coincide with a natural feature of the part—a decorative trim line, for instance. We will deal with the practical details of FRP mold making in Chapter 11.

PLASTER TRANSFER MOLD-ING

It is frequently necessary to make one or more intermediate moldings when working toward a production mold or even a one-off product. For instance, if you are able to obtain a shape which is close to your needs, it is sometimes more practical to reproduce that shape in plaster, rather than to mold off the original. This may be because the shape, while close to the desired contour, nevertheless needs some modification. If the original is highly valuable or borrowed, or both, it obviously should not be messed with. Or the material from which it is made (or at least its surface) may be such that it cannot safely be exposed to polyester—a piece of bodywork with a fresh enamel paint job, for example. Sometimes it is simply more convenient and/or faster and/or cheaper to do it this way.

There are some drawbacks to plaster noted in Chapter 12. However, the difficulties arising from variations in the hardness of the surface are essentially eliminated by the

"There remains the labor issue."

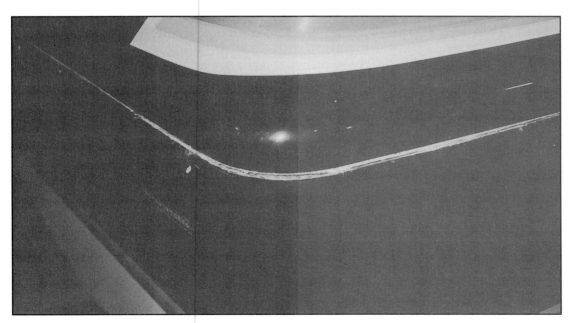

Flash lines and part registration are some of the drawbacks encountered with multi-piece molds. Photo by Michael Lutfy.

Even simply shaped parts sometimes need a split mold. The "joggle" in these Indycar body panels required for a flush fit with adjacent bodywork are formed by the loose mold piece visible on the left. Photo by Jack Gladback.

"For our purposes, something called Hydrocal B-11 is top notch."

"one-shot" molding technique described below. Besides, this is a *molding* process—the basic surface should be defined by the original part to be copied, and shouldn't need extensive re-working. If you are going to carve a completely new shape from the plaster dupe, you should probably consider starting from scratch with a more manageable plug material.

Procedure

Start by cleaning the original thoroughly, then apply a coat of petroleum jelly as a parting agent; it can be rubbed on with your fingers. You shouldn't leave great gobs of the stuff on the surface; on the other hand, it should be thoroughly covered. (I have long been intrigued by the possibility of using PAM™—a vegetable oil in a spray can used in non-stick fry pans—as a release medium for plaster, but I never had the nerve to actually try it!)

Plaster Material—There is a wide variety of plasters available: some harden quickly, some slowly; when dry, some have very hard, almost stone-like surfaces which sand relatively cleanly; others are quite soft and chalky. For our purposes, something called Hydrocal B-11 is top notch. It sets to a stone-hard surface, and though it costs a lit-

tle more than regular Plaster of Paris, it is still ridiculously cheap. Many craft and art supply houses carry Hydrocal, as do some building supply outfits; if you can't find it, any old plaster will do.

Mixing—Now, mix up a batch of plaster. Fill a container of suitable size (say a small plastic pail) about 1/2 to 2/3 full of just lukewarm water, and start sifting the plaster into the water. Just dip into the bag, grab a handful, and sift it through your fingers into the water. (You should apply a barrier cream to your hands before doing this—plaster dries out your skin terribly.) As you keep adding plaster, you will notice that it sinks out of sight but, pretty soon, "mountains" of plaster begin to persist above the "lake" of water. Assuming the container is about as high as it is wide, you've got the right amount of plaster when the area of the mountains and lakes are about equal. Do not stir this mixture; just let it sit for a very few minutes, then stir just once or twice, and immediately begin splashing the plaster onto the working surface.

The Technique—It takes a bit of practice to master this technique, but it consists mainly of grabbing a handful of the "mud" (which should be left to thicken until it forms a loose glop, so it's just barely capable of being held in the hand), then flicking it onto the surface with an underhand/backhand motion, a bit like tossing a Frisbee. Part of the trick is to spread your fingers wide at the same instant you flick. With practice, it is possible to lay a shell of plaster between 1/4 inch and 1/2 inch thickness all over the greased surface.

Before this first splash has hardened, pre-cut scraps of burlap sacking (say post-card sized) should be dunked in a fresh batch of plaster and the surplus removed by squeegeeing between thumb and forefinger. These wetted scraps are shingled all over the surface, then more plaster slopped on and roughly leveled out with hand and/or trowel. The idea is to get a shell which is no thicker than necessary, to avoid excessive weight, shrinkage and distortion. This takes some practice. Before the plaster is completely set, edges can be cleaned up with an assortment of tools.

Surface Finishing—Quite quickly, the plaster will begin to harden and get cool; once it cools, the mold is ready for removal. Now you can repeat the whole process to come up with a plaster duplicate of the original part. Unless you are an Olympic class plaster-splasher, however, you will discover an assortment of flaws in the surface of your intermediate plaster mold. Chief among these are little craters formed by air bubbles trapped against the original surface (that's part of why the "hurling" technique is important), and rills and laps, where the first splash of plaster ran down the surface before getting hit with the next. If these craters are bigger than, say, a pencil eraser, mix up a little extra plaster and fill them in, but do not raise a bump on the surface—a little low is better than too high. If they're really tiny, don't worry about 'em, just smear a little more petroleum jelly onto the surface, making sure the bubble craters are filled in. Don't overdo the grease job, though—you don't want too much petroleum jelly transferred onto the dupe part, as you're going to

want to paint it eventually. Follow the above directions about technique, and you will soon have a duplicate original with a uniformly hard surface, workable within the limits of plaster, albeit with a number of ridges and bumps. The surface will also have a residue of parting agent on it. Wipe off the grease with a paper towel as best you can, finishing off with just a little acetone or lacquer thinner, then give it a day or two to harden up. After that, hand sanding with about 120 grit garnet paper will get rid of the bumps and ridges, the remaining petroleum jelly, and shallow bubble craters. You'll clog up quite a bit of sand-paper at this stage, but the work should go pretty quickly.

If you have modifications in mind that require removal of material, you can hack and scrape away at the plaster surface with any of the usual plaster working tools. If you want to add material, then by all means work with polyester auto-body filler. You shouldn't just slobber filler onto the raw plaster surface, however; first roughen up the area where you intend to fill, so as to provide a substantial key for the subsequent filling. Then spray on several coats of primer, first making certain that you've vacuumed all the sanding dust off the surface and have wiped it over with a tack cloth. It's wise to also cover the "back" side of the plaster with primer, as you're eventually going to wind up wet-sanding, and you need

> *"Part of the trick is to spread your fingers wide at the same instant you flick."*

Inward projections on a part that forms mounting flanges are produced by securing a flat "return" to the mold edge. Aerodine Composites prefers sheet metal for this job. Photo by Jack Gladback.

"The eco- nomical use of material and the pro- vision of a rigid support can both be achieved by a technique borrowed from art cast- ing, called mothering."

to avoid accidentally soaking the plaster with water. Once the primer is on and light- ly sanded or *brown-bagged* (see Chapter 12), you can start working free-hand with filler, making sure you squeeze it well down into the previously roughened surface. At this point you can also use spot-putty to fill the remaining rills and bubble craters. From here on, the procedure is exactly the same as described for finishing the surface of a plug—see Chapter 12.

FLEXIBLE MOLD-MAKING MATERIALS

There are a few situations which call for a flexible material. One, obviously, is when you're trying to produce a flexible molded part. Another is when a small, complex part—normally requiring a split mold—has to be molded in one piece, without any flash line. Finally, you may want to produce a shape which would be a helluva lot simpler to make if only you could produce a straight one first, and then somehow bend it. For example, some pretty intricate shapes can be milled into a piece of wood, molded using a flexible material, and then the rubber dupe curved in one or more planes, from which a production mold can subsequently be pro- duced.

Drawbacks

There are three drawbacks to flexible molding materials: compatibility with the resin system later used to make parts in the mold, cost, and the need for some sort of stiff support to contain the molding surface. As to compatibility, note that silicone rubber may inhibit the cure of polyesters—some- times completely! Beware! Urethane rub- bers seem to work fine, but unless treated there is sometimes a problem with release, so use mold release wax, and experiment with small samples before committing your- self.

Cost can be minimized by using as little

material as possible, and by recognizing that this process is in practice limited to small parts. The economical use of material and the provision of a rigid support can both be achieved by a technique borrowed from art casting, called *mothering*. The mother is a split plaster shell or flask, in which an eco- nomically thin flexible molding surface is contained. In practice, the plaster mother is made first, and then liquid rubber poured into the space between the mother and the sample part.

Flexible Mold Procedure

Working from a finished original, the pro- cedure is as follows. First, a blanket of mod- eling clay, say a quarter inch thick, is wrapped over the outside of the original. A parting line is identified on the outside of the plasticene, and thin metal shims knifed care- fully into the surface, to set up a parting flange. Using the splash-coat/burlap rein- forcement method detailed above, the plas- ter mother can then be produced in two halves—one at a time. In the clay blanketing operation, one or more risers have to be pro- vided—just extra knobs of clay, strategical- ly located—so that you will have holes to pour the rubber in and vents for air to escape. The metal flashing which forms the parting line should be stripped away as soon as the plaster is set enough to permit, and then dents pressed into the exposed flange surface (if you get the timing right, you can just poke your finger into the soft plaster) so that the second half of the mother will have corresponding bumps. The bumps and dents later provide remarkably accurate indexing of the two flask halves.

Once the two halves of the mother are fully hard and ready to use, one half of the clay blanket is stripped away, the job reassembled, and the liquid rubber material poured through the pre-formed riser into the space previously occupied by the clay. Once the rubber is cured, a few keystone shaped pieces are cut out of the flanged edge of the rubber molding, to ensure that the two halves will later register properly, and the operation is repeated on the other side. After the second half of the rubber mold is cured, the flask can be dismantled and the rubber mold carefully removed from the original.

MOLDLESS CONSTRUCTION

Although (as stated at the beginning of this chapter) it is far more common to form FRP products with molds, the truth is that the first experience most people have with FRP involves *moldless* construction. When you patch a rust-hole in a fender by draping a piece of resin-saturated glass cloth over the gap there is no mold involved, at least for the portion that actually spans the opening. A similar "free-forming" technique has also been used for the manufacture of simply shaped goods like lawn furniture—saturated fabric is just draped over a primitive wire frame and allowed to cure. The shapes that can be achieved in this way are limited, but there are other, more versatile techniques for producing FRP goods which likewise do not involve the use of a separate, re-usable mold.

The Expendable or Sacrificial Mold

One is a technique for making tanks of all sorts by carving a chunk of foam to the desired shape, wrapping it entirely with resin-saturated reinforcement, and then dissolving out the foam plug with a suitable solvent once the shell has cured. This is undeniably an intriguing technique, but there are a few intrinsic limitations: the foam must be unaffected by the selected resin system; the resin must be impervious to the solvent used to purge the core; the thickness of the wrapping may need to be taken into account when shaping the core; and the outer surface of the finished tank necessarily has the texture of the fabric used.

Styrene Foam—Styrene foam can be dis-solved by styrene monomer (vinyl benzene—see Chapter 3), yet is impervious to epoxy resin, which itself is quite unharmed by the styrene monomer. Conversely, polyester resin contains styrene monomer, and thus gobbles up the foam at a brisk rate. (In youthful innocence and ignorance, I once attempted to make a gas tank for a motorcycle in this way, using a hand-carved form of styrene foam wrapped with glass cloth and polyester resin. After the styrene in the resin had its way with the foam plug, the wrinkled, knobby result looked remarkably like the brain of some large animal!)

Polyurethane Foam—A different problem attends the use of polyurethane foam. It is impervious not only to epoxy and polyester, but also to virtually everything else, and cannot be satisfactorily dissolved by any commonly available solvent! The best that can be achieved after prolonged saturation in acetone is a sort of spongy mess, which can only be extracted from the surrounding shell with great difficulty.

There are few instances where construction of this sort would, by itself, be acceptable for a gas tank—most race sanctioning bodies would demand a fuel cell. Nevertheless, there are surely situations where it would be handy to be able to make a custom tank to hold the mandated fuel cell, and it is reassuring to know that the epoxy will remain unaffected by any gasoline that might contact it. One caution here is that the styrene foam plug should be painted with a coating of resin, and the resin allowed to gel, before any reinforcement is applied—if the fabric is applied dry, there may be areas in contact with the plug that do not get completely surrounded with plastic.

Disposal—Another consideration is responsible disposal of the mixture of styrene monomer and polymer, after the form has been dissolved out of the tank. The quantity of this toxic waste (and the amount of styrene monomer needed to do the dissolving) can be greatly reduced by con-

> *"After the styrene in the resin had its way with the foam plug, the wrinkled, knobby result looked remarkably like the brain of some large animal!"*

> *"Of course, for strictly one-off construction it is more economical in terms of materials to produce a male molding over a plaster plug, then to break the plaster out, than it is to go through the whole male plug/female mold/part sequence."*

structing the plug in the form of a hollow box; if it won't hold its shape without help, it should be possible to "tack weld" the separate sheets together with just the tiniest dab of solvent. Finally, it would be irresponsible to use this form of construction for a tank intended to hold potable (drinkable) water. As pointed out in Chapter 6, while fully cured epoxy is completely harmless stuff, with hand-mixed epoxy it is impossible to be certain that there isn't at least a little uncured resin lurking about, and that is potentially very nasty indeed if it is ingested.

While it is probably impractical for an individual or a small shop, it is worth bearing in mind that the styrene beads that are the raw material for the making of (white) bead foam are commercially available, and that they can be foamed by heating with steam. If formed in a split mold, shaped blanks could be quickly and cheaply produced, for use as either captive or dissolvable formers for any number of applications. I once contemplated producing a handful of fuel tanks for a particular class of race car, using such foam plugs as sacrificial molds for the process described above.

Plaster—A more common material for the production of such expendable molds, however, is plaster. Air ducts of complex shape are made for aircraft in this way, the plaster being cast to shape in split molds, then broken out of the cured FRP molding by simply bashing on the outside of the duct with a hammer. (It helps to incorporate coiled wire or stout cord into the plaster casting, to assist in the removal.)

Of course, for strictly one-off construction it is more economical in terms of materials to produce a male molding over a plaster plug, then to break the plaster out, than it is to go through the whole male plug/female mold/part sequence. This way of working will usually result in an unsatisfactory final result—the problem is the amount of very nasty grinding and sanding work, plus the weight of the filler required, if the "up" sur-

face is to brought to a satisfactory level of finish. Nevertheless, there are situations where it is justified. In those cases, while the male form is usually referred to as a plug, it is certainly used as a mold, so this process of male molding over a disposable plug is really just another instance of the use of an expendable mold.

The Gossamer Albatross—In the production of the Gossamer Albatross—the man-powered aircraft that successfully crossed the Straits of Messina—there was a particularly clever application of a sacrificial mold. The main wing spar was formed by hand laying unidirectional carbon fiber pre-preg onto the outside surface of an aluminum tube. The lay-up was then spiral wrapped with a ribbon of heat shrink plastic, then hot oil was piped through the aluminum tube. The heat both provided the temperature needed for the ETC epoxy resin system to cure properly and also caused the shrink wrap to contract tightly onto the laminate, serving the purpose usually provided by a vacuum bag and autoclave. Once the laminate was cured, the aluminum tube was dissolved out with acid and the shrink wrap was peeled off, leaving an exceptionally strong, stiff, and light hollow carbon fiber tube. Ingenious!

The Captive Mold

When it is not necessary to provide a hollow space in the interior, it is of course possible to employ the fiberglass-over-foam method described above, and just leave the foam former in place; perhaps the best known application of this procedure is in the field of home-built kit aircraft. The technique involves precisely cutting high-density styrene foam to the required shape using a hot-wire cutter guided by templates, then covering the resulting blanks with a combination of bi-directional and unidirectional reinforcement saturated with epoxy resin. The texture of the fabric weave on the exposed outer surface is then filled with a syntactic foam (see Chapter 15) of microballoons mixed into more epoxy resin, applied with a squeegee.

The resulting skin-foam-skin sandwich yields a light yet strong and stiff structure, while the all-of-a-piece construction and the opportunity to produce smooth three dimensional curves produces a more precise and more slippery aerodynamic shape than the usual arrangement of aluminum sheets, curved in a single plane and riveted together. Yet all of this can be achieved by complete amateurs with no prior experience, having negligible facilities, and using the sorts of tools you would find in your kitchen drawers.

Applications—This ingenious and elegant technique was probably invented by a member of the surfing community; the first application I am aware of was in the production of fiberglass surfboards, and it is still used for making both them and sailboards. However, these more commonly use polyester resin for its lower cost and easier handling characteristics. In that case, of course, styrene foam is useless; a urethane foam core is commonly used in these applications.

As for its first application to aircraft, if it was not pioneered by the brilliant aircraft designer Burt Rutan, it was certainly his series of VariEze aircraft which popularized it. Other kit plane makers have since adopted the technique, and it is also used in the manufacture of certain Lotus sports cars. Lotus at one point considered using inflatable rubber bladders to form the molding surface for certain box sections in the composite chassis-body assembly of that car, but that plan was rejected because of concerns about the possibility of a punctured bladder. A negligible weight penalty was incurred by using a captive foam filler instead.

Another instance of a captive or incorporated mold is in the construction of certain types of boats. A canoe, for instance, can be built that has the appearance of convention-al cedar-strip construction, but which gains additional toughness, strength and durability by a covering of glass cloth and clear epoxy resin over both inside and outside surfaces. The cedar strips, with a modified tongue-and-groove arrangement at their edges, are temporarily nailed or stapled to the outside of a skeleton armature, each strip being edge glued to the next. Once the glue has dried, the staples are removed, the surface smoothed, and the glass cloth and epoxy applied. Once it has cured, the assembly is removed from the armature and the inside is then covered in the same way.

And here's a dandy way to make a battery box—just envelop the cardboard box the battery came in with food wrap, to serve as a parting agent, then lay up glass fabric and resin (polyester will do fine) on the outside of that. Once the laminate has cured, the cardboard can be ripped out. Do not leave the battery in the box while you're doing this, though; when this was attempted in my shop, the cardboard did not crush to accommodate the shrinkage, as we had expected, and the result was a splendid battery box... and a cracked, useless battery!

Finally there is the use of a captive mold in the filament winding process. As noted in Chapter 9, filament wound goods with partially closed ends require that either the mandrel (which serves as the form) be made in sections so it can be dismantled and removed, or else left in place. In one instance of the latter, a high performance racing bicycle frame is made which employs carbon fiber filament wound onto a light gauge aluminum tube. While it would be possible to dissolve this out, it is actually left in place, where it contributes a little to the structural performance and may in fact ease some of the problems associated with the winding pattern (as mentioned in Chapter 9) by taking care of loads that are off-axis from the carbon's point of view. ∎

> *"This ingenious and elegant technique was probably invented by a member of the surfing community; the first application I am aware of was in the production of fiberglass surfboards, and it is still used for making both them and sailboards."*

11

FRP MOLDS

Each part perfectly captures the surface texture of the mold it is made in. The mold, in turn, is a mirror image of the original master pattern or "plug," which must have a flawless finish to avoid having to rework every part made in the mold. Mold for an Indycar wing end plate, on right, is produced from plug on left. Photo by Jack Gladback.

As mentioned in the previous chapter, the actual process of construction of a FRP mold is generally similar to the method of making a part in that mold, as described in Chapter 7. There are some differences, however, and unlike an individual part, the mold will eventually represent all of the grief and sweat that went into the making of the plug, as well as the labor and materials in the mold itself. Also, the ease or otherwise of making parts in the mold, and the quality of every one of those parts, will depend on the quality of the mold. This, then, is no place to cut corners.

At this stage, we assume that we are building a female mold of medium size (bigger than a breadbox; smaller than a Buick), that it will be built using polyester resin, and that either a plug or an original part (perhaps in metal) is at hand, and finished to perfection.

(A detailed description of plug making is provided in the next chapter.) Whether plug or prototype part, the working surface must be slick, smooth, hard, and made of something that will not be affected by the resins and other chemicals that are about to contact it. In most cases that surface will be paint.

PAINTED SURFACES

On no account work over fresh enamel paint! I have twice had the experience of customers bringing in apparently flawless prototype parts with automotive enamel paint surfaces, for production of a mold and subsequent duplicate pieces. In one case it was assured that the surface was acrylic lacquer; it wasn't. In the other case, it was admitted that the paint was enamel, but that it was many months old and had been out

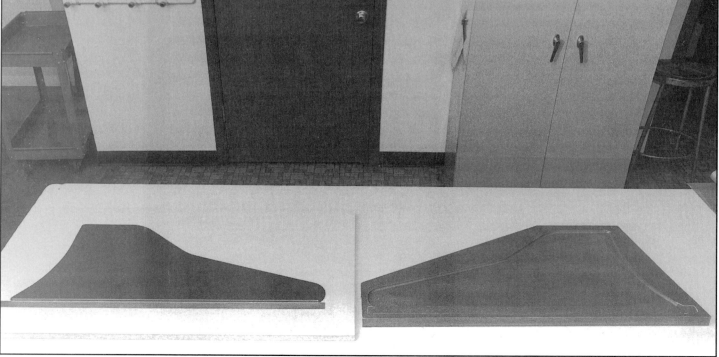

A flawless plug surface is only achieved by painstaking smoothing by hand. Aerodine Composites worker does final finishing on plug surface with #1500 grit cloth. Photo by Jack Gladback.

"In both cases, after countless hours of painstaking work, not only was the resulting mold garbage, so was the finish on the sample part."

baking in the sun a lot, etc., etc., so there shouldn't be any problem; there was. In both cases, after countless hours of painstaking work, not only was the resulting mold garbage, so was the finish on the sample part. (Naturally, not only did they not want to pay, they also expected their "terrific" original paint job restored!)

Lacquers

Of course, the only way to be completely sure about the surface is if you produced it yourself. The old nitrocellulose ("straight") lacquers or the newer and more common acrylic lacquers are fine, *if they are fully dried*, as are polyurethane and epoxy paints. There are also coatings based on furane resin purpose-made for this application. A factory automotive paint job is fine—they're baked. With others, you take your chances. (Once fully hardened, body shop enamel may also be OK, but I never intend to find out.) Assuming further, then, that you are absolutely satisfied on this point, you should sniff the surface. No kidding. If your nose is jammed up with shop fumes, drag the thing and yourself outside into the fresh air, and be completely sure that there is absolutely no hint of solvent odor.

PROCEDURE

The usual way of proceeding is as follows. First, ensure that the plug (or prototype part) is securely anchored, so it won't move around or fall over while you are working. This may seem obvious, but bear in mind that the mold will add a considerable weight as it is being built, perhaps all at one end or on one side, and what seems solid now may become increasingly unstable as you add material. Indeed, sometimes the order in which mold sections are made has to be based on this consideration.

Surface Prep

Now you wax the surface thoroughly, three or four times, and thoroughly buff after each coat. The wax used should be specifically identified as mold release wax, as noted in Chapter 7; this is not the time to take a chance with ordinary automotive or domestic waxes. A thick application of wax is neither necessary nor desirable, but it is absolutely essential that all of the surface is coated; the point of doing it several times is

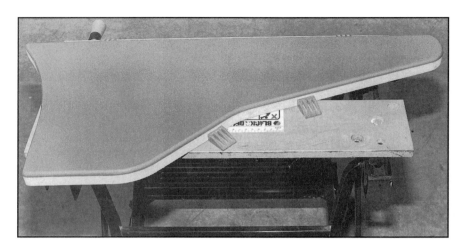

Some way must be found to hold the work securely. Changing it to sawhorses is one solution. Photo by Jack Gladback.

"A product called 'FomeCor,' which consists of two paper facings separated by a thin layer of foamed plastic, is lighter than Masonite and easier to cut accurately."

to be sure to cover any spots you might have missed with the first application. In most cases waxing and polishing by hand is completely satisfactory, and proves to be an agreeable way to ease yourself into the project; terry cloth toweling works well for both waxing and buffing. If the object is large—say the size of a boat—waxing and buffing by hand can become tedious; a power polisher fitted with a lambswool bonnet can speed the process. If the buffing is done by machine, however, be sure that it is a low speed polisher, not just a polishing pad installed on an electric drill—excessive speed will overheat the wax, causing it to soften and smear.

Flanges

Even if the finished part has a shape that can be produced in a one-piece mold, the mold should be provided with flanges around its edges to provide stiffening (and perhaps to form a surround for securing the edges of a vacuum bag—see Chapter 8). There is also the fairly common case, mentioned in the previous chapter, where the "other" section of a multi-piece mold consists simply of a piece of flat stock of some sort, intended to form turned-under mounting/stiffening flanges for a part that could otherwise be made in a true one-piece mold. In all of these situations the plug or pattern is probably flat on the bottom, and so will sit flush on a horizontal surface. In that case, an appropriate piece of sheet stock placed under the plug or pattern will serve both as part of the support structure and as the flange molding surface. A sheet of melamine board set on a pair of sawhorses works well, but be certain to secure the plug to the melamine board, and the melamine board to the sawhorses. (Melamine board is just particle board with a thin coating of melamine plastic, and is used for making cheap kitchen cabinets, etc. It is available from most building supply stores).

In the case of true multi-piece molds, you will next have to model flange(s) right onto the surface of the pattern along the part line(s), to allow fastening the mold sections together once they are complete. Begin by using a crayon or wax pencil to carefully mark the parting line(s) on the surface. (You should have thought about where these junctions between mold sections will wind up during the design and planning process; if you've postponed this decision 'till now, you just ran out of time!)

Flange Materials—A variety of materials and techniques may be appropriate for these flange patterns, always bearing in mind that they become, in effect, part of the plug or pattern, and thus must possess the same characteristics as the plug itself—a slick, firm surface that is unaffected by the resin and that will not interfere with the cure. Among the most suitable materials is tempered "Masonite." It is easy to cut with a jigsaw, can be rasped to an approximate fit and, once coated with a film-forming parting agent like PVA (see below), it makes a serviceable molding surface.

A product called "FomeCor," which consists of two paper facings separated by a thin layer of foamed plastic, is lighter than Masonite and easier to cut accurately. It can be worked precisely and quickly with a sharp utility knife. The fact that both the paper facings and the foam core need a coating of something impervious is not as much of a drawback as it might appear, since you are probably going to be spraying the entire working surface, including both the plug and the flanges, with PVA (see below). FomeCor is widely used by graphics designers, and is available at suppliers for that trade. It is rather more expensive than Masonite. Any of the above materials can be tacked in place on the "wrong" side with a hot-glue gun.

Flange models made from heftier materials, like melamine board, will need some sort of structural support, which may be fastened either to whatever is holding the plug off the floor or else to the surface of the plug itself. In this latter case, it is important that the points of attachment are accessible later, so that any resulting damage to the surface can be repaired before proceeding with subsequent sections of the mold. The off-cuts from the material used to make the plug station templates (see Chapter 12) will often prove useful as ready-made brackets for locating and securing these flange patterns. (The light weight of FomeCor might allow it to be simply stuck onto the surface of the plug at a right angle along the marked part lines, without the need for any kind of support structure beneath.)

There remains in every case the inevitable misfit between the surface of the plug and the cut edge of the flange model. Anything other than a sharply defined line here will exaggerate the subsequent problem of flash lines on the finished part, so it is worth going to some pains to ensure a clean junction between the plug and the flange pattern.

Here we can kill two birds with one stone. After temporarily jigging the flange material in the right position with tape, the gap can be filled and the flange secured to the surface of the plug at the same time by dribbling molten wax into the gap. (*Micro-crystalline wax*—see below—is better than ordinary paraffin wax for this purpose.) Once this has solidified, any fillet of wax that spoils the sharp right angle intersection can be carefully cleaned up by hand. A wooden

coffee stir stick will do, with a sharp working edge and corner whittled into it for this purpose; even better are the small wooden tools used by clay sculptors. These come in a wide variety of styles; you will find an assortment at art supply stores.

Modeling clay, also called *plasticene,* is another candidate material for this job; this is simply fine clay, bound together with an oil of some sort. It is certainly easier to work than wax, and many report success with its use. However, there are certainly some combinations of types and brands of resin and plasticene that are not happy with each other; I have seen polyester that remained uncured when in contact with modeling clay.

Another possibility is to make the flange models entirely out of a slab of wax. There is a material used in arts and crafts (you're going to become well known at an artists' supply store!) called *micro-crystalline wax,* which has a more gradual transition from solid to liquid than ordinary paraffin (candle) wax, and is also softer when it is hard, so it can be shaped more easily. It comes in slabs which can be *hot wired* (see Chapter 5) to produce rectangular planks which can be pieced together end to end and gently worked by hand (perhaps with a little judicious heat from a hair drier) into the required profile. A final quick pass at the contacting

"There remains in every case the inevitable misfit between the surface of the plug and the cut edge of the flange model."

An example of a flange attached to a section of a boat mold. Note how the gap has been filled in. Photo by Michael Lutfy.

The most common parting agent (mold release) is wax. On small parts, this is most conveniently applied by hand. Photo by Jack Gladback.

"This, then, argues for omitting the PVA and working directly on the waxed surface."

edge with the hair drier will soften it sufficiently to allow the "plank" to be stuck directly on the surface of the plug. One great beauty of this stuff is that it will come cleanly off the surface later, and any residue polished away—it is, after all, wax. It is a tad expensive but, provided any contamination is cleaned off the surface, it can be re-melted and re-used indefinitely. An electric crock pot serves admirably for storage, re-melting and dispensing of the stuff, and any sort of channel-shaped metal vessel will serve as a mold for casting fresh bricks.

To PVA or Not?

At this point, you have a serious choice to make. The conventional option is to spray a coat of PVA over the entire surface of that part of the plug, including the flange models, which will form the first piece of the mold. This provides a valuable back-up to the wax and, as long as the film is continuous and the plug surface is finished to the standard described in the next chapter, it is pretty much guaranteed that you will get a serviceable mold off the plug. It may not be easy and you may trash the plug, depending on what it is made from, but the mold should come off intact. The drawback to this way of

proceeding is that the slight orange peel texture of the PVA will be captured on the surface of the mold.

It is not particularly difficult to restore a brilliant smooth gloss to the mold by wet sanding, followed by polishing with rubbing compound, and this is the way most people work most of the time, but there is a catch: a mold surface re-worked in this way is usually inferior to an untouched, virgin surface. The reason has to do with the way the fillers and pigments in gel coat distribute themselves in the sprayed film. At the undisturbed surface, each microscopic granule is totally surrounded with plastic; sanding off this surface begins to expose these particles. Subsequent polishing with rubbing compound and glazing material will produce a surface that may look flawless to the naked eye, but at the microscopic level it is nevertheless rougher than a pristine sprayed surface. The consequences are not usually seen for some time, but while a virgin mold surface may be good for the production of several hundred parts, one re-worked in this manner may start to cause grief after, say, a few dozen.

This, then, argues for omitting the PVA and working directly on the waxed surface. Sadly, that in turn greatly increases the difficulty of removing the mold from the plug, and the probability of damage to the plug, which may or may not be a problem. Worse, it also greatly increases the risk of a truly stuck (i.e. junk) mold. In general, it is probably wise to reserve this technique for duplicate molds—those made from a master part produced, in turn, from an existing well-seasoned mold, without the use of PVA.

It is maddening that full advantage cannot usually be taken of the immaculate surface of the plug the first time around. After all, by the time the first part is made in the mold, the shape will have been translated twice— once to make the mold, a second time to make the part. Going through this process all over again to make a master part, and then a second mold, is probably just not worth the trouble, unless you are planning to make a heck of a lot of parts in that second, production mold. The only exception to this might be when you know in advance that the first part produced in the mold is itself a prototype, subject to some re-working and modification before the production mold is made from it in turn. In that case the original mold may be constructed with rather less care than the painstaking steps we are spelling out here, using PVA both on the plug during mold making and in the mold during the making of the master part, then re-finishing the surface of that part to visual perfection. In most cases, though, we're stuck with PVA. (Uh, perhaps we should avoid the word stuck here!)

Applying PVA

To proceed then, strain the PVA, vacuum the surface and go over it with a tack rag. Then, using moderate air pressure and the fluid flow just barely cracked open, fog on a very light mist coat of PVA. After a few minutes to allow this mist coat to dry, turn out the fluid screw a bit and lay on a slightly wetter coat of PVA. Continue in this way until the PVA flows together into a uniform glossy green film. The object is to get a film thick enough that it will peel off in a continuous sheet; practice on a waxed scrap surface like a piece of melamine board or "Arborite." (As suggested in the next chapter, it is definitely preferable for the plug or pattern surface to be colored white, to provide a color contrast that will assist in judging the thickness and evenness of the PVA, and of the gel coat which will follow.) If you get the PVA on too wet, especially at first, it will gather up into a severe orange-peel, or else run and tear. PVA will "crawl" away from any contamination on the surface, such as a fingerprint, so if the plug needs to be handled at this stage, use cotton work gloves. If you screw-up the PVA, you simply cannot touch it up; just mop it all off

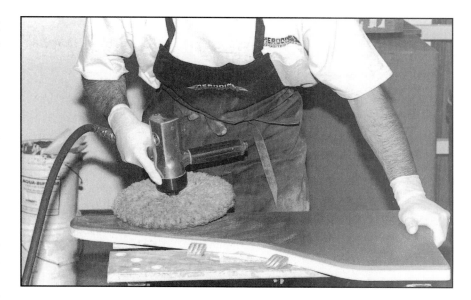

A power polisher can also be used to buff the wax. Beware excessive speed—do not overheat the wax. Photo by Jack Gladback.

with warm water, a sponge and paper towel, and start again. If you do have to abort the first PVA job, you may want to throw on another coat of wax before you re-spray. PVA dries quite quickly, provided the atmosphere is dry; a lunch break is usually time enough. In humid weather you may want to hasten the process; a hair drier works well.

Gel Coats

I noted in Chapter 4 that a distinction is usually made between *general purpose* (GP) gel coat, which has a proportion of flexibilized polyester in it to resist cracking under flexing and vibration, and *tooling* gel coat, which is more brittle but harder. Another feature of tooling gel coat is that it is usually supplied unfilled—it does not contain any of the finely divided filler particles that add impact resistance to GP formulations, and also reduce its cost. Thixotropic agents to reduce sagging on vertical surfaces are usually included however, but the silica gel particles that impart this "body" are extremely small and are soft and fluffy. For mold making, then, you definitely want tooling gel coat.

Color—Perhaps surprisingly, you should also give thought to the color. First, you want a contrast between the color of the gel

> *"If you screw-up the PVA, you simply cannot touch it up; just mop it all off with warm water, a sponge and paper towel, and start again."*

"Now comes the scary part—shooting the gel coat. Before you start, have an ear to the weather forecast; if rain is predicted, forget it—you've got a day off."

coat and that of the plug surface, to allow gauging by eye the thickness of the applied coat. A color contrast between the mold and subsequent parts is also desirable, for the same reason. This is why most mold gel coats are either black or orange. But here's a consideration that brings us back to the issue of whether or not to use PVA: the material used to make black pigment is *lamp black*, also called *carbon black*, and its particles are inherently much, much finer than those of any colored pigment, no matter how finely ground they may be. Thus, if you have decided to play it safe (and unless you have quite a bit of experience at this business, you certainly should—nothing will ruin your enthusiasm faster than having to chop up the whole shebang with an ax after you discover your brand-new mold is permanently welded to the plug), then you are committed to PVA on the plug, followed by refinishing the mold once it is thoroughly aged. A mold surface made from black tooling gel coat can be brought up to a finer micro-finish than any other color. (It means, however, that making black colored parts in the mold will give you headaches.)

Applying Gel Coat—Now comes the scary part—shooting the gel coat. Before you start, have an ear to the weather forecast; if rain is predicted, forget it—you've got a day off. Otherwise, be sure everything you need is at hand, that the shop and all the materials are at 65-75F—preferably at the warm end of that range, and set to work. Get into your protective coveralls, mask and gloves; get your spray equipment organized; be sure the compressor, all air lines and the water trap are drained; thoroughly mix the gel coat and, according to your equipment, dispense or mix in the catalyst. You're not quite ready yet to work on the critical surface. Take a moment to ensure, first, that the separate spray patterns for the resin and the catalyst are mixing properly. As noted in Chapter 5, you may have to carefully plan your progress across the surface, paying par-

ticular attention to this matter of the convergence of the resin and catalyst spray patterns. Refer to that chapter also on the matter of catalyst ratio—you want a cure fast enough to minimize contamination of the exposed gel coat surface, but not so fast as to cause pin holing, shrinkage, or any other grief. In general, it is better to work a little slower all round than when making parts. Do a practice shoot against a piece of scrap to confirm uniform catalyst distribution and overall gel time. Use the minimum air pressure that will ensure complete atomization of the resin spray. Excess pressure will cause the material to bounce back off the mold surface, creating overspray (material splattering everywhere), and will tend to cause material already deposited onto the surface to be pushed around, making it more difficult to achieve a uniform thickness. If all is well, face the plug, take a deep breath... and pull the trigger.

Spray Technique—You should try to keep the spray pattern perpendicular to the surface; spraying at a large angle will make the material flow across the surface, which risks trapping air bubbles and makes it impossible to maintain uniform thickness. While the color contrast between white plug (with green PVA over it) and black gel coat will prove a boon in indicating the extent and uniformity of coverage, you must not count on eyeball judgment alone—you must measure the thickness of the applied film at various points on the surface from time to time. You are aiming for a rather thicker coat than you would apply for a part; 20-25 mils (.020-.025 inch) is about right. The gel coat should be sprayed on quite thickly (this is not paint), ideally in three or four passes with each successive coat at right angles to the previous, but again note the cautions in Chapter 5 about the matter of the shape of the spray patterns. Measure the thickness with a gel coat gauge after each pass, and try to correct variations in thickness on the next pass. Then check again.

PARTING AGENTS
How to Avoid Getting Stuck

Although wax and PVA, alone or in combination, are by far the most common mold releases or parting agents, there are some others that should be noted. First are some synthetic polymers that are used in the same way as waxes but which are claimed to offer superior performance. These are especially useful for ETC curing systems, where the heat might cause ordinary carnauba wax to melt, destroying the protective film. They are also claimed to offer superior releases with room temperature cures.

Then there are internal mold releases—they are mixed right into the resin. The companies that market this stuff are not resin brewers or formulators, and there is some debate between these groups about the potential effects the release agent—probably a metallic soap of some kind—might have on the cure. The resin manufacturers say they can't guarantee their products if unknown substances are added to them; the internal release makers won't say just what it is. These formulations can be used for either molds or individual piece parts.

Some sheet materials make a suitable release film for certain special applications. Saran™ food wrap is completely impervious to polyester and vinylester, and is surprisingly tough and stretchy. I once had considerable success using Saran wrap on a small run of male-molded equipment enclosures that, in truth, had insufficient draft, and the first few had caused grief on de-molding when wax and PVA were used. The fix was to stretch the Saran over the mold and tape it into place using "invisible" mending tape, which is also immune to styrene.

After the seemingly endless process of surface preparation, this part of the operation goes surprisingly quickly; but almost all of the quality of the job consists in those preparations, as professional auto body painters will fully appreciate. Once finished with the spraying, there is not much to do beyond cleaning up the equipment and yourself. The gel coat will not be ready to work on for at least a couple of hours, so it often proves handy to do all of the waxing and other prep work in the morning, let the PVA dry over lunch, set up and shoot gel coat in the afternoon, then let it sit overnight. Twelve hours is not too long to leave the gel coat exposed, provided you minimize the risk of contamination by dust. And don't forget to leave the heat on in the shop!

Laminating

The following day, the gel coat should still squeak when you drag a clean fingertip across it, though it may not leave a print. At this point you're ready to start laminating the structural part of the mold. The general procedures are as described in Chapter 7 for making a part, with the exception that the first layer of material contacting the gel coat should always be mat; you do not want any kind of fabric texture printing through to the working face of the mold. As well, you will want to fill the sharp inside corner that occurs where the flanges meet the main part of the mold. There are two ways to tackle this. First is just to mix up a batch of polyester-based auto body filler and carefully trowel it into this sharp right angle bend with the rounded end of a tongue depressor or coffee stick. Alternatively, some folks lay a bundle of roving, saturated in catalyzed resin, into the corner. The object is to avoid having to force the reinforcement that follows into too sharp a radius, thereby running the risk of having it bridge over the corner, leaving unsupported gel coat.

By all means try to time the laying up of the mold to avoid both an excessive thickness of laminate curing at one time, which will cause excessive exothermic heat, and the need to leave the job incomplete for an extended period (such as over a weekend), which will impair the adhesion of subsequent layers.

The mold needs to be built heftier than the

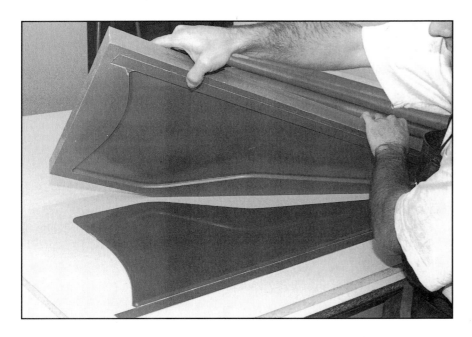

It is customary to provide wide margins at the edges of molds for stiffening and, as here, to provide a mounting flange for a vacuum bag. Photo by Jack Gladback.

Shaping of wax or modeling clay fillets is eased with a shaped wooden spatula as used by sculptors. These are available from art supply shops in a variety of styles. Photo by Jack Gladback.

stiffening sections and/or ribs can be added. Once the basic shell of the mold has been built up to, say, six ounces of reinforcement per square foot, almost any material—cardboard channels, lengths of rope, plastic hose split lengthwise—can be laid on the surface in the form of a rough grid, and further lamination applied over the top. The extra depth provided by these inclusions will add hugely to stiffness without a corresponding increase in weight, cost, and labor.

Stiffeners

If a plug has been made according to the methods described in Chapter 12, it is particularly economical, convenient and elegant to make the stiffeners or reinforcements from the scrap left over from making the plug station templates; these remaining bits will have been pre-cut to something very close to the required shape.

It is very important to allow the basic shell to thoroughly cure and harden on the plug before these stiffeners are added, otherwise the shrinkage of the resin used to stick them to the outside of the mold will cause distortion (sometimes severe) of the mold surface in the vicinity of the attachment. In Chapter 7, I cautioned against applying fresh laminate over the top of a fully cured surface, because of the doubtful security of this secondary bond; this is one place, though, where following that counsel will get you into trouble.

Solution—There are two techniques that help in dealing with this damned-if-you-do, damned-if-you-don't situation. One is to use several small scraps of reinforcement to just tack the stiffeners in place, using a very slow cure rate resin (reduce the catalyst ratio), to minimize shrinkage. Although these little "spot welds" are quite weak, what we're after is not strength but stiffness, and in this respect they work well. Better, perhaps, is to use epoxy to attach the stiffeners; if a slow curing combination of epoxy and curing agent is used, it shrinks less than polyester,

parts it produces, though many people overdo this. Certainly it needs to be thick enough that it doesn't distort or "oil-can" while you're rolling out the laminate which, for small (air scoop sized) molds, means a bare minimum of six ounces of reinforcement per square foot. Greater overall stiffness than this would provide is usually needed, especially for a large mold (say the size of a hood), but this requirement is better met by selective stiffening than by building up to enormous thickness.

Local stiffening of the edges is provided inherently by the edge flanges; elsewhere,

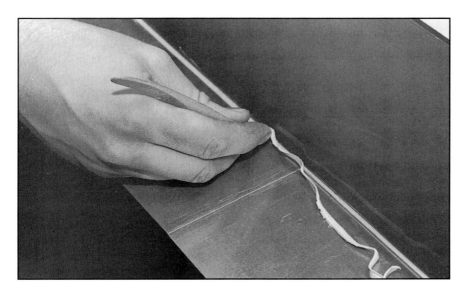

and will permit the use of a continuous stripe of reinforcement to form the joint. Epoxy is also a better adhesive than polyester and so will bond better to the cured polyester laminate beneath. In either case, if the basic shell has thoroughly cured, grind all the shine off it in the area of the attachments, vacuum off the dust, and give it a quick scrub with acetone before attempting to stick anything to it. Be careful with the grinding, though—excessive vibration may cause premature separation of the mold surface from the plug in places.

The above really only applies if the stiffeners themselves are plywood, or something similar. If the material is foam, cardboard, etc., then once in place, the stiffening ribs will have to be covered with a couple of extra layers of reinforcement, overlapping at least a couple of inches onto the semi-finished shell. Of course, if these ribs are made from styrene foam, then epoxy *must* be used. (Actually, even if they are some other kind of foam that is unaffected by polyester, like urethane, use epoxy anyway; those wide bands of reinforcement will likely cause trouble with the print-through distortion we've been talking about if polyester is used.)

Sandwich Construction

An alternative to local stiffeners is to use sandwich construction, as described in Chapter 15. This will eliminate any risk of telegraphing the pattern of stiffeners onto the working surface of the mold. An inch or two of plaster added to the back of an FRP mold can also be used to add stiffness and heft, though this technique is now regarded as rather old-fashioned. This plaster-on-plastic construction was used for the first set of production molds for the 1954 Corvette.

When fitting stiffening ribs to the mold shell, another thing to think about is how well they will support the mold when it is inverted, as it will have to be when making parts. Depending on the size and shape of

the mold, it may be convenient to arrange for the mold to sit stably in three attitudes—flat on its back and on either side. That will permit working in it later without constantly having to jury-rig some way to hold it where you want it.

Trimming

Apart from trimming the edges, you're done. And unlike trimming parts, which is often most conveniently done while the resin is at the gelled stage, the trimming of the mold should probably be left until it is fully hard, to avoid any risk of distortion. Indeed, if what you have just produced is just one part of a multi-piece mold, it is likely best to leave this first section in place on the plug, and to leave the edges only roughly trimmed, for a couple of reasons. First, any damage which might occur to the plug while removing this first section may make it difficult or impossible to replace it in the correct position later, when the time comes to make the next section. And you do want the first piece in place when making the second, to ensure correct registration of the two mold sections and their mating flanges. Leaving the edges of the first piece—the flanges—wider than their finished size permits tidying up minor damage that might occur where the lamination of the flanges of the second piece overlap and adhere.

Removal

There is an almost irresistible temptation to rush the removal of the mold from the plug, to relieve the anxiety about the state of the gel coat and to enjoy the satisfaction of just quietly sitting and admiring a well done piece of work. Resist it, though, even if there are to be no additional sections and the mold is now complete. The mold should be left on the plug for as long as practical, but certainly a couple of days at least. This is called resting the mold; what you're really waiting for is for the cure to progress further down the line toward full hardness before subject-

Gelcoat after sanding; magnified 1,000 times

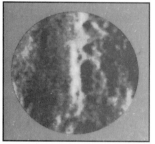

Gelcoat after compounding; magnified 10,000 times

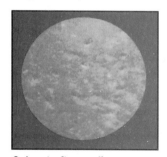

Gelcoat after sealing; magnified 1,000 times

Gelcoat after waxing; magnified 10,000 times

"Smoothness" depends on how closely you look. These microphotographs show a mold surface in various stages of preparation. Photo courtesy TR Industries.

> *"Depending on size and shape, it may be necessary to somehow lash the two together temporarily (rope? tape?) before calling in several strong helpers to wrestle the whole business onto its head."*

All molds require more stiffening than their thickness alone provides; flat molds like this one for the IMSA WSC car undertray made by Aerodine Composites needs extra help. Note egg-crate stiffeners, and diagonal struts to prevent racking. Photo by Jack Gladback.

ing it to the sometimes considerable stresses it will endure in getting it off the plug.

If additional mold sections are to be made, sections of the flange models need to be removed before proceeding, so that the flanges on the first piece can serve as the molding surface for the flanges of the next. Depending on just where the part lines are, this may require inverting the whole assembly of plug and partial mold. This is where Murphy's Law can step in with a vengeance: it is a curious thing, but it seems that a mold will release from the plug much more easily when you want it to stay stuck than when you're aiming to get it off! Depending on size and shape, it may be necessary to somehow lash the two together temporarily (rope? tape?) before calling in several strong helpers to wrestle the whole business onto its head. Judicious arrangement of the shape of the stiffeners can sometimes permit gently rolling the assembly over, but in any case beware of the protruding flanges—it is all too easy to apply forces that pry them outward, breaking the contact of the first mold section with the plug.

However you have gained access to the flange patterns, they should now be removed, again taking pains to avoid prying the mold section away from the plug, and for the first time you will get a view of the working side of the gel coat on the now visible faces of the flanges. Damage to the remaining exposed surface of the plug, whether from rough handling during the overturning or from spots where it was necessary to tack support brackets for the first set of flange patterns, can now be repaired. Once that is done, you're ready to repeat all of the above operations to make the next section of the mold. Fun, eh? ∎

12

PLGS

To make molded parts, you need a mold. That leaves the issue of how the mold is formed in the first place. Again, there are various alternatives, but usually an FRP mold is made in much the same way as an FRP part, using a master shape or pattern as the "mold-for-the-mold." That master pattern—called a *plug* or *buck*—could be an original part that is to be reproduced. But for an original design, the plug has to be built from scratch by hand. Since the mold will exactly duplicate the shape and surface texture of the plug, and since the parts will likewise precisely copy the contours and surface features of the mold, any flaws or inaccuracies in the plug will be reflected in every finished part. Except in cases where only one part will

ever be made (and often even then), it will prove easier to make sure the plug is perfect than to re-work either the mold or every one of the finished products.

STATION TEMPLATES

For such objects as pleasure boats, automobile bodywork and light aircraft parts, the traditional method of plug construction is to cut a number of *station templates*, typically out of plywood, each of which represents the cross section of the finished product at a particular point. These templates—corresponding to top, side, and end views of the object—are then located correctly in space and secured to an *armature* or *base plate*, also usually of wood, forming an "egg-

An example of a traditional egg-crate armature, with station templates. The gaps must be filled in to complete the plug.

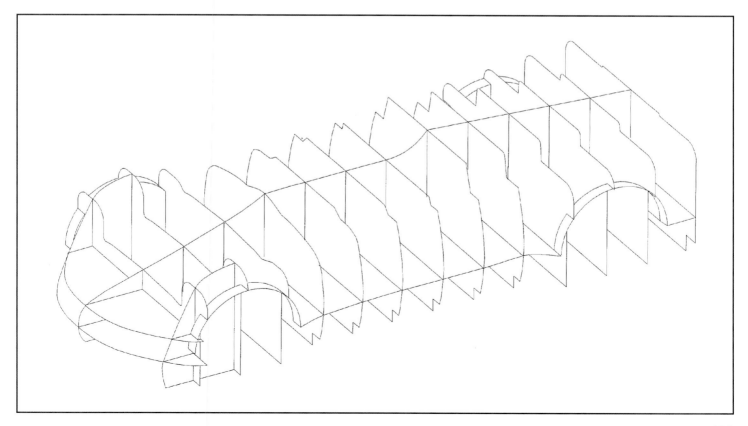

crate" pattern. For something like an automobile body part or a boat—which may be anywhere from 5 to 50 feet long, this method may require anywhere from a handful to several dozen such templates. The spaces between these templates then need to be filled in.

PLASTER PLUGS

The classical (i.e. old-fashioned) way is to staple chicken wire across the gaps, somewhat below the eventual surface, then to weave strips of plaster-soaked burlap through the chicken wire. Next, more plaster is mixed up and trowelled into place and roughly graded to contour with a long flexible spline (an aluminum yardstick, for example), using the station templates as a guide. The problem of producing a decent surface remains.

Surface Finishing

There is one classic publication on the subject of mold making which glibly passes off the entire operation of surfacing a traditional plaster plug by advising the craftsman to "finish in the usual way." This must have been meant as a joke, as the surfacing of a plaster plug is an absolute swine of an operation, which takes far longer than the building of the armature, the template cutting, and the rough plastering and splining operations all put together. Compared with the flawless surfaces we are accustomed to in modern products, Michaelangelo himself could not produce a plaster surface which would pass muster.

Common Problems

One of the basic problems with plaster seems to be variations in the hardness and texture of the surface, made worse by any attempt to improve the surface in localized areas with extra applications of fresh plaster. To get truly smooth surfaces, free of waves and ripples, all of the surface must be of

equal hardness. Ultimately, this uniform surface can be achieved with lots and lots of black paint. In the meantime, getting from an obviously rough and inadequate plaster surface to one that seems to be worth a first coat of paint (gloss black, so you can see the surface irregularities from reflections) will drive you to tears.

All in all, you may wonder why anyone would even bother with plaster. Actually, it has considerable utility for specific applications. If the end product does not demand a first-rate surface, and especially if it is very large, the low cost of plaster and the *relatively* little work it takes to get a *mediocre* surface may justify the use of plaster. It is also very well suited to transfer molding— see Chapter 10. On the whole, though, it is a pain.

Body Filler

To provide a more manageable surface to work with, the plaster may be made deliberately undersize, and then a decent slathering of body filler troweled all over the surface. The polyester-based filler is much more pleasant stuff to work with: it shreds cleanly and quickly with a cheese-grater when it reaches a *green cure*, and can be further worked with a body file before it's fully hard; it sands more quickly, more uniformly and with much less dust than plaster; and local patches and improvements can be mixed up, applied and cured in minutes, versus hours or days for plaster. But if we're making the surface out of polyester filler, why bother with plaster at all?

STYROFOAM™

Nearly everyone is familiar with Styrofoam™—the rigid polystyrene foam used as insulation in house-building. It comes in the form of boards from one half to four inches thick, and its low cost and light weight, plus the ease with which it can be shaped, make it a natural replacement for the older methods. In fact, it allows us to re-think the entire section-template/armature business.

Some years ago, it was my ambition to build a limited production sports car using stressed skin construction in FRP. Though the project eventually sank out of sight in a sea of red ink, it progressed as far as the construction of various plugs and molds. The greatest challenge was producing a plug for the outer surface of the car.

Having previously produced a number of plugs for paying customers using the old-fashioned, chicken-wire-and-plaster system, I was certain there had to be a better way. The procedures described below are the ones we actually used (they can be applied to objects of any size, from plant pots to sailing yachts), while the accompanying photos show the progress of work on that doomed sports car project.

The technique involves tracing cross-section drawings onto the surface of a sheet of Styrofoam, cutting around the outline, and then stacking these section templates together to form an approximation of the desired shape—in effect using the foam as both templates and gap fillers at the same time. The cutting can be done by hand with a keyhole saw, jigsaw, or even a bread knife, or with a powerband saw or sabre saw. All of these methods produce a highly irregular edge and an amazing quantity of foam crumbs which are fairly harmless (except as a minor fire hazard), but maddeningly difficult to clean up. An alternative is a hot-wire cutter, which melts its way through the foam, producing a very clean and precise edge, but also some acrid smoke, which must be guarded against. Adequate ventilation and a reactive cartridge mask must be used. Hot-wire cutters can be purchased, but most are home-made. Details about a variety of types are found in Chapter 5.

Smoothing—After the foam slabs are assembled, the steps between sections are then rasped down to provide a smooth tran-

Modern materials ease plug construction. Styrofoam blanks hot wired to profile are assembled to form a close approximation to the finished shape. Steps between foam slabs, visible at left, are hand rasped with a cheese grater to form a smooth contour, as on the right.

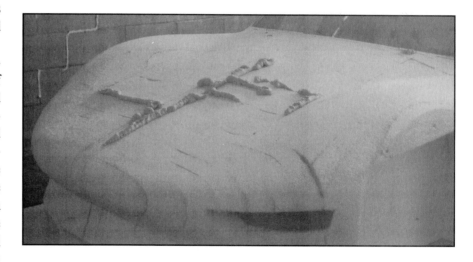

Gaps that appear can be filled with insulating spray foam (above) then rasped smooth again (left).

Once all foam is smoothed, there remains the problem of forming a hard surface.

To protect the foam from attack by the polyester resin in body filler, it is sprayed with exterior latex house paint. The surface can now have body filler applied.

> *"You can just slather it on and hope for the best, but there are a couple of tricks which help keep the application evenly thick."*

sition from one section to the next. The best tool for this part of the job is an item known to body shop workers as a *cheese-grater* and is sold by the Stanley Tool Co. under the trade name "Surform." Using the cheaper, lighter white foam, there's not much that can be done to improve the surface beyond this cheese-grater step; with high-density (blue) Styrofoam a surprising improvement can be accomplished with an ordinary mill file. Nevertheless, the problem of achieving a really first-class, hard surface finish remains.

Using Filler w/Foam

Ordinary automotive body filler cannot be used directly over styrene foam—the styrene content in the polyester-based filler attacks the foam, which promptly turns into a sticky, spongy mess. What is needed is either a surfacing material which does not attack the foam, or else a barrier of some kind between the foam and the polyester filler. Epoxy fills the bill on both counts, although it is expensive, and controlling costs by applying a thin shell over the soft foam blank is not a good idea, as the shell may very well crack and break up under handling. But a thick epoxy shell is even

more expensive. Also, although special epoxy mold making materials are available, they generally do not work as easily as ordinary automotive type polyester filler.

House Paint—So, that leaves the idea of a barrier between the foam and a surface of polyester filler. Somewhat surprisingly, there is a material which is cheap, generally available, and effective for this purpose. The secret is ordinary exterior latex house paint! It must say "alkyd" somewhere on the label—interior latex paint is unsuitable. And the paint must be sprayed—brushing leaves a glossy surface which interferes with adhesion of the body filler. Since most alkyd latex paint is intended for brushing, it is a bit thick for spraying, so thinning with a little water may be necessary. While it may be possible to get away with fewer coats, three sprayed coats of alkyd latex, with ample drying time between coats, will ensure an adequate barrier. Once the last coat is fully dry, polyester-based filler can be safely applied right onto the painted foam surface.

After stripes of filler of controlled thickness are applied, the spaces in between can then be filled.

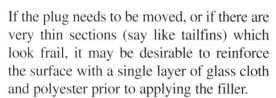

A drywall knife works well for this operation.

If the plug needs to be moved, or if there are very thin sections (say like tailfins) which look frail, it may be desirable to reinforce the surface with a single layer of glass cloth and polyester prior to applying the filler.

Applying Filler—The object is to get a uniformly thick layer of filler applied. You can just slather it on and hope for the best, but there are a couple of tricks which help keep the application evenly thick. One is to apply a first batch of filler with a notched trowel, thereby leaving a series of raised ridges of fairly uniform height all over. The second application of filler is intended to be thick enough to mostly cover these ridges. Subsequent rasping with a cheese-grater while this second application of polyester is partly but not fully cured (somewhere between five minutes and an hour, depending on shop temperature, amount of catalyst, thickness of coat, etc.), until the ridges, contrasting by their hardness, just barely appear all over. (A little pigment of a contrasting color can be mixed into the second batch of filler, to further aid in establishing just where the ridges are). It obviously helps if the tracer ridges have been applied in a regular crisscross pattern.

The variation on this trick is to cut one long notch out of the middle of a scraper, leaving little feet sticking down at each end, so that as you draw the scraper across the surface the feet contact the surface under-

neath, leaving a wide stripe of soft filler. Keep these stripes fairly close together and roughly parallel and a little later, after the stripes are hard enough, you can go back and fill in the trenches in between them, using a normal straight scraper (a drywall knife works well) and a new batch of filler. Local blurts and bumbles can be quickly carved down with a cheese-grater, provided you don't let the plastic harden up too much, and then the grater marks flattened out with a conventional body file. Don't worry about digging an edge of the body file into the surface—it's bound to happen and you just regard it as another local defect to be later filled and rasped and filed.

The body filler is then sanded until it seems approximately smooth.

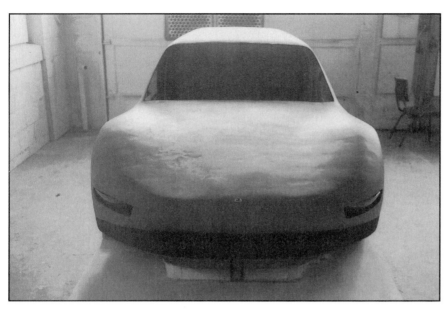

A coat of glossy paint reveals just how much work remains to be done!

Repeated sanding and painting is needed, as well as countless local repairs with spot putty. This work can prove gruelling.

heart-breaking round of sanding and painting and sanding and painting and on and on until either you've got the most perfect surface the world has ever seen, or you can't stand it any more and call it quits somewhere short of perfect. Cheer up, it could be worse: you could be starting the same job with plaster!

O.K., mask on? Fan running flat out? Sandpaper tight on the sander? So, get to it. Don't try to erase local humps by growling away continuously at one spot—you will overheat the filler, causing it to soften and gum up the paper; use long, sweeping strokes. At first you will only be able to level out the most obvious unevenness; you just can't judge the surface by eye, as it is too matte and dull for vision to be of much help. You can feel a surface like this more easily than you can see it—just lightly draw your palms and fingertips across the surface, and a whole new world of dips and bumps and wobbles becomes known to you through your sense of touch. After hours of sanding and feeling and sanding and feeling, you will get to the point where it doesn't seem to be getting any better. Stop. Now paint the thing black.

Plug Painting

To be more exact, first sweep the floor, then vacuum everything in sight. Using a small amount of acetone and a paint brush, lightly scrub the surface with acetone. Don't allow the acetone to pool or even sit on the surface too long—mop off any residue at once with paper towel. Now, set up to paint (air-lines drained of water? lacquer-based primer thinned according to supplier's instructions? paint thoroughly strained?) and lay on several coats of primer. The first couple of coats will soak right into the filler surface. After you get this stage over, apply at least two more full coats. Once the primer is dry, take an ordinary brown paper bag, crumple it up, and scrub over the whole surface. This is a quick and effective alternative

Final Finishing

However you arrive at it, you should now have a fairly uniformly thick layer of polyester body filler over the painted foam. Now all you have to do is turn all of that "fairly uniform" stuff into absolute perfection ("Finish-in-the-usual-way," indeed!) You are going to need a lot of #120 grit sandpaper, a power sander, a fresh set of dust filters for your mask, a huge shop vacuum, and a fridge full of cold drinks—to cut the dust, you know. You are about to start on a dismal, to wet sanding. Wipe the surface with a tack cloth, then lay on two or three coats of ordinary black lacquer, leaving the last coat quite wet (use the maximum recommended proportion of thinners, select a slow drying thinner, and apply the coat as thick as you dare without risking bad runs and sags), so as to give a decently glossy finish. Now, wash up, go outside, have a breather, and brace yourself for the next step.

Sanding—That glossy paint will reveal that we have a lot more work to do! At this stage you should be working with wet-or-dry sandpaper of about #240 grit, keeping the surface wetted with a sponge. Be sure to use a sander with an orbital action, take long sweeping strokes, keep at it for a while, and eventually you will have a "dappled" finish—low areas still glossy black and blotchy high areas where you went right back to the filler. Depending on how low the low spots are, you may want to fill them in by troweling on spot putty (really just very thick lacquer paint). Certainly you will want to apply spot putty to the surprising number of medium sized nicks and pits and gouges you will discover, but don't expect spot putty any thicker than about 1/8 inch to dry in less than a day. Sand some more to flatten out the spot filling, then vacuum again and thoroughly wipe over the whole surface with a tack cloth. And paint it black all over again.

This process will need to be repeated several times, achieving several things at once. The glossiness of the black surface permits a visual check on subtle waves; the even slickness of the paint aids in judging other kinds of flaws by the "Braille" method; the dapple effect dramatically indicates high and low spots by obvious color contrast; and each successive paint job itself adds two or three mils all over, which can then be sanded off the "hills," leaving the "valleys" alone. Eventually you will achieve a surface which is as good as a lacquer paint job can be when applied over a surface worked with #240 paper. So then you go to a finer grade of

With sufficient work, something close to perfection emerges. With windows simulated with black paint and some details in place, for review purposes, we may now permit a brief period of rejoicing!

paper.

Be sure to allow at least overnight for drying/hardening time on this last coat of lacquer and, if you're absolutely satisfied with the way things look, wet sand all over with #400 grit wet-and-dry sandpaper by hand, until all the gloss is gone. You don't need to raise any kind of gloss on the by-now flatted lacquer surface, because you're going to paint it again. White, this time, (to provide a color-contrast to the PVA—polyvinyl alcohol—which will follow) and just four or five coats. After at least a weekend break, wet sand again with #400 paper until the surface is again completely flatted, then go over the whole thing with #600 paper, still wet-sanding, until you feel a characteristic change in the drag of the paper across the surface, which tells you that the #600 has erased all the micro-scratches the #400 left.

Now get some rubbing compound and about an acre of cheese-cloth and start rubbing. If you didn't get impatient, and you got everything right and didn't leave some problems in the vague hope that they would go away, you should now have a super white lacquer paint job. There! You're finished! ■

> "*This process will need to be repeated several times, achieving several things at once.*"

13

MATERIALS & STRUCTURES

MATERIAL STRENGTH

Everything will break if you pull on it hard enough. If you make a part bigger, you will have to pull proportionally harder to break it, so the strength of the part has increased, but when we talk about the strength of the material the part is made from, rather than the part itself, we have to take account of the fact that there is more material in the larger part. That's why the strength of materials is expressed in pounds per square inch—the number of pounds tells us how much force we are applying, the number of square inches tells us how much stuff we are applying the force to. To permit comparisons between one material and another, it is customary to talk about the force it takes to break one square inch of the material.

The high strength-to-weight ratio of FRP materials make them especially suitable for race cars. Without them, many drivers would most likely not walk away so easily as they often do today. Here, Jimmy Vasser's 1993 Indycar is placed "on the hook" after bouncing off a concrete barrier. It only received minor damage. Photo by Michael Lutfy.

Tensile Strength

Take, for example, a slat-shaped piece of material, say one-half inch thick and two inches wide—like a fence picket. If we pull lengthwise on this, the force will be passing through one square inch of material (one half inch times two inches), all the way from one end to the other. If it takes a force of 10,000 pounds to break the slat by pulling on it in this way, then it is said to have a *tensile strength* (strength measured when in tension) of 10,000 pounds per square inch—10,000 psi. (One thousand psi is often abbreviated ksi, so our fence board material would have a tensile strength of 10 ksi.)

Note that this is a property of the material, not the fence board. If we cut another board twice as thick, the same 10,000 pound force would be acting on twice as much material, so the material would only be working half as hard; it would take twice as much force—

20,000 pounds—to break the board. But since that force would be acting on two square inches, rather than one, the figure for the tensile strength of the material would remain unchanged; 20,000 pounds divided by two square inches is exactly the same as 10,000 pounds divided by one square inch—10,000 psi, or 10 ksi.

Tensile Stress

If we apply a smaller force to the board, say half the amount needed to break it, the material will still be "working," but only half as hard—the force acting on each square inch will be reduced by half, to 5 ksi. This relationship between the force applied and the area it is acting on is called *stress*; we would say that the tensile stress on the material was 5 ksi. Note that stress and strength use the same units; the tensile strength is simply a statement of the tensile stress it takes to break the stuff.

Compressive Strength

So far, so good. But if we push on the board, rather than pull on it, something awkward happens—it buckles sideways, so we're no longer able to push on it straight lengthwise. Depending on how long the board is and what kind of material it is made from, we might be able to spring it into a "C" shape by pushing on the end; we might even be able to force the "C" to close to form an "O," and we still might not break the board.

We'll return to this important issue of buckling later, but for now let's suppose we cut a short piece off the board and try the same imaginary tests again. When we pull on it, we get the same result as before—it takes a stress level of 10 ksi to break it. When we push on it, though, it is less prone to buckle because it is shorter, so we can imagine that if the piece we cut off is short enough, we could push on it until it actually breaks. This push is called a *compression load*, and we would express the stress in the material the same way as for tension—the

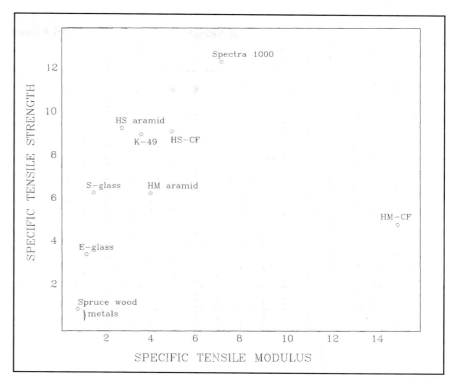

size of the push, in pounds, divided by the area the push is acting on, in square inches. The compressive strength—the stress needed to break the material in compression—may be similar to the tensile strength, or it may not, depending on the material. For most metals and composite materials, the tensile and compressive strengths are similar. Some materials, though, show much better results when loaded one way compared to the other. Cast iron and concrete, for example, are much stronger in compression than in tension; wood, magnesium, and aramid laminates have the opposite characteristic.

Ductility vs. Brittleness

When we crush our short piece of board by exceeding its compressive strength, we would expect it to splinter and break, and so it would if it were made of wood. Concrete, glass fiber and carbon fiber laminates, cast iron, and many other brittle materials would do the same. If the material were a Kevlar or Spectra fiber laminate, however, or mild steel or aluminum, and if the test piece were

The tensile strength-to-weight ratio and strength-to-stiffness ratio of various fibers are compared here, together with spruce wood and metals. The further to the right a material appears, the stiffer it is in relation to its weight; the higher up the chart it appears, the stronger it is in relation to its weight. Note that all structural metals occupy the small triangular area at bottom left.

"This phenomenon, called yielding, is what makes it possible to bend and contort metals into shapes like coat hangers and lamp shades, and why a dented fender stays dented."

short enough in relation to its thickness that it didn't buckle, it would likely squash like putty, rather than shatter. Materials that flow under load like this are said to be *ductile.*

And if we were to repeat the tension test with chunks of the same variety of materials, we would discover that the cast iron and concrete pieces, and all the strong fiber laminates, would resist the stress right up to the bitter end, and then let go with a bang. With the mild steel, aluminum and magnesium samples, though, something very curious would happen as the stress started to approach the ultimate tensile strength. To explain it, we have to step back for a moment.

Strain

For all the materials, we would discover that when we try to stretch it, we succeed—the test piece grows longer in proportion to how hard we pull. If we relax the force, the piece springs back to its original length. Now, the amount of stretch we're talking about here is so small that, with most solid materials, it is imperceptible. Still, the effect is real, and becomes visible in the case of materials like rubber. This change of length in response to an applied stress is called *strain*; the way most engineers would put it is that all materials respond to stress by straining. For the kind of strong materials that we make structures out of, this strain never exceeds one or two percent of the original length (and usually much less), before the tensile strength is exceeded and the piece breaks. For many materials, the strain is completely reversible up to that point—if we remove the load, the part returns to its original length, so the extension in response to the load is called elastic strain... which brings us back to the strange thing that happens when we pull on a structural metal.

Yielding

In the case of steel or aluminum, and most

other strong metals, the strain is perfectly elastic—the extension is proportional to the stress... up to a point. But once the stress level exceeds some substantial fraction of the ultimate tensile strength (say two thirds), some of the stretch becomes permanent—the test part will spring back, but not all the way. In other words, at some critical stress level the material changes from an elastic solid to something that flows like a thick fluid. This phenomenon, called *yielding*, is what makes it possible to bend and contort metals into shapes like coat hangers and lamp shades, and why a dented fender stays dented.

Yield Strength—This ability to yield is one of the basic distinctions between metals and composites, and is seen as a valuable safety feature, favoring metals. For example, if an aircraft suffers a severe overload in flight, say from a violent updraft of air, its wing spar might be loaded so heavily that the stress exceeds the *yield strength*—the stress level at which it begins to yield, but not the ultimate strength. At that point, the wings would bend upward somewhat, and stay bent. While this is not a great thing to have happen, it is still preferable to having the wings snap off. Likewise, a steel tube front wishbone on a race car may crumple in a wheel-banging duel on the track, leaving a crippled car to limp around to the pits. A carbon fiber suspension arm, though, would snap off, maybe leaving the driver with tire marks on his helmet...and we pray nothing worse. This is one reason why designers worry a lot about applying composites to critical structural parts—there's no question they are strong enough, but look what happens when you overload them. We talk more about this in the next chapter. For now, though, note that the tensile yield strength of a composite is indistinguishable from its ultimate tensile strength—the load from which it cannot recover to its original length is the same as the load required to break it.

Shear

When we pull lengthwise on a piece of material, we are applying a tensile stress to the molecular bonds that hold the material together—we're trying to tear them apart. When we stress the same part in compression by pushing on it, we are trying to squash the molecules closer together. About the only other thing we can do to stress these bonds is to try to slide the molecules apart, sideways. This is called a shear force; it is the kind of load that tries to rip the ball off a trailer hitch. Another way to express the same thing is to visualize the direction the force acts, in relation to the long axis of the test piece. Tension and compression loads act along that line, though in opposite directions; shear loads act at right angles.

Shear forces also arise when you attempt to skew a rectangular plate into a diamond shape by grabbing two opposite edges and shoving them in opposite directions. The same thing is going on in a thin panel in an aircraft or race car chassis under load—in stressed skin construction, the largest stresses are in shear. Shearing forces also crop up in beams; even though people talk mostly about the bending or flexural stresses in a beam, there are significant shear stresses, too, and these become a major consideration in composite structures, as discussed later and in Chapter 14.

Fatigue

The strength figures for various materials quoted in engineering handbooks and supplier's brochures refer to the stress levels a new sample of material will tolerate in one test. If we were to repeatedly subject the material to that same level of stress, it would soon fail. This loss in strength with repetitive loading is called *fatigue*, and the severity of the effect depends on the material itself, on how large the cyclic load is, and how frequently it is applied. It also depends on whether the load is removed completely part of the time, or cycles between a *major*

and a *minor* stress. Paradoxically, all materials fatigue less if they are prevented from relaxing completely between applications of the peak, major load; likewise, all materials suffer worse when the cyclic load fully reverses—that is, if it varies from tension to compression and back.

Fatigue Resistance

While all materials fatigue, some resist it much better than others. And there are differences between materials in the way strength diminishes under *fatigue loading*—some lose strength fairly rapidly at first, then the effect tends to level out. In the case of steel, for example, there is an *endurance limit*—a stress corresponding to about half the static strength can be repeated virtually forever without failure. This characteristic is comparatively unusual, however, so to ensure a useful life for a structural part, it needs to be sized based on the strength remaining after whatever pattern and frequency of loading it is expected to experience in use. When only a single figure is specified for the strength remaining after fatigue loading, rather than a chart or table showing the pattern of fatigue, 10,000,000 stress cycles is generally used as a benchmark figure.

An advantage of composite materials sometimes touted in print is that they do not fatigue. This is simply not so, though it is true to say that the fatigue resistance of composites is generally superior to that of metals. Unidirectional laminates using Kevlar retain about three quarters of their static strength after ten million cycles of loading in tension (though they do less well when the loading reverses between compression and tension); similar carbon fiber laminates keep perhaps two thirds of their original strength; glass fiber composites are down to about half by that point.

Stiffness

We said above that materials respond to

> *"An advantage of composite materials sometimes touted in print is that they do not fatigue. This is simply not so, though it is true to say that the fatigue resistance of composites is generally superior to that of metals."*

> *"When you make something out of FRP you are not just making a part, you are also making the material it is fabricated from."*

stress by straining—they "spring" very slightly in the direction of the load, and if that load lies within their normal working range, they will spring back. This relationship between stress and strain determines the stiffness of a material. A stiffer material deflects less under a given load than one less stiff. Note that stiffness has nothing directly to do with strength. Nylon rope, for example, is strong, but lacks stiffness—it extends conspicuously under load; a ceramic bathroom tile, on the other hand, is stiff, but weak. The number that expresses the stiffness of a material is its *modulus of elasticity*, often shortened to just "modulus" (it is often signified by the capital letter "E" in tables.)

It is quite common for a part to be *stiffness critical*—if made from enough of any common structural material to have adequate strength, it may nevertheless deflect too far to be useful. This is usually the factor that governs the design of aircraft control surfaces and race car monocoque chassis. In other structures, considerable deflections can be tolerated, but ultimate strength is paramount. This is the case with many aircraft primary structures—the parts that hold the wings on, but is seldom an issue in race cars, except around localized areas where loads are very tightly focused—at bolted connections, for instance.

Specific Strength

We have already remarked on the obvious—a part can be made stronger by making it bigger. The problem with this is that a larger part is also heavier. In situations where weight is important (and there are few places in race cars and aircraft where it is not), then what we are concerned about is the *strength-to-weight* ratio or specific strength of a candidate material.

The quest for materials with a high specific strength accounts for a large part of the composites revolution. Even the humblest structural laminate—woven E-glass fabric

in a matrix of polyester resin, the sort of thing you could make in your backyard—matches all but the most exotic "high-tech" metals in specific strength, and comfortably beats any conventional metal that might be formed into a thin panel. A state-of-the-art composite—a unidirectional aramid/epoxy laminate, for instance—blows the doors off all metals in this respect.

Specific Stiffness

Bigger parts are not only stronger, they are also stiffer, simply because there's more stuff there to resist the load. Again, though, they are heavier, so what we're after are materials that are very stiff in relation to their weight. This relationship, *specific stiffness,* is an area where composites vary widely, straddling the properties of metals. Woven E-glass fiber in polyester falls far short of metals in this regard; unidirectional S-2 glass in epoxy approximately matches them; a unidirectional aramid/epoxy pre-preg offers roughly twice the specific stiffness of aluminum or steel; and a unidirectional high modulus CF/epoxy pre-preg is, incredibly, about nine times as stiff in relationship to its weight as any common metal!

Consistency of Material Properties

When you make something out of FRP you are not just making a part, you are also making the material it is fabricated from. Unlike working with metals, where you purchase a raw material whose strength and stiffness can be predicted with a high degree of accuracy, the mechanical properties of reinforced plastics depend on the basic properties of two raw materials—resin and reinforcement—but also on the kinds of processing methods used to work them into a finished product, and on the skill and care of the individuals doing that work. Comparatively small differences in, say, resin-to-reinforcement ratio or workshop temperature, can result in large variations in

PANELS OF EQUAL BENDING STIFFNESS

Relative Weight	Relative Thickness		
1.00	1.00		Steel
0.65	1.22		Titanium
0.55	2.29		E-glass/epoxy
0.48	1.44		Aluminum
0.36	1.66		Magnesium
0.31	1.88		Aramid/epoxy
0.21	2.97		5-ply Douglas fir
0.19	3.77		Aramid/foam sandwich

"Even with the best of intentions and technique, there will inevitably be a wider scatter of material characteristics from one composite part to the next, than with metals."

the strength of a laminate.

Even with the best of intentions and technique, there will inevitably be a wider scatter of material characteristics from one composite part to the next, than with metals. In the aerospace industry, exquisite pains are taken to minimize this variability in performance. When composites are used in structural applications by aviation manufacturers, they tend mostly to be in the form of pre-pregs, as described in Chapter 8, partly because pre-pregs can be stronger and stiffer than wet lay-up fabrications, but also because of the much more consistent results obtained. (To give some idea of the exertions dedicated to safety in the aviation industry, which depends on predictable material properties, the maker of the pre-pregs will have been required to perform confirming tests on all incoming resins by means of liquid chromatography, infrared spectroscopy, and other equally arcane and expensive procedures!)

STRUCTURES

The relative merits and drawbacks to using FRP as a structural material is covered in the next chapter. However, a brief overview is necessary here. A structure is a deliberate arrangement of material intended to resist external loads, so the response of a structure to loads depends partly on the material, and partly on how that material is disposed. An ideal structure is one that uses the least amount of material to do the job, so the structure will be as light as possible. For something like a rope, the strength and stiffness of the structure depends only on the material, but structural loads seldom line up with structural parts so that the material is stressed straight-on from end-to-end; most real world situations involve loads acting at right angles to the structure.

For instance, most FRP moldings are in the form of thin sheets or panels. These panels often form parts of a tube-shaped structure loaded in torsion—the loads try to twist the tube from end to end. This torsion in the tube as a whole takes the form of shear loads in the surface that makes up the tube—any small section of the tube wall is being stressed as if two opposite edges were being forced in opposite directions, so as to make it distort from a rectangle to a diamond shape. Sometimes, too, these thin panels are loaded sideways, such as by aerodynamic forces, or ordinary handling. Either way, a

"Nevertheless, engineering handbooks and materials textbooks give figures for the 'bending' strengths of materials (sometimes called flexural strengths), for good reasons."

thin panel loaded in this way will likely buckle long before the material is stressed to anywhere near its breaking point.

Bending

When you impose a load on a beam—say, by standing in the middle of a plank set across a pair of sawhorses—the beam (the plank) will bend. Even a very poor engineer could easily calculate the bending force and the bending stress in the plank, if you told him its length, width and thickness, and how much you weigh. Yet from the point of view of the material that the plank is made from, there is no such thing as a bending force; all it knows is tension, compression and shear.

Nevertheless, engineering handbooks and materials texts give figures for the "bending" strengths of materials (sometimes called *flexural strengths)*, for good reasons. As remarked earlier, while some materials have "symmetrical" characteristics—their behavior is the same in both tension and compression, others do not. In a symmetrical concrete beam, for example, we need never worry about the face that is in compression, it is the tension side that is going to fail first, so the "bending" strength of the beam is limited by its tensile strength. A wood beam, on the other hand, is limited by the comparatively low strength of the material on the compression side. So, to permit quick and easy calculation of the ability of a chunk of stuff to act as a beam, we invent the concept of a "bending stress."

The stress in the material of a beam varies through its depth, changing smoothly from a maximum in tension right at the surface of the tension face, through zero at the middle of the beam, to a maximum in compression at the opposite surface. The peak stress in the material occurs at the outside surfaces. Meanwhile, the material at the center is essentially unloaded—it is just along for the ride, which makes a simple rectangular beam extremely inefficient. A common solution is to concentrate most of the material at

the surfaces and remove as much of the rest as possible, as in an "I" beam, which consists of two thick flanges that carry most of the load, separated by a thin web that does little more than hold the flanges in place. A hollow rectangular tube, though less efficient than an "I" beam, is another approach to eliminating as much of the material from the center of the beam, while still leaving some material there to stabilize the compression face against local buckling.

Though FRP is not often used to make the webs and flanges of an "I" beam, it is common to form the material into hollow rectangular box sections which are loaded as beams. In that case, the face that is in compression when the beam is loaded will be just like any thin panel that is subject to bending forces—it will tend buckle, to "run away from the load." And we have already noted that shear forces, common in FRP structures, also cause thin panels to buckle long before the strength of the material becomes a consideration. In both cases, these buckling loads amount to forces acting across the thickness of the panel, in effect stressing it as a beam.

Now, the strength and stiffness of a beam depends on what it is made out of, but also on the depth of the beam. Greater depth not only spreads the load over more material, it also gives the beam more leverage to resist the bending. When a thin panel is forced to be a beam by forces acting at right angles to its faces, the depth of the beam is the thickness of the panel, and it can be shown that the resistance of the panel to buckling—whether from a compressive load applied to opposite edges or from a shear load—depends on the basic stiffness of the material and on the cube of the panel's thickness. A small increase in thickness therefore makes up for a sizable reduction in material stiffness. The low density of composites compared to metals puts them at an advantage here, a point we will return to in the next chapter. ∎

FRP AS STRUCTURAL MATERIAL

14

With a few exceptions, composite parts are not made as thick chunks; they are usually formed into panels that are very thin in relation to their area. Because the materials themselves are strong, such a plate or sheet will firmly resist being pulled on. If we push on it, though, it will buckle at a fraction of the load it would take to break it in tension. I mentioned in the previous chapter that the load it takes to buckle a thin plate being pushed on edgewise depends on the cube of the thickness of the plate. That means that if you have a choice between two materials that have the same strength and stiffness in proportion to their density but one is less dense than the other, then the same weight of material will produce a thicker part when the lighter material is used. Even though their tensile strength and stiffness will be identical, that extra thickness will greatly

increase the resistance to buckling of the piece made with the less dense material, compared with the other.

COMPARING FRP TO METAL

I also noted in the previous chapter that composites often have a specific stiffness (stiffness-to-weight ratio) that matches or exceeds that of metals. They are also generally less dense than metals—carbon- and glass-based laminates are about the same density as magnesium; Aramid and Spectra fiber laminates are even lighter. What that means is that a panel or plate made from such materials will be substantially thicker than a panel with the same area and weight made of, say, aluminum, and will gain in buckling resistance as a result. That is one reason why composites are so well suited for making weight-efficient thin shelled struc-

High performance cars require high performance materials. The series-dominating performance of this Toyota IMSA GTP car is as much due to its advanced composite construction as to the power of its engine, or the skill of its driver.

Strength and stiffness of a laminate produced using a "balanced" fabric are roughly equal measured along the warp and the fill, but note that both strength and stiffness are much lower when measured at 45 degrees.

"First, composites are not isotropic—unlike metals, they do not have the same strength and stiffness in all directions."

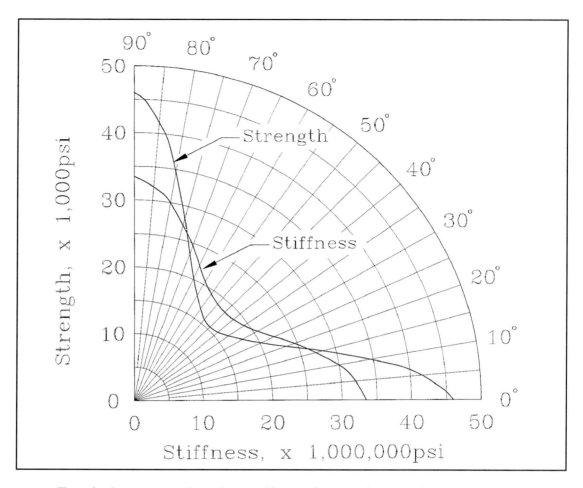

tures. (Even in those cases where the specific stiffness of the composite is inferior to metals—common E-glass laminates, for example—if the minimum weight of the part is set by buckling resistance, then the greater thickness of the FRP part usually goes some way to offsetting the deficiency in specific stiffness.)

Specific Strength & Stiffness

When we compare both the specific strength and the specific stiffness of composites with those of competitive metals, we find that the specific strengths of composites exceed those of metals to a greater extent than do their specific stiffnesses. It is fairly safe to say, then, that a properly made composite part, using any high performance reinforcement, that is as stiff as the metal part it replaces will have a formidable

advantage in strength. And we have suggested that in most automotive applications stiffness is more critical than strength—though not more important. That does not mean, however, that we can design a safe, lightweight part based purely on the published figure for the specific stiffness of a laminate similar to the one we intend to make, then setting the thickness based on the weight of a comparable metal part. This issue of the differences between metals and composites was touched on in the previous chapter, but there is more that needs to be said.

How They Differ—First, composites are not *isotropic*—unlike metals, they do not have the same strength and stiffness in all directions. Fabrics with a balanced weave—the same yarn count per inch in both warp and fill—will have equal strengths measured along the warp and along the fill, but they will be less strong when measured at 45

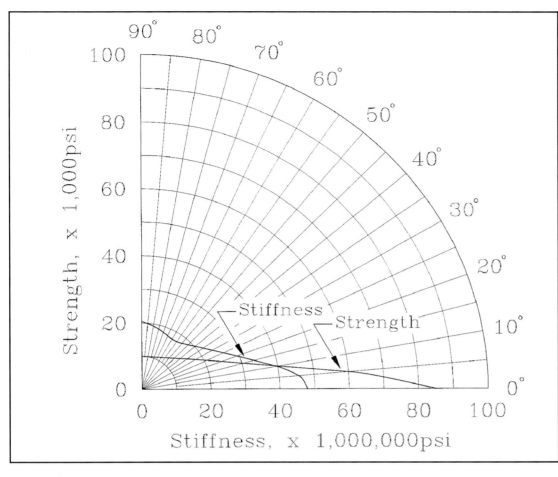

"Composites are also anisotropic (not isotropic) in another direction."

degrees. And unidirectional laminates, while enormously strong measured in the direction the fibers lie, have negligible strength "across the grain." In short, the mechanical properties of composites are directional.

Design Problems—This can pose some agonizing design problems. On the one hand, arranging the laminate so most of the fibers are aligned with the anticipated loads will lead to sensational performance; on the other hand, misjudging just where the loads are coming from will create a disaster. Yet hedging the bet by providing fibers running in multiple directions may unacceptably increase the weight of the structure. Likewise, when it is known that the loads will come from many directions, a weight penalty will have to be accepted. This is not the case with metals. In truth, if any of the advanced fibers are used, the performance is still likely to exceed a similar part made

from, say, aluminum. However, a laminate using woven glass as reinforcement—perhaps the most common kind—will almost certainly be heavier than its aluminum counterpart if the two are to have equal stiffness.

Shear

Composites are also anisotropic (not isotropic) in another direction. The shear strength and stiffness of composites varies hugely, not just between one kind of reinforcement and another, but also depending on whether the forces act across the fibers, or try to separate them from each other. Then there is *inter-laminar shear*—forces that act to slide the layers of a laminate over each other. These forces arise in any multi-layered laminate that is being bent, in the same way that the pages in this book slide past each other when you bend the book as a whole. Because there is usually little or no

*"The maxi-
mum load
the entire
joint can
carry, then, is
the one that
will shear off
those end riv-
ets, or rip
one or the
other of the
sheets right
at the rivet
hole."*

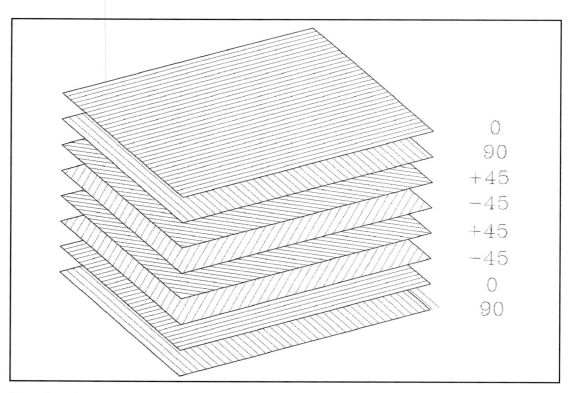

To provide adequate resistance to "off axis" loads around bolt holes, etc., composites need additional plies of material applied with the fibers running at various angles. This typical laminate sequence for a CFRP composite suggests how much extra material is needed.

fiber lying in a direction that would oppose this effect, the interlaminar shear strength depends almost entirely on the properties of the resin matrix. This problem is usually worst for very thin laminates made from very fine weave cloth. (Note, though, the use of a layer of mat or chop to help key layers together, as mentioned in Chapter 2.)

Stress Concentrations

Another major consideration when contemplating the use of composites for jobs traditionally done by metals is the business of *stress concentrations*. The ability of metals to yield provides them with an ability to deal with local overloads—the overstressed material can warp somewhat, relieving the load on itself by throwing part of the load onto adjacent material. If two sheets, for example, are joined together by a row of rivets, and a load arises that acts along that row, the usual textbook assumption is that almost all the load is carried through the two indi-

vidual rivets at each end of the row. The maximum load the entire joint can carry, then, is the one that will shear off those end rivets, or rip one or the other of the sheets right at the rivet hole. This is quite true when the materials are perfectly elastic, but when the material can yield, then either the overloaded rivets or their holes will distort, until some of the other riveted joints take up a larger share of the load.

Note that some of this deformation is permanent. This means that the next time the same sized load gets carried across that same row of rivets, the critical ones are less highly stressed. This will also have another effect over time, as the reduced peak and average loads at these yielded areas will improve the fatigue life of the whole joint. In a sense, the structure has adaptively redesigned itself.

This example of a rivet hole is a useful one, for another reason. The stresses around the edges of the holes in a bolted or riveted joint are not only higher than in the surrounding material, they are also directionally complex—even though the force may be a simple pull from end-to-end, some of the stress at the edge of the hole will act at various angles to that straight pull. The amount of additional material that needs to be added around the bolt hole to deal with this stress concentration depends on the particular material being used. A carbon fiber laminate, for example, requires twice as many fibers running at plus and minus 45 degrees as in the direction of the load; aramid fiber requires only half as much as that.

Point Fastenings—Rivets, bolts, screws—all create stress concentrations in all materials, and that means more material, and thus more weight, is needed than if the object were made in one piece. Connections, then, reduce the efficiency of all structures, but the inability of most composites to yield makes the situation worse. (Aramid's comparatively good showing on this score can be attributed to the fact that it and Spectra fiber do behave in a ductile way when overloaded, though only in compression.)

One of the advantages of composites is the ability to produce very large, complex shapes in one piece that could only be reproduced in metal by joining together multiple separate sections. Actually, any attempt to mimic fabricated metal construction using composites is likely to result in an even more inefficient structure. One reason cited for the commercial failure of the Learfan aircraft was the decision to make the airframe from composites, but to make it in discrete panels, secured to separate frames (also of composite construction) by means of point fasteners. The result was a structure that could arguably have been executed in metal at a comparable weight—and far lower cost. Still there are places where sections of a structure need to be detached—perhaps to allow for servicing or repairing of whatever they cloak, or to simplify the problem of replacing damaged sections—and so

How FRP Composites Carry Loads

Many people believe that the strength of a FRP laminate is necessarily reduced whenever any of the fibers in it are broken. This is definitely not so. It is equally untrue that a fiber has to extend from one end of a load carrying part to the other, in order to contribute to the strength of the laminate.

First, realize that a fiber, by definition, is something that is many times longer than its diameter. Now, in a properly constructed laminate, all of the surface of each fiber is firmly attached to the resin that surrounds it, and the area of that contact is many times greater than the cross sectional area of the fiber. Now, imagine a small zone within the laminate where two fibers, "A" and "B," lay side-by-side, fairly close to each other, but only partly overlapped in length, so one is closer to one end of the laminate, overall, and the other closer to the opposite end.

If we anchor one end of the laminate and pull on the other end, there will be a tendency for the two fibers to slide past each other. Each, however, is stuck to the surrounding resin, so the interface between fiber and resin is stressed in shear–the fiber is trying to slide through the resin; likewise, the resin between the two fibers is also stressed in shear. Thus, each fiber passes the load into the resin, and the resin "hands off" the load to the next adjacent fiber. Provided each fiber is long enough in relation to its diameter, then even though the shear strength of the resin is a mere fraction of the tensile strength of the fiber, there will be so much more resin carrying the shear load than there is fiber carrying the tension load that the fiber (or the bond between the fiber and the resin) will break before the plastic does.

There is some minimum length of fiber for which this will be true, and that is why a laminate made with, say, short chopped strand reinforcement will not be as strong as one using longer fibers. On the other hand, if the minimum length criterion is met, longer fibers will not make the laminate any stronger. Equally, any more resin than is needed to pass the load from one fiber to the next does nothing to increase the strength of the laminate and just adds weight.

Another way to look at it is on the basis of the tensile stresses. In the previous chapter, we saw that any material which is pulled on lengthwise will stretch somewhat, or *strain,* and that the amount of this strain depends on just two things–the stress (the load per unit of cross section area) and the elastic modulus of the material. So, if we know the stress, we can easily calculate the strain, or vice versa. Now, when a composite is stressed, all of it grows longer–the fibers and the resin have equal strains. The fiber, however, is many times stiffer than the resin, so assuming that half the volume of the composite is fiber and half is resin (a representative figure), then the stresses in the two will be in the same ratio as their elastic moduli–about 25:1! Clearly, the matrix is lightly stressed, even when the fibers are carrying a very large load, and since the area of contact between the fiber and the plastic extends over the whole surface of the fiber, the matrix has no problem transmitting the load from one fiber to another.

> *"There is also the issue of quality control. It is worth repeating that the composite manufacturer is not just making a structure but is also making the material from which it is fabricated."*

point fasteners are required, and more attention needs to be given to the material immediately surrounding the hole when that material is a composite as opposed to metal.

Sandwich Structures

Although covered in much more detail in the next chapter, something should be said about sandwich structures. These present particular problems around bolted connections, and anyplace else where loads are highly localized. One technique for dealing with this is to remove the core in the area surrounding the attachment, and bring the two skins together, locally reinforced with additional layers of laminate. It is common for at least some of this extra material to be a thin sheet of aluminum, to take advantage of its isotropic, ductile nature.

Surface Bonding—Provided the surface is properly prepared, aluminum will bond securely to an epoxy laminate. One surface treatment that works is to dissolve a small amount of epoxy resin in a solvent like acetone, then to thoroughly scour the aluminum with Scotchbrite™ while keeping it immersed. The scouring removes the layer of oxide on the surface of the aluminum; the residual trace of epoxy prevents the oxide from re-forming, and provides a chemical link between the metal and the epoxy resin/adhesive used to adhere it to the composite.

Resin Filling

An alternative method, used more often with foam or balsa cores than with honeycomb, is to rout out some of the core material below and around the hole in the skin, leaving a cylindrical void. A filled epoxy resin is then squeezed into this hole. For some light duty fastenings, a bolt or other fastener can be embedded in this resin—a process called *potting*. Alternatively, and especially where the loads are substantial, this plug of filled resin can be drilled to finished hole size, and a bolt passed right

through. The hole routing can be done with a nail or screw, with its head bent over, chucked into a power drill.

Other Considerations

Composites require thinking differently in other ways, too. For one thing, their service temperatures are much lower than those of metals. (There are exotic resin systems used in military and aerospace applications that will tolerate very high temperatures—as much as 500 or 600 F, it is rumored. Apart from their very limited availability and their cost, most of these resins produce by-products as they cure and so require processing at high pressures.)

Quality Control—There is also the issue of quality control. It is worth repeating that the composite manufacturer is not just making a structure but is also making the material from which it is fabricated. Not only is the next part you make likely to differ in strength from the last one, both of them may be far from the "book" figures for the strength of a laminate using exactly the same combination of reinforcement and resin. In aviation and aerospace work, a high level of consistency is ensured by eliminating hand work wherever possible, such as by using pre-pregs instead of hand lay-ups, and by constant testing of both incoming materials and finished parts. Without these tests, any assumptions about material properties are essentially guesswork. There are test labs all over the continent that will provide hard numbers about the strength of the parts you make, usually based on coupons cut from a part of the laminate that would be trimmed off anyway. If someone's life may depend on the strength of the parts you make, it would be irresponsible not to take advantage of these facilities. The tests are not outrageously expensive, and even if the absolute numbers are not of particular interest, the scatter in test results between a number of supposedly identical parts will prove educational. ∎

FRP SANDWICH CONSTRUCTION

15

In Chapter 13, we noted that when thin-shelled structures are loaded in bending or torsion, compression and shear forces are induced in the surfaces of these shells. Such loads in turn tend to cause the thin walls to buckle—effectively, each section of the skin is loaded in bending. Now, the resistance to this buckling depends on the stiffness of the material the panel is made from, but it depends even more strongly on the thickness of the panel. Mathematically, the stiffness varies with the cube of the thickness, so if we double the thickness, we get eight times the resistance to buckling, for just twice the weight.

While that represents a favorable exchange of added stiffness for added weight, we cannot forget that the material in the panel, no matter how thick or thin, is not being well used when it is loaded in this way—while the surfaces are highly stressed, the middle of the thickness of the panel is mostly dead weight. What we need is some way to increase the thickness without increasing the weight in proportion. The solution is *sandwich construction*—two widely spaced strong skins separated by a material of very low density.

SANDWICH THEORY

Sandwich construction is analogous to an "I" beam—the two skins serve as the flanges, while the lightweight filler, the *core*, acts as the web, stabilizing the skins by carrying the lateral forces that threaten to start them buckling. Since these loads run at right angles to the plane of the facings, they act toward or away from the core, so the core is exposed to a combination of compression and shear, or tension and shear, depending on whether the skin is trying to buckle toward or away from the core.

For a given weight, this division of mater-

Workers construct honeycomb cored composite sandwich that forms nose section of deHavilland Dash 8 aircraft. Guy Levesque photo courtesy deHavilland Inc.

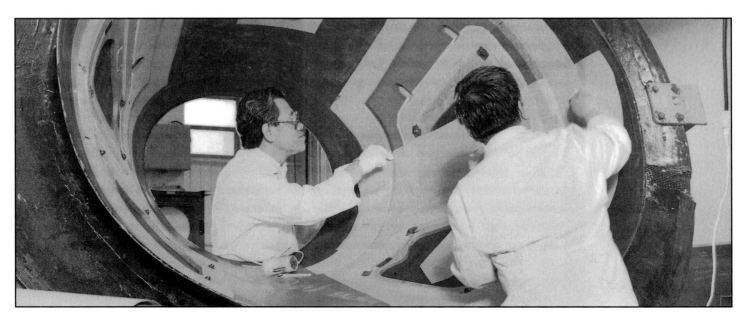

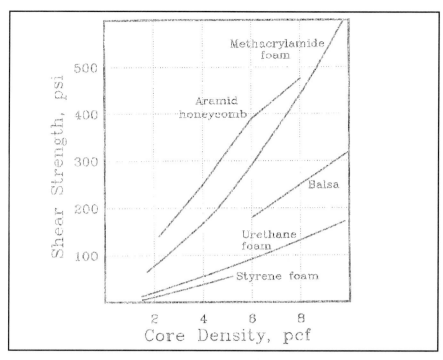

Shear strength of core materials varies almost linearly with density.

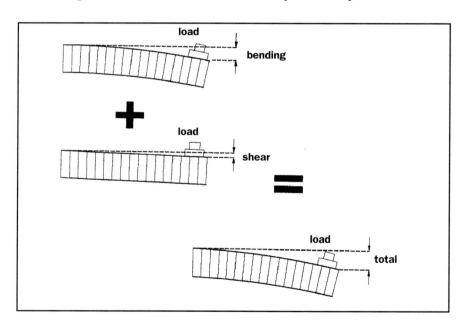

How sandwich beams work.

"high-tech" applications. Very often an FRP panel needs to be made far thicker than is necessary for any practical purpose, and thus heavier and more expensive, simply to avoid its feeling cheap and flimsy. This is not so much of a problem on small parts, or ones having a complex shape with curvature in multiple directions, but flat panels, even quite small ones, may "oil-can" noticeably in normal use. Even if they aren't exactly frail, the drumming and fluttering that results from this lack of stiffness can cause premature fatigue, causing hair-line cracking in the resin, especially in gel coat, and the constant fidgeting can wear out fastener holes.

Sandwiches can be made from many skin and core combinations. Metal skinned sandwiches using a variety of cores are common in the aerospace industry, and a highly efficient structure can be made using plywood skins over a balsa wood core. Our attention here, though, is on the use of FRP skins. That still leaves the core material to consider.

SANDWICH CONSTRUCTION CORES

The core accounts for most of the overall thickness of the panel, so unless a material of very low density is selected it will represent a significant fraction of the total panel weight. At the same time, the core must be strong enough to sustain the forces generated when the skins are tempted to wrinkle. It is the job of the sandwich designer to strike the optimum trade-off between the weight and thickness of the core and that of the facings. Among other things, that decision depends on the relationship between the density of the core material and its strength in tension, compression and shear. The heat tolerance of the core, how easy it is to cut to shape, its durability in service, cost, and compatibility with the adhesive used to adhere it to the skins are other factors that have to be taken into account. For example,

ial into three separate zones, and the use of very low density material for the core, can give many times the stiffness and strength of a single thin panel. Needless to say, it sees widespread application in aircraft and race cars, but also in boats, sporting goods, and even house doors.

As the last example suggests, sandwich construction is not limited to highly loaded styrene foam is easily shaped using a hot wire (see Chapter 5), but dissolves in polyester or vinylester resin.

Balsa

One of the most successful aircraft of World War II—the Mosquito bomber—employed sandwich construction throughout. The sandwich in this case was formed of thin birch plywood skins spaced apart by a balsa wood core. Immediately after the war, sandwich construction was adopted by the dawning fiberglass boat-building industry, as a means of dealing with the low stiffness of single skin construction in GFRP; balsa was usually selected as the core material, no doubt partly because of the shortage of alternative materials.

As in the Mosquito, the balsa was applied with the grain running perpendicular to the facings. (It still is, since balsa, like all woods, is much stronger along the grain than across it.) Because even large balsa trees are only a few square feet in cross section area, end-grain balsa is supplied in the form of small square "tiles." To simplify covering a large area, these tiles are available in sheets with the individual blocks spaced slightly apart (to allow the sheet to be curved) and glued to a light, open weave fabric called scrim. Balsa sold for use in sandwich construction is available in densities from five to sixteen pounds per cubic foot, and is kiln dried and treated with a fungicide.

Structural Properties—Compared to other potential core materials of equal density, balsa has excellent compressive strength and stiffness, but inferior shear strength. Its service temperature limit, while greater than most foams, is restricted to the boiling point of water (212F), which makes it compatible with some but not all ETC resin systems. Balsa is unaffected by polyester and vinylester resins.

Uses—Although it has been replaced in many applications by honeycomb (see

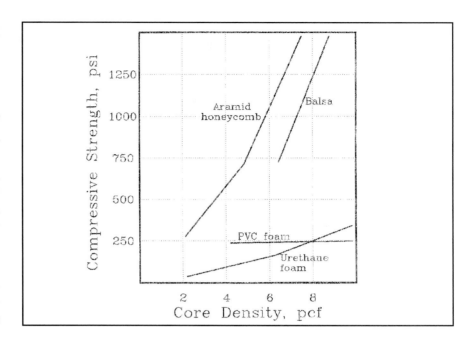

below), end-grain balsa is still used in the sandwich floor panels of many commercial aircraft, and offers many advantages to the do-it-yourself sandwich builder, including modest cost, wide availability, and ease of working.

Foams

Any material that can exist both as a liquid and as a solid can be foamed. The trick is to introduce bubbles of air or some other gas into the liquid, then arrange for it to solidify. You make a foamed thermoset of a sort when you do an inadequate job of getting all the air bubbles out of a laminate. The kinds of foams used in sandwich construction, though, are usually *thermoplastics*—they soften when heated, and melt to a liquid if they get hot enough. That's how they get the bubbles in, but it also sets an upper limit to the temperature that a foam cored sandwich can be exposed to. The strength and stiffness of foams, particularly in shear, are proportional to their densities—a foam of, say, one quarter the density of the parent material in solid form will have roughly one quarter of its shear strength and stiffness.

Other foams available in the form of boards and used for sandwich cores are

Compressive strength of various cores compared on the basis of density.

> *"The trick is to introduce bubbles of air or some other gas into the liquid, then arrange for it to solidify."*

"But there are some difficulties involved with the use of hand-poured urethane foam in this way. First, it proves difficult in practice to control even the average density of the foam, and quite impossible to obtain uniform density throughout the part."

methacrylamide and polyvinyl chloride (PVC). Methacrylamide foam is a brilliant, sparkling white color. It has superior heat resistance to most other core foams, and is strongly resistant to solvents. Both it and PVC foam exhibit slightly better mechanical properties than other core foams, though at higher cost. Some versions of PVC foam can be tailored and fitted into complex contours by careful use of a heat gun.

Polystyrene Foam—Nearly everyone is familiar with the rigid plastic foams used as insulation in house-building; the most common of these is polystyrene foam or Styrofoam™. It is important to distinguish between the two forms of polystyrene foam—the white expanded bead foam used in beer coolers, and the true closed cell foam, which is blue in color. Bead-foam is unsuitable as a structural core material, but closed cell polystyrene foam is successfully used as a sandwich core in many light aircraft structures.

Polystyrene foam comes in the form of boards from one half to four inches thick, and in large billets sold as flotation foam for boat docks, etc., in densities ranging from about 1.6 pounds per cubic foot (pcf) to more than 5 pcf; the ones used in structural sandwich construction tend toward the higher end of that range. Common Styrofoam SM™ insulating boards are about 2.0 pcf. Polystyrene foam softens noticeably above about 140-170 degrees F and can be easily and accurately shaped using a hot-wire cutter; freehand shaping is quickly achieved (cold) with a Surform™ tool, and the resulting surface can be brought up to a remarkably smooth finish using an ordinary mill file. Polystyrene foam is about the cheapest core material, though its shear strength and stiffness are inferior to many alternative materials of comparable density and, as noted, it dissolves in polyester and vinylester resin.

Polyurethane Foam—Polyurethane foam is also widely used for thermal insulation, as

well as for packaging for delicate items; like polystyrene, it is sold in boards and slabs. Polyurethane foams can be rigid or flexible—much "foam rubber" is, in fact, urethane foam; our only interest is in the rigid foams, which come in densities from 3 to 60 pcf. The grades used for sandwich cores are taken from the lower half of that range. Urethane foams can tolerate from 175 F to 250 F, and are strongly resistant to solvents; they are therefore safe to use with polyester and vinylester resins. On the other hand, urethane foams create extremely toxic smoke when exposed to heat, so they must not be hot wired.

Liquid Polyurethane Foam—Polyurethane foam can also be created on the spot by mixing two liquids, which froth up and expand to twenty to forty times their original volume, and rapidly harden to a solid. This immediately suggests the use of this pour foam for production of sandwich cores, especially ones requiring complex contours, that are formed in place by pouring the liquid into the space between two molded skins, and this is indeed how the flotation chambers on some fiberglass boats are made. But there are some difficulties involved with the use of hand-poured urethane foam in this way.

First, it proves difficult in practice to control even the average density of the foam, and quite impossible to obtain uniform density throughout the part.

Polyurethane Foam Problems—This problem seems not to be specific to "low-tech" operations; even when purchased as pre-manufactured boards or slabs, urethane foams exhibit a density gradient through the depth of the slab, a matter which the various manufacturers acknowledge. For critical structural parts that are designed on the basis of a detailed stress analysis, the unpredictable mechanical properties of the foam, and the variation in those properties from part-to-part, makes this a very dicey business indeed. Of course, where a sandwich is designed "by the seat of the pants" for an application that is not part of a primary structure, these are minor considerations—such a part will almost certainly be stiffer for the same weight (or lighter for the same stiffness) than if made as a single, thicker skin. Still, there are problems.

First, the foam develops very large expansion forces as it rises. If the two-part liquid is poured into a cavity formed by unsupported thin skins, these expansion forces will surely distort the part badly, and may even burst it. Even if the part is confined in a mold, the mold itself will be stressed to a degree that is hard to imagine until you have seen it. The first time I tried it, I very narrowly avoided destroying a mold for a race car wing in this way. Disaster was barely averted by furious wrench twirling to dismantle the two-piece mold, and a valuable lesson was learned. Do not attempt to confine the foam as it expands; give it somewhere to go.

Even when there appears to be plenty of room for the foam to rise without running into the "roof" of an enclosure, urethane is extremely sticky stuff, so the foam tends to stick to the laminate surface even as it is rising. This causes the rising *bun* to tilt sideways, trapping large voids between the foam and the skins. This same sticking also tends to make the upper part of the rising bun form a plug or stopper that restricts the expansion of material lower down. The space the liquid is poured into must be wide and shallow if this is to be avoided; do not pour into narrow, deep crevices. (When foam-in-place urethane is used in industrial applications, it is pumped into deep cavities using a long wand, which is slowly withdrawn as the material is injected. This apparatus is generally adapted to urethanes that expand to a very low density—too low to be of much use as a core.)

Microballoons—A foam is nothing more than something full of holes, so rather than buy a material that is "pre-filled" with holes,

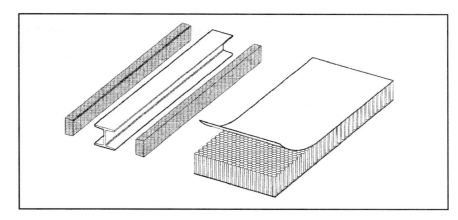

you could buy the holes themselves, and mix them into a liquid resin like polyester or epoxy! The "holes" are actually microballoons of phenolic plastic (purplish maroon in color) or glass (white), which are available in sizes from 1/8 inch down to a few thousandths of an inch in diameter, though the larger sizes are not seen much. When these microballoons are mixed into a liquid resin, anything from a slight thickening effect to a frothy light paste with the consistency of whipped cream can be had, depending on the quantity added. This combination of hollow spheres of one substance in a matrix of an altogether different material is called *syntactic foam*.

Honeycomb

Foamed plastics are seldom used as a core material in the aviation industry, or in race cars, and balsa is used only to a limited extent. The preferred core material for critical structural applications is *honeycomb*—an arrangement of hexagonal cells (though they can be triangular or other shapes), like a cross section of a bee hive. Honeycomb is the highest performance core material, but it is also the most costly.

Honeycomb was first developed during World War II, as a replacement for balsa in the making of radomes—the balsa itself was transparent to radar, but became opaque if it got soaked in water. The material used then was made from ordinary paper, dipped in phenolic resin for waterproofing. Now, the

In the same way the "web" of an "I" beam stabilizes the "flanges" against buckling, honeycomb stabilizes thin skins against wrinkling, while reducing weight by eliminating under-used material.

"Disaster was barely averted by furious wrench twirling to dismantle the two-piece mold, and a valuable lesson was learned."

Honeycomb is available in a variety of materials and not all cells are hexagonal. Note the overexpanded honeycomb second from bottom and second from top; the distorted cell structure allows the honeycomb to be more easily curved, at least in one direction. Guy Levesque photo courtesy deHavilland Inc.

paper is most often made using Nomex™ (DuPont) fiber, rather than wood fiber.

Design—It is produced by printing stripes of adhesive across sheets of the material. Multiple sheets are then stacked together with the glue lines on alternate layers staggered and, after the glue has hardened, the stack, called a *bole*, is cut into *bole slices*, which are drawn apart to yield the finished product. (This stuff is called *expanded honeycomb*, to distinguish it from *corrugated honeycomb*, which is made by running aluminum sheet or foil through corrugated rollers to form half-cell shapes, then gluing multiple layers together.)

The design decisions facing the specifier of a honeycomb cored sandwich include the weight-and-thickness-of-skins versus density-and-thickness-of-core dilemma faced when using other core materials, but they go even beyond that. A given core density can be arrived at using large cells with comparatively thick walls, or more smaller cells of thinner material. The upper limit to the size of an individual cell is set by the tendency of the skin to buckle between cells but, if weight is not to be increased, smaller cells would need to have thinner walls, which would be more prone to buckling themselves. Thankfully, the makers of honeycomb offer detailed design guidance to help resolve these troublesome issues.

Wet Lay-Up—When honeycomb core is used in wet lay-ups, it is common to first produce one skin, then for the core to be set down on the still wet laminate, so the laminating resin serves as the adhesive for this connection. The second skin is more problematic. If a wet lay-up is applied over the core to produce the second skin, there will be a tendency for the resin to drain out of the reinforcement and into the cells. About the only practical alternative is to produce the second skin independently, then to assemble it to the core using a film type adhesive. This obviously demands closer than typical control over the shape and dimensions of both core and skins.

Pre-Preg—When the facings are produced from pre-pregs, this problem is avoided, and the choice then is between separate production of the two skins, allowing them to fully cure, followed by assembly to the core using film adhesive, or by letting the resin in the pre-preg serve as the glue and completing the assembly before either skin is cured, a technique called co-curing. Notably, the force required to peel the skin away from the core is different for the "up" surface than for the "down" side. This occurs because of differences in the shape and size of the fillet of resin that forms at the junction between each cell and the skin, in turn caused by the flow of the resin under gravity during the cure. ■

INDEX

BIBLIOGRAPHY

Adams, A.A. "Composite structures for automobiles - Lotus experience," in: *ASM Advanced Composites Conference Proceedings, December 2-4 1985.*

Agranoff, Jeff (ed). *Modern Plastics Encyclopedia.* McGraw-Hill. N.Y., 1976.

Benjamin, B.S. *Structural Design With Plastics.* Van Nostrand Reinhold. N.Y., 1969.

Binks Manufacturing Co. *Plural Component Spray Systems,* Binks publ'n #TD 16-1R-3. Binks Manufacturing Co., Franklin Park, IL, 1990.

Binks Manufacturing Co. *Airless Spraying,* Binks publ'n #TD 11-1R-2. Binks Manufacturing Co., Franklin Park, IL, 1986.

Cacoutis, S. & L.K. John & K. Young. *Development and certification of the de Havilland Dash-8 aircraft cabin interiors to meet the FAA's improved flammability standards.* 39th Int'l SAMPE Symposium & Exhib'n, Anaheim, CA, April 11-14th, 1994. Society for the Advancement of Material and Process Engineering.

CIBA-GEIGY. *Epoxy Plastic Tooling Manual.* REN Plastics, Lansing, MI, 1978.

Crandall, Michael S. "Extent of Exposure to Styrene in the Reinforced Plastic Boat Making Industry." US Dept of Health and Human Services, National Inst. for Occupational Safety and Health, publ'n. # 82-110, 1982.

Delmonte, John. *Technology of Carbon and Graphite Fiber Composites.* Van Nostrand Reinhold. N.Y., 1981.

Dietz, Albert G.H. (ed). *Composite Engineering Laminates.* MIT Press. Cambridge, MA, 1969.

DOW Plastics. *DERAKANE Epoxy Vinyl Ester Resins Technical Product Information,* DOW publ'n #125-00016-1293 SMG. The DOW Chemical Co, Midland, MI.

DOW Plastics. *Fabricating Tips DERAKANE Epoxy Vinyl Ester Resins,* DOW publ'n #125-00082-1004 AMPM. The DOW Chemical Co, Midland, MI.

Du Pont Co. *Technical Symposium V.* E.I. Du Pont de Nemours, Inc., Industrial Fibers Division.

Du Pont Co. *KEVLAR — Data Manual for Kevlar 49 Aramid.* E.I. Du Pont de Nemours, Inc., 1986.

DuPont Co. *KOREX Aramid Paper Honeycomb Core,* DuPont publ'n #H-47663. E.I. Du Pont de Nemours, Inc. Wilmington, DE.

DuPont Co. *Design and Fabrication Techniques for Honeycomb of NOMEX Aramid Sandwich Structures,* Du Pont publ'n #H-14475. E.I. Du Pont de Nemours, Inc. Wilmington, DE.

DuPont Co. *Kevlar 49 Aramid for canoe, kayak, and small boat construction,* DuPont publ'n #E-43688. E.I. Du Pont de Nemours, Inc. Wilmington, DE.

DuPont Co. *Kevlar 49 Aramid for Boat Hull Construction,* DuPont publ'n #A-88946. E.I. Du Pont de Nemours, Inc. Wilmington, DE.

Gill, R.M. *Carbon Fibres in Composite Materials.* Iliffe. London, 1972

Gordon, J.E. *Structures.* Pelican. Harmondsworth, Middlesex, 1978.

Gordon, J.E. *The New Science of Strong Materials.* Pelican. Harmondsworth, Middlesex, 1974.

Gougeon Brothers, Inc. *WEST System Technical Manual & Product Guide.* Gougeon Brothers, Inc. Bay City, MI, 1994.

Kiefer, W.R. et al. *Fabrication of automotive body components in GrFRP.* SAE 790028.

Lacovara, Bob. "Troubleshooting Tooling," in: *Professional Boatbuilder,* no. 21, February/March 1993, and no. 22, April/May 1993.

Lannon, Maurice. *Polyester and Fiberglass.* Maurice Lannon & Gem-O'-Lite Plastics Corporation. North Hollywood, CA, 1969.

Loken, Hal and Martin Hollmann. *Designing With Core—Materials and Analysis.* Aircraft Designs, Inc. Monterey, CA, 1988.

Marshall, Andrew. "Composite Basics," (a series of articles appearing in *Homebuilt Aircraft* between February, 1983 and August, 1984).

Marshall, Andrew. *Practical Sandwich Structures/Advanced Composites.* Marshall Consulting, Inc. Walnut Creek, CA, 1982.

Morgan, Phillip. *Glass Reinforced Plastics.* Iliffe & Son. London, 1955.

Noakes, Keith. *Build to Win.* Osprey. London, 1988.

Noakes, Keith. *Successful Composite Techniques.* Osprey. London, 1989.

O'Rourke, B.P. "The use of composite materials in the design and manufacture of Formula 1 racing cars," in: *Proceedings of the Institution of Mechanical Engineers.* v. 204 part D.

Owens-Corning. *Pro's Guide to Pultrusion Troubleshooting.* Owens-Corning Fiberglas Corporation. Toledo, 1990.

Owens-Corning. *Pro's Guide to Filament Winding Troubleshooting.* Owens-Corning Fiberglas Corporation. Toledo, 1990.

Owens-Corning. *S-2 Glass Fiber.* Owens-Corning Fiberglas Corporation. Toledo, 1993.

Petrick, Paul J. *Fiberglass Repairs.* Cornell Maritime Press, Inc. Cambridge, MD, 1976.

Pfund, Bruce. "Mold Releases," in: *Professional Boatbuilder,* no. 12, August/September 1991, and no. 13, October/November 1991.

Pfund, Bruce. "Post Curing," in: *Professional Boatbuilder,* no. 14, December/January 1992.

Pfund, Bruce. "The Changing Face of Polyester Resins," in: *Professional Boatbuilder,* no. 8, December/January 1991.

Pfund, Bruce. "Light-Curing Resins," in: *Professional Boatbuilder,* no. 18, August/September 1992.

Pfund, Bruce. "Secondary Bonding," in: *Professional Boatbuilder,* no. 19, October/November 1992, and no. 20, December/January 1993.

Premo, E.J. "The Corvette plastic body," SAE paper #212, 1954.

Roark, Raymond J. and Warren C. Young. *Formulas for Stress and Strain.* McGraw-Hill. New York, 1975.

Rosato, B.V. and C.S. Grove Jr. *Filament Winding: Its development, manufacture, applications, and design.* Interscience Publishers. New York, 1964.

Shell Chemical Co. *EPON Resins,* Shell publ'n #SC227-90. Shell Chemical Co.

Shell Chemical Co. *EPON Resin 828,* Shell publ'n #SC235-91.828. Shell Chemical Co., 1991

Shell Chemical Co. *EPON Resin 862,* Shell publ'n #SC772-92. Shell Chemical Co., 1991

Sonneborn, Ralph H. *Fiberglas Reinforced Plastics.* Reinhold Publishing Co. New York, 1954.

Van Iden, Byron. "More power for your air tools," in: *Stock Car Racing,* v.29, no.4, March 1994.

Warring, R.H. *The New Glassfibre Book.* Model and Allied Publications. Kings Langley, Hertfordshire, 1971.

Wiley, Jack. *The Fiberglass Construction and Repair Handbook,* 2nd ed'n. TAB Books. N.Y., 1988.

Wills, John A. *Gel Coat Compounding for Industrial and Marine Products.* John A. Wills. Valley Center, CA, 1984.

Wills, John A. *Industrial Resin Puttys.* John A. Wills. Valley Center, CA, 1984.

Wills, John A. *Glass Fiber Auto Body Construction Simplified.* Dan R. Post Publications. Arcadia, CA, 1965.

Wood, Richard. *Car Bodywork in Glass Reinforced Plastics.* Pentech Press, London, 1980.

OTHER HP AUTOMOTIVE BOOKS

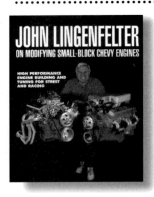  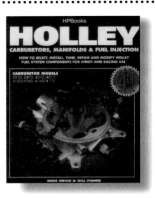 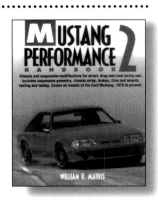

HANDBOOK SERIES

Auto Electrical Handbook
Auto Math Handbook
Automotive Paint Handbook
Baja Bugs & Buggies
Brake Handbook
Camaro Restoration Handbook
Corvette Weekend Projects
Fiberglass & Composite Materials
Metal Fabricator's Handbook
Mustang Restoration Handbook
Mustang Weekend Projects
Off-Roader's Handbook
Paint & Body Handbook
Sheet Metal Handbook
Street Rodder's Handbook
Turbochargers
Turbo Hydra-matic 350
Understanding Automotive Emissions Control
Welder's Handbook

CARBURETORS

Holley 4150
Holley Carburetors, Manifolds & Fuel Injection
Rochester Carburetors
Weber Carburetors

PERFORMANCE SERIES

Big-Block Chevy Performance
Camaro Performance
Chassis Engineering
How to Hot Rod Big-Block Chevys

How to Hot Rod Small-Block Chevys
How to Hot Rod Small-Block Mopar Engines
How to Hot Rod VW Engines
How to Make Your Car Handle
John Lingenfelter On Modifying Small-Block Chevy Engines
Mustang Performance
Mustang Performance 2
1001 High Performance Tech Tips
Race Car Engineering & Mechanics
Small-Block Chevy Performance

REBUILD SERIES

Rebuild Air-Cooled VW Engines
Rebuild Big-Block Chevy Engines
Rebuild Big-Block Ford Engines
Rebuild Big-Block Mopar Engines
Rebuild Small-Block Chevy Engines
Rebuild Small-Block Ford Engines
Rebuild Small-Block Mopar Engines
Rebuild Ford V-8 Engines

GENERAL INTEREST

Auto Dictionary
Car Collector's Handbook
Fabulous Funny Cars
Guide to GM Muscle Cars

TO ORDER CALL: 1-800-223-0510
HPBooks
The Berkley Publishing Group
200 Madison Avenue
New York, NY 10016